A World in Transition

Women, Family, and Child Care in India

A World in Transition

SUSAN C. SEYMOUR

CAMBRIDGE
UNIVERSITY PRESS

PUBLISHED BY THE PRESS SYNDICATE OF THE UNIVERSITY OF CAMBRIDGE
The Pitt Building, Trumpington Street, Cambridge, United Kingdom

CAMBRIDGE UNIVERSITY PRESS
The Edinburgh Building, Cambridge CB2 2RU, UK   http://www.cup.cam.ac.uk
40 West 20th Street, New York, NY 10011-4211, USA   http://www.cup.org
10 Stamford Road, Oakleigh, Melbourne 3166, Australia

First published 1999

Printed in the United States of America

Typeface Palatino 10/13.5 pt.   *System* DeskTopPro$_{/UX}$®   [BV]

*A catalog record for this book is available from
the British Library*

Library of Congress Cataloging-in-Publication Data
Seymour, Susan C. (Susan Christine), 1940–
Women, family, and child care in India : a world in transition /
Susan C. Seymour.
p. cm.
Includes bibliographical references (p. 305–14) and index.
ISBN 0–521–59127–9 (hardcover). – ISBN 0–521–59884–2 (pbk.)
1. Women – India.   2. Women – India – Social conditions.   3. Family –
India.   4. Child care – India.
HQ1742.S438   1998
305.4'0954 – dc21   98–26768
                                 CIP

ISBN 0 521 59127 9   hardback
ISBN 0 521 59884 2   paperback

To the memory of my mother and father,
Helen Rosalie Close Seymour (1909–1996)
and
Kent Osborn Seymour (1902–1984),
in appreciation for their inspiration and unrelenting support
of all my endeavors
and
to the memory of my surrogate parents,
Ruth Seymour Close (1885–1979)
and
William Henry Close (1904–1997),
teachers and collaborators in adventure and travel

Contents

Illustrations

Tables and Figures

Tables

Figures

Acknowledgments

First I want to thank all those families in Bhubaneswar, Orissa, India, who not only allowed me to invade their homes for research but also made me a long-term friend and surrogate relative. There are not words adequate to express my appreciation. I can only hope that those who read this book will recognize some of what they taught me and will not be offended by my representations and interpretations of their lives such as I have come to understand them.

I am appreciative of the institutions and agencies that have supported my research in Bhubaneswar over the years. The National Institute of Mental Health supported my initial fieldwork in 1965–67. My subsequent trips in 1976, 1982, and 1987 were made possible by research awards from Pitzer College. And a Senior Scholar Fulbright Fellowship enabled me and my family to reside in Bhubaneswar in 1989.

Many others have contributed to this book. I particularly want to thank friend, colleague, and collaborator Carol Chapnick Mukhopadhyay. The theoretical work that we did for our book, *Women, Education, and Family in India* (1994), helped to frame this book as well, and that collaborative effort was a continual stimulus for this endeavor. I also want to thank friend and colleague Sheryl Miller, with whom I have co-taught Women, Culture, and Society for many years at Pitzer College – a course in which I tried out ideas for this book as well as early versions of some of its chapters. Professor Miller and the students in that class have provided me with invaluable feedback and support. I also want to thank Usha

Menon, another friend and colleague, who helped with some of the final translations of mother/daughter/grandmother interviews.

Finally, my husband and son deserve not only immeasurable appreciation but also a great deal of the credit for this book. They were both active and passive participants in my research and writing: They tolerated my absences when I traveled to India without them. They accompanied me to Bhubaneswar in 1989 and fully participated in our joint family life there. And they put up with me subsequently as I endeavored to write this and other books while engaged in full-time teaching and administration.

Preface

My marriage was fixed twenty-one days after my birth. I moved to my father-in-law's place when I was twelve. I was literate; I had five to six years of school.

(Excerpt from an interview with a seventy-year-old Indian grandmother)

How, as Westerners, do we respond to this matter-of-fact response to my inquiry about an elderly woman's marriage? How can we even imagine a sociocultural system in which such practices not only were considered normal for many women but also resulted in satisfying lives for them? I refer here to *their* perception of satisfaction, not ours. This book will address such questions by introducing readers to a system of family and gender that is based upon cultural assumptions and structural principles that are very different from those characteristic of most contemporary Western societies.

The grandmother quoted in the opening excerpt is someone I have known for thirty years. She and her husband, children, and grandchildren have participated in my long-term study of changing family organization, child-rearing practices, and gender roles in India. Her statement here is not a complaint, but a matter-of-fact response to a question from me about the timing of her arranged marriage. For a high-caste village woman, born some seventy years ago, it was not unusual to have one's marriage arranged at birth. What was unusual about this woman's marriage was that the groom was a fellow villager, so that at age twelve she was not forced to move to a totally strange village and household. Furthermore, she was unusual in having received some education at a time girls were rarely sent to school. Her literacy enabled her to tutor her own children and grandchildren, to be sensitive to her daughters' educational ambitions, and to occupy herself in old age by reading the Hindu epics.

Although in some respects this Indian grandmother is unusual, in most respects her life is an outgrowth of a family and gender system that many Western women would view as oppressive. Ideally, this is a family system that keeps sets of related men together in multigenerational households, known as "joint families," by sending daughters away and bringing in outside women as wives and daughters-in-law through a complex system of arranged marriage. Women are the moving pieces in an exchange system that creates extensive webs of kinship. Is this a hardship for them? Yes, for they must leave the security of their own family and join a different family. Do they find it oppressive? Sometimes, but not generally. Indian women are socialized to expect a dramatic transition at the time of marriage and to assume new responsibilities in their husband's household. Whereas early socialization for gender roles is a necessary ingredient, the degree of satisfaction that the women who are described in this book express – and that I have witnessed over many years – cannot be reduced to socialization practices alone. It emerges from a much broader sociocultural system in which women, though structurally disadvantaged, are expected to fill critical family roles associated with power, authority, and respect. Furthermore, this familial system is enmeshed within a cultural system in which feminine powers are writ large: Within Hindu theology and practice females are believed to possess great power (*shakti*). Male deities cannot act without their female counterparts – their source of creative power – and female deities are widely worshipped in their own right.

Their general satisfaction with life does not mean that some Indian women cannot either imagine or desire change. In fact, change has arrived for many of the young women I have known since their early childhood. Unlike their mothers and grandmothers, they have had considerable schooling. Most have completed primary and secondary school, and some have completed college and even gone on to acquire graduate degrees. Some have established careers outside the home, whereas many of their mothers and grandmothers still observe purdah (female seclusion). Has this new generation of educated women forsaken arranged marriages? No. Although the time of their marriage has been dramatically delayed for women (and men), most women continue to accept parental authority in marital planning and express a preference for arranged marriages. They generally distrust what are known in India as "love marriages" – that is, marriages based upon personal desire and self-selection. As one highly educated young woman I have known since she was an infant put it, "I don't want to take any such project [marriage] on for myself because I know my parents are very capable in this matter."

To comprehend why this young woman and others accept parental choice and authority in such a critical matter requires Western readers to set aside their own cultural assumptions and preferences and enter a different familial system – one that emphasizes the collective well-being of all members over the personal desires of any one member. In this system, "self-realization," for example, is not a cultural ideal. To describe how this system is conceptualized and structured, how children are socialized into it, and how, in particular, the lives of women are affected by it is the goal of this book. To make understandable to readers that systems of family and gender are always dynamic and adaptive to forces of change – in this case, to the forces of recent urbanization and modernization – is another goal. Just as debates about what a "family" is and should be, and about what women's and men's roles and statuses are and should be, are rife in contemporary America, so too are they in India. In the United States such debates have coincided with the nation's transition from an industrial to a postindustrial society. Similarly, as India – the world's largest democracy – adjusts from being primarily an agrarian society to an increasingly urbanized and industrialized one, debates and tensions around the future of the joint family, of child care, and of women's roles are to be expected.

Note on Transliteration

To make this book accessible to a broad audience, I have used a minimum of Indian terms and have Anglicized spellings for most of the Hindi and Oriya terms that I do use. Accordingly, the Hindu deity is presented in Anglicized form, Shiva, rather than as Siva. Some less familiar Hindi terms are italicized, such as *Jati*, and presented according to the conventional system of transliteration.

CHAPTER ONE

Introduction

January 1989

At 5:30 a.m. I awaken to the sound of coughing and retching just outside my window. In the cool Bhubaneswar winter people suffer from respiratory problems. Mr. Misra, my landlord, has arisen early to go out to buy fresh food for the day (traditionally, a man's task). Before going out to shop, he needs to cleanse himself for his morning worship, and this requires a cleaning of the respiratory system. As the coughing and throat clearing die down, I hear the familiar sound of running water against a bucket followed by the sloshing of water poured by hand over a lightly clad body in the early morning cold. Mr. Misra is purifying himself before entering the family "worship room." These sounds of water mingle with the cries of egrets, red-waddled lapwings, and turquoise kingfishers as they move into the rice fields behind our house. The muffled sounds of bells and the chanting of priests rise from the ancient temple across the road and mix with the early morning traffic in front of our house. Soon the chanting and ringing are echoed and magnified. Mr. Misra is in the "worship room" just on the other side of our bedroom wall. He waves a bell and offers food and prayer to an array of pictures and statues representing Hindu gods and goddesses.

Other sounds of life begin in the courtyard. Someone is washing last night's cookware. I can hear the outdoor water tap running again and the sound of brass and stainless steel pots and pans being scrubbed on the concrete floor of the courtyard. It is time to rise and begin my own morning ablutions and prepare for breakfast. Soon the aroma of Mrs. Misra's cooking from next door will begin. The astringent smells of onion, garlic, chilies, and other spices being cooked in

1

mustard oil will waft into the house. As my husband says, "India fills *all* of one's senses." The morning has barely begun and the senses already seem full, but most of Bhubaneswar's sounds, smells, and sights are yet to be taken in.

My husband, our twelve-year-old son, and I are living not far from the neighborhood where my time in Bhubaneswar, Orissa, India, began nearly twenty-five years ago. What began as a two-year study of changing family organization and child-rearing practices has become a long-term witnessing of social transformation. I have been following the lives of the 130 children and their extended kin, whom I first studied in 1965–67, and have returned this time to focus upon women – the mothers, daughters, and grandmothers that I have known for so long – in order to learn firsthand from them about the changes that they have seen and experienced as residents of a rapidly urbanizing town and center of government and education. Change for women in this part of India in the past quarter of a century has been dramatic.

In 1946, Bhubaneswar – an ancient temple town in eastern India dating back to the early centuries B.C.E. – was selected to become a new seat of government (Figure 1). Thus began its transformation from a small agricultural town renowned for its medieval Hindu temples to a new capital city. The British had created Orissa as a province in 1946. With India's independence from Great Britain in 1947, Orissa became a state and Bhubaneswar a full-fledged capital city. In the 1950s, land to the east of the old temple town (the "Old Town") was bulldozed and on it government offices and housing were constructed, creating the "New Capital." Within a decade, Bhubaneswar's population swelled from about ten thousand to nearly forty thousand residents. By 1965, when I began research there, its population had grown to about fifty thousand. By 1989 it had jumped to four hundred fifty thousand.

Within four decades Bhubaneswar grew from a large village, where the same families, which for generations had resided in caste-based neighborhoods, knew one another, to a sizable city, with many of the institutions of modern urban life as well as its social anonymity. In growth of population alone Bhubaneswar experienced dramatic change. The change, however, has gone far

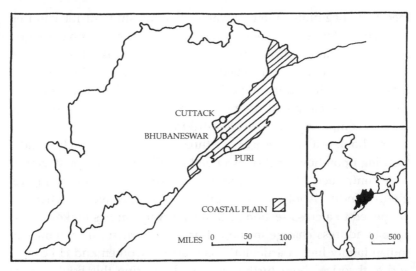

Figure 1. Map of Orissa

deeper than mere demographics would indicate. The establishment of schools – from the kindergarten to the postgraduate university level – has provided both old and new residents potentially transformative educational opportunities. Along with schooling have come new job opportunities, ranging from all levels of government service to the many kinds of work that go into building an urban infrastructure, for example providing transportation and lodging, moving and selling food and other goods, and supplying a multitude of services such as clothes washing, house cleaning, and cooking. An age-old agrarian way of life has had to come to terms with a modern life based less upon ascribed caste status and temple rituals and more upon achieved status through education and new forms of secular employment.

Because of its rapid growth and transformation Bhubaneswar was an ideal microcosm for observing the impact of urbanization and modernization upon traditional Indian principles of family structure, gender roles, and socialization practices. I began examining those processes of change in 1965 when, as a member of the Harvard-Bhubaneswar Project,[1] I spent two years studying family organization and child-rearing practices. At the time I never imag-

3

ined I was beginning a long voyage – that my study of 130 children and their extended families would evolve into a thirty-year study of changing family structures and gender systems. However, my initial two-year stay enmeshed me in the lives of Bhubaneswar families and whetted my appetite to understand better the forces of change in a society that resembled my own in its degree of socio-cultural complexity but was also strikingly different.

This book is a synthesis of my three decades of research in India focusing upon how a set of extended families have adapted as they have confronted life in a rapidly urbanizing and modernizing re-gion of India. Applying a longitudinal perspective to what has happened to a cross section of Bhubaneswar families makes it pos-sible to address change in the cultural and structural dynamics of Indian family life – particularly as it affects women and children – and to theorize about further change. In writing this book, I have had several goals. The first, and most basic, is to introduce Ameri-can readers to a system of family structure and gender roles based upon strikingly different cultural assumptions and structural prin-ciples than those predominant in the contemporary United States. In doing so, I also want to give readers an empathic understand-ing of the Indian system so that they can comprehend why, despite the restrictions such a system imposes upon them, most Indian women find it satisfying. Nonetheless, this is a family and gender system undergoing dramatic change. Will it, as Western social scientists once predicted, come to resemble that of the West?[2] Will multigenerational extended households based upon kinship ties traced through men be replaced by two-parent nuclear house-holds?

Another of my goals is to describe a variety of households so that readers will understand that the ideal patrifocal joint family system in India is no more monolithic than is the nuclear family system in the United States. Although in both societies there is a culturally ideal system that predominates and motivates people to behave in certain ways, also in both societies family and gender systems vary by class and caste status, ethnic and religious identity, rural versus urban residence, and regional location. Just as there are diverse family structures in the United States, the joint family in India can take a variety of forms. It can range from as few as four to over twenty-five members living together, and it can vary dramatically with respect to the constraints that women experience. How are these different families, which vary by caste and class status and by Old Town–New Capital residence, adapting to the forces of urbanization and modernization? Are there discernible patterns of adaptation and change? These are some of the questions I shall address.

One way to garner insights into a particular family system and its underlying cultural premises is to examine its child-rearing practices. In every society, adults try to produce, through a set of conventional child care practices, children who will fit either their society or their subculture of society. In India, for example, mothers are expected to sleep with their young children rather than with their husbands. Why, compared with much of the Western world, is the mother-child relationship in India given priority over the husband-wife relationship in this and other respects? Different principles of personhood and gender identity underlie Indian child care practices and distinguish them from predominant American practices. What happens, then, when a society undergoes fundamental change, such as India is experiencing as it moves from a predominantly agrarian base to an industrial one? Will changes in child care practices accompany changes in India's family and gender systems as they adapt to such transformations?[3] My longitudinal research in Bhubaneswar provides some answers to these questions.

In describing India's predominant family and gender systems and their associated child-rearing practices, I have chosen to focus upon the lives of women. By following daughters from early childhood to adulthood and comparing their lives with those of their mothers and grandmothers, I hope to make the texture of women's lives in Bhubaneswar accessible to American readers and to challenge some Western stereotypes of South Asian women. Americans often assume, for example, that a family system that practices early arranged marriage and female seclusion must force women into passivity and powerlessness. From an outside perspective, these women appear to be victims of an unjust patriarchal order. And yet in India a woman rose to be the head of state, women are governors, and women constitute a greater percentage of the mathematics, science, and medical students than in the United States. How can we reconcile such examples with stereotypes of female passivity and powerlessness?

I approach this and other such questions with some caution, recognizing the dangers inherent in trying to speak for or to represent the lives of women of another society, particularly a formerly colonized one. The synthesis of women's lives that I shall present, however, is based upon what Bhubaneswar women of all ages have taught me over a long period, and I shall use their voices as much as possible to represent their attitudes and perspectives. I am convinced that they would want me to try to correct misperceptions that women in the "first world" have of women in the "third world." Furthermore, that they are proud of their society, their families, and their ways of life, does not mean that they cannot imagine or desire change.

A final goal of this book is to expand its readers' concept of what is "normal" by examining certain assumptions about culture and human development. For example, much of Western psychological research treats the individual as central, and the tendency is to focus upon individual self-development. Accordingly, the individual's acquisition of the cognitive and affective skills that will enhance that person's independence and achievement of goals is emphasized. Self-reliance and self-realization are the expected outcomes of child development, and close dyadic bonds between mother and child, for example, are considered part of the normal developmental process. What happens, then, in a society such as India's, where the preference is to rear children collectively – that is, where there are many "mothers" – and where close dyadic bonds are discouraged and even considered dangerous? And what happens when children are taught that familial, not individual, goals are primary and that independence from the family is not desirable? Among different societies conceptions of personhood may vary dramatically, as may the outcomes of different socialization practices and expectations for children. Through an in-depth examination of family life in India, I shall try to expose some of the cultural assumptions that underlie Western conceptions of human development, interpersonal relationships, and intrapsychic processes, while explicating some of those cultural assumptions that are characteristic of India.

January 1989

It is the dry, cool season in Bhubaneswar, the season of weddings and the season when I first arrived in Bhubaneswar twenty-four years ago. Up the road taped music blasts from a neighbor's house for everyone to hear and to know that another family is about to celebrate its daughter's wedding. For this purpose numerous loudspeakers have been installed outdoors. I listen for other indications of the momentous event, and it is not long before there are distant sounds of drumming. The drumming, together with untuned blasts of horns, gradually grows closer and closer in the darkness of late evening. The bridegroom's party is nearing the bride's house and, along with other bystanders, I go out to the road to watch.

The entourage is led by a band – a somewhat bedraggled set of outcast musicians who walk, only in a semblance of order, while playing their instruments. Their irregular, staccato sounds are punctuated by occasional blasts of firecrackers. Behind them are the "merry makers," friends and relatives of the bridegroom. In the 1960s a bridegroom's party consisted only of men, but tonight there are also young women dancing in the streets. There are 75–100 young men and women surrounding the bridegroom, who rides in an automobile decorated with garlands of flowers – strings and strings of jasmine and marigolds. The scent of flowers mixes with other night smells – those of dust, cows, diesel fumes, and spices mixed with dung-fire smoke and people crowded together. Formerly arriving on horseback, the bridegroom now travels perched high on the back of an open automobile. He, too, is bedecked with garlands of flowers that cover his white robes and gold crown. Accompanied by friends and relatives, he is on his way to collect his bride who, together with her family and friends, awaits him and the beginning of the wedding ceremony and feasting that will fill much of the night. Soon the groom's family will gain a daughter-in-law and the bride's family will lose a daughter, but only after much lavish celebrating. First, it must be made clear to everyone that she comes from a family of status and constitutes a sacred gift. A new stage in the cycle of the family is underway.

7

Weddings in India mark a highly significant moment of family transition – the moment when two extended families come together not only to celebrate their union through marriage but also to transfer a girl from one family to another. To provide a context for subsequent chapters of this book it is important first to introduce some of the principal structural features and accompanying ideology of India's predominant family and gender systems and their implications for child-rearing practices and women's lives. This is followed by a brief description of contemporary Bhubaneswar, its recent transformations and its long legacy as an administrative and cultural center in this part of India.

Patrilocal Family Structure and Ideology

In contrast to an American cultural system that tends to emphasize the individual and to idealize the autonomous nuclear family unit – which is just one segment of a potentially much larger family unit – India's culturally idealized family system places the welfare of the collective extended family above the interests of the individual; traces descent and inheritance through males (patrilineality);[4] encourages sets of related men to reside together and bring wives in from the outside (patrilocal residence); gives males authority over women; and bases family honor, in part, on the sexual purity of women, using such institutions as early arranged marriage and purdah to control female sexuality. This extended family unit, commonly referred to as the "joint family," is male oriented in both its structure and associated beliefs and values; hence, my use of the term "patrifocal family structure and ideology."[5]

Although India's contemporary patrifocal family system is unique in some respects, its patriarchal heritage is not. Over thousands of years India, like other state-level societies based upon intensive agriculture, evolved a system of social stratification and a set of dominant structures and beliefs that give precedence to males over females – to sons over daughters, fathers over mothers, husbands over wives, and so on.[6] Although they are more pronounced among upper castes and classes than among lower-status ones

8

and are more predominant in North India than in South India, these male-oriented structures and beliefs nevertheless constitute a sociocultural complex that profoundly affects women's lives throughout India.[7]

Ideally, a set of related men – a father and his sons or a set of brothers – and their wives and children constitute a joint family. Wives are outsiders who enter the family through marriage, whereas daughters are born into the family but must marry out. Because sons remain within the family, inheriting the family property and producing the next generation, they are preferred over daughters. Daughters not only leave the family when they marry, but their marriages may drain the family of economic resources. To arrange a daughter's marriage often requires that a dowry, or substantive gifts, be given to the groom and his family. However, to give away his virgin daughter in marriage is also considered a man's most sacred gift, and thus it is important to have daughters as well as sons.

In the past, a girl's marriage might be arranged when she was an infant or a young child and be consummated at puberty, at which time she would move to her in-laws' house and village. Two principles would have been operative: to marry off a girl before she is sexually mature and to marry her to someone older than herself. The latter principle would help to affirm the gender hierarchy and authority system that should prevail in the joint family, whereas the former would protect a girl's family from the potential dishonor that a sexually mature girl could produce if she were to have contact with inappropriate men outside of marriage. Both principles are still operative today, although in a somewhat changed form. Accordingly, from puberty on girls are increasingly protected until they marry and move to their husbands' and parents-in-law's household. Ideally, the girls are socialized to be obedient, self-sacrificing, and hardworking so that they will adjust well and contribute positively as wives and daughters-in-law in their new households. It is important to emphasize, however, that such qualities do *not* imply passivity; an initially shy, respectful wife and daughter-in-law must one day become a forceful mother, mother-in-law, and grandmother.

Shifts in women's roles are dramatic in India and are associated with significant changes in status and responsibility. At marriage, for instance, a girl leaves her natal family and comfortable position as a daughter to become a wife and daughter-in-law in her husband's household. She must abruptly switch from a relatively high status and reasonably carefree position in a familiar setting to a potentially low status and heavily work-laden position in a strange household. It is motherhood that marks a significant improvement in her position and a rise in status, particularly if she produces sons. Furthermore, with sons a woman will someday become a mother-in-law with authority over a set of daughters-in-law, and she will become a grandmother to her sons' children. Familial roles are particularly critical to a woman's identity and status in India.[8]

In describing India's patrifocal family system in a context of change I have, for several reasons, chosen to focus upon the lives of women. Although the literature on Indian women has improved, there is still very little that addresses women in urban settings and that focuses upon processes of modernization.[9] In Bhubaneswar I have had the opportunity to witness dramatic change for many young women as its first set of highly educated daughters has come of age. On the whole, the change has been more profound for women than for men and has raised serious questions about the relationship of women's education to marriage, dowry, and economic security – issues that will be explored in subsequent chapters. Furthermore, my initial focus on child-rearing practices provided me with an intimate perspective from which to view these women's lives. For two years I spent most of my time in the inner courtyards of peoples' homes watching children and their principal caretakers, mostly women – mothers, grandmothers, aunts, older sisters, and female cousins. As a woman doing research among women and children, it is not surprising that I tended to develop particularly close ties with women in Bhubaneswar.[10]

There are also theoretical reasons for my concentrating on women. When I began research in Bhubaneswar, the most recent women's movement in the United States had not yet begun. There was little of feminist consciousness and no feminist anthropology. I returned, however, in the late 1960s, to a country torn apart by the

Vietnam War and in the throes of a civil rights movement that helped stimulate a women's movement. That movement, during the past twenty-five years, has profoundly affected most academic disciplines as well as given rise to a new discipline, women's studies. There has been an outpouring of literature in this field, both descriptive and theoretical, that has stimulated me to reexamine my early research in Bhubaneswar as well as to undertake further research there and in other parts of Asia.

When I first went to India I had received training in such areas as kinship and social structure, child development, and theories of modernization, but with no mention of gender as a critical category. Women were essentially invisible. Ironically, I was to spend the next two years primarily with women in a highly sex-segregated, male-dominated society, and I was to watch principally women socialize the next generation of men and women. Despite the paucity of relevant theory, I was forced to think extensively about women's lives in relationship to men's and in relationship to the prevailing patrifocal family system in which the women were enmeshed. As I observed women and children and became involved in their lives, a dialogue began: Just as I wanted to learn about them, they wanted to know about me and about women's lives in the United States, about our family systems, and our ways of rearing children. A long-term conversation and friendship ensued.

To be more precise, I should say *dialogues* because my relationships have been with a diverse group of women and their families. In many respects Bhubaneswar encapsulates, on a small scale, aspects of India's contemporary social complexity. For example, although it is a predominantly Hindu town, other religious groups are also represented. In the Old Town, a hierarchy of caste Hindu communities – from several categories of Brahmin priests at the top to outcaste Washermen and Bauris (landless laborers) at the bottom – still exists. (India's caste system as it operates in Bhubaneswar is described in Chapter 3.) By contrast, the New Capital is dominated by a hierarchy of government servants who range from high-ranking administrators at the top to government-employed Sweepers (janitors by caste) at the bottom. Of course, numerous nongovernment communities help to sustain this burgeoning city. They range from wealthy merchants, on the one hand, to impoverished rickshaw wallas (bicycle "taxi drivers"), on the other hand. Family structure and systems of gender vary among these different communities, and therefore women's lives must be examined within the context of diverse family forms and systems of social stratification.

My initial two-year study of family organization and child-rearing practices required selecting a cross section of Bhubaneswar households – i.e., sets of family members residing together under one roof – which would represent some of that town's diversity.[11] Accordingly, I selected a caste-stratified set of Old Town households to observe and, in the New Capital, a set of households ranked by status in the government bureaucratic hierarchy (Chapter 2). I focused my 1965–67 study on twenty-four households altogether – half from each side of town – with 130 children under the age of ten together with their caretakers. The total population of these households at that time was 240 persons. Given that Bhubaneswar is predominantly a Hindu town and that my sample was small, I selected only Hindu families to study. In the intervening years I have returned regularly to Bhubaneswar and have remained in touch with all but one of my original sample of families.

My longitudinal research among these diverse families has made it possible for me to watch a set of young girls mature into young women and to see how their different family and community contexts have helped to shape their roles, their interpersonal relationships, and their attitudes. During this period, some of these girls have acquired an extensive education, while others have not. Some have married young, although rarely as young as their mothers and grandmothers had, while others have remained unmarried. Some, after marriage, have resided with their parents-in-law and continued to observe such practices as purdah; others have not. Some have become employed outside of the home – almost unheard of in the 1960s – and plan to remain employed even after they are married and have children. A few have even left unhappy marriages, a highly controversial and radical action in contemporary Bhubaneswar and one that their mothers and grandmothers would never have considered.

In addition to watching a set of young girls and their brothers grow up, I have been able to talk with parents and grandparents over an extended period about their daughters' changed circumstances. In a family system in which parents and grandparents hold authority and collective concerns generally outweigh individual ones, such attitudes are critical. Furthermore, the reflections of mothers and grandmothers about their own lives in light of their daughters' and granddaughters' new opportunities are both intriguing and illuminating. Their perspectives, together with those of the younger generation, may offer significant insights into the future of India's patrifocal family system.

Bhubaneswar: A City of Change and Transformation

I began this chapter with a brief description of some of the early morning sounds and aromas to which I awakened in the winter months of 1989. Now I want to provide readers with other glimpses of life in Bhubaneswar – evoking both place and time – to make more visible the settings for my subsequent examination of family life and gender roles.

The house in which I lived with my husband and son in the winter and spring of 1989 epitomized the rural and religious legacies of Bhubaneswar and the town's recent growth and development. The house was new, but two of its sides abutted rice fields, symbols of Bhubaneswar's rural and more bucolic past. The third side opened onto our landlord's and his brother's shared compound. And a fourth side faced the Cuttack-Puri Road, a two-lane paved road connecting Bhubaneswar with Cuttack, Orissa's largest city to the north, and Puri, a sacred town to the south. In 1965–67 this road had been adequate for the kinds of traffic that then existed: occasional buses and automobiles, a rare motorcycle, a moderate number of bicycles, and numerous bicycle rickshaws and bullock carts – the principal means by which farmers brought their

produce to town. (Although bullock carts have not altogether disappeared, most local produce is now brought in strapped to bicycles and motorcycles while more distant produce comes by truck or
train.) The Cuttack-Puri Road, which in the 1960s, with its sparse
traffic, I felt I could safely navigate on my small Jawa motorcycle,
had by 1989 become a dangerous quagmire of motorized vehicles
continuously blasting their horns and weaving their way at high
speeds through heavy pedestrian, bicycle, and rickshaw traffic. Ac-
cidents are frequent and severe.

Directly across this heavily traveled road are reminders of the
even more distant past: two of Bhubaneswar's beautifully sculp-
tured "beehive" temples dating from the tenth century. Muktesvara
Temple is my favorite among Bhubaneswar's hundreds of temples.
Often referred to as the "gem" of Orissan temples, it is small in
scale, carved like lacework from top to bottom, and covered with
small figures of river goddesses, naked ascetics, and lions. Despite
its location just off the main road, it engenders quietude and repose,
and for many years I have found it a restful retreat. A small number
of local residents come to it for daily worship, and hundreds of
Hindu pilgrims visit it weekly – another of the many reminders
that urban growth and modernization are not necessarily linked to
secularization. Indeed, with growth in transportation and local ac-
commodations many more pilgrims have been able to visit Bhubaneswar.

Muktesvara Temple is just one of approximately five hundred
temples that remain from Bhubaneswar's medieval period of Hindu
revivalism when some seven thousand temples and shrines were
constructed. Bhubaneswar has been a cultural and administrative
center at least three times over a two thousand-year period. Its
most recent "rebirth," as the capital of the new state of Orissa, is
only the latest transformation the town has experienced. I use the
imagery of rebirth both to mark Bhubaneswar's Hindu, Jain, and
Buddhist heritage – a heritage in which time is conceived of as
cyclical and events as recurrent – and to place that heritage within
a historical context of repetitive change and transformation. "Modernity" thereby becomes a relative term and Bhubaneswar's cur-

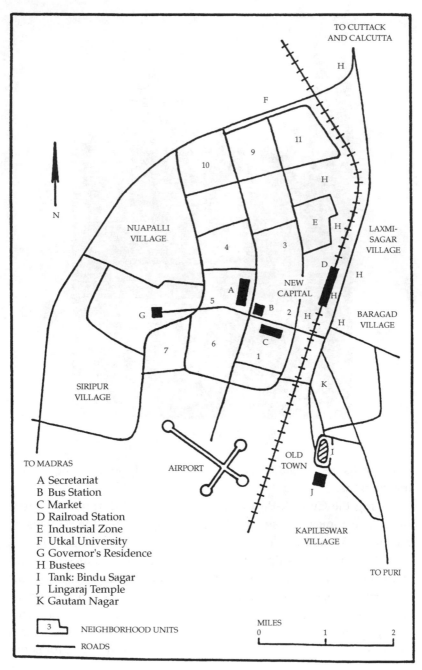

TO CUTTACK
AND CALCUTTA

NUAPALLI
VILLAGE

LAXMI-
SAGAR
VILLAGE

NEW
CAPITAL

BARAGAD
VILLAGE

SIRIPUR
VILLAGE

TO MADRAS

AIRPORT

OLD
TOWN

KAPILESWAR
VILLAGE

TO PURI

A Secretariat
B Bus Station
C Market
D Railroad Station
E Industrial Zone
F Utkal University
G Governor's Residence
H Bustees
I   Tank: Bindu Sagar
J   Lingaraj Temple
K Gautam Nagar

3   NEIGHBORHOOD UNITS

ROADS

MILES
0   1   2

Figure 2. Map of Bhubaneswar

15

Plate 1. Muktesvara Temple

rent status as a state capital just one of several significant incarnations.

Taking the Cuttack-Puri Road south of the Old Town for a few miles, one comes to a small village built up against the remains of an ancient walled town known as Sisupalgarh. Sisupalgarh represents Bhubaneswar's first known transformation. It dates from the third century B.C.E., when King Ashoka, one of the principal rulers of North India, conquered the town and made it a provincial capital in his new Buddhist empire. Ashokan edicts, carved in stone and dating from this period – among India's earliest inscribed records – are located near the road a few miles further south. Thus, for some

Plate 2. Close up of female figures on Muktesvara Temple

seven centuries before Bhubaneswar became a religious center for Hindus, it was a Buddhist center.

Predating Bhubaneswar's Buddhist incarnation, however, is its Jain heritage. Archaeological, historical, and linguistic evidence suggests that during the fourth and third centuries B.C.E. Bhubaneswar was a center for Jain religion and the capital of the Kalinga kingdom. Jain monastic caves dating from that period are still found in hillsides to the north of the New Capital. Thus, the hundreds of Hindu temples and shrines that today are scattered throughout the Old Town represent Bhubaneswar's third major incarnation. They date back to the sixth century, when the town experienced a period of Hindu revivalism and became the cultural center of the Utkal kingdom with a flourishing of the regional language, Oriya. Between the sixth and twelfth centuries Bhubaneswar was transformed into one of India's major Hindu temple towns,[12] becoming a center of pilgrimage and learning that in legend is compared with Varanasi.[13]

Bhubaneswar thrived during this medieval period. Its many temples and shrines attracted throngs of pilgrims who had to be housed, fed, and assisted in performing rituals giving rise to numerous monastic institutions, many of which continue to this day.[14] People were also attracted to the town's sacred waters. An underground river that was famous for healing physical and spiritual illness wells to the surface near Lingaraj Temple, creating a large sacred lake known as Bindu Sagar and filling several smaller pools and tanks that were used for drinking and bathing. By the late nineteenth century, however, when the town's ancient sculptures were surveyed by an official chronicler for the British Raj, the majority of Bhubaneswar's temples had been deserted.[15] Nonetheless, Lingaraj Temple, originally known as Tribhuvaneshwar (Lord of the three worlds) Temple, from which Bhubaneswar gets its name, remained in use, and it continues to be the Old Town's principal temple complex.[16]

Glimpses of the Old Town, 1989

Not far from Muktesvara Temple – several blocks by meandering dirt paths – lies Bindu Sagar, the sacred lake that marks the physical and symbolic center of the Old Town. It continues to be associated with Bhubaneswar's principal temple complex, Lingaraj, which, as a non-Hindu, I am not allowed to enter. Each morning local residents bathe in Bindu Sagar: young children who laugh and play in the water as they soap themselves and shampoo their hair; men – often sadhus – Hindu ascetics or holy men who sit by the side of the water in meditation after bathing; and clusters of lower-status women who chat with one another as they wash themselves and their clothes. These women are highly adept at changing from the clinging wet sari in which they bathed to a fresh dry one without improperly exposing themselves. Bindu Sagar is both the sacred and the social center of the Old Town. By about 8:30 a.m., however, most of these activities are over for the day, and it becomes a place for pilgrims and tourists to visit and perhaps to immerse themselves in its sacred waters.

Spiraling out from Bindu Sagar like the spokes of a wheel are highly congested, caste-based residential neighborhoods, together

Plate 3. Aerial view of the Old Town with Lingaraj Temple in the foreground and Bindu Sagar in the background

with monastic institutions (ashrams), temples, and shops. Only two roads entering the Old Town can accommodate motorized vehicles. Most Old Town roads are narrow paths that wander through local neighborhoods and can be used only by foot and bicycle traffic. As I traverse these meandering lanes, I wonder in what ways things

Plate 4. One of the bathing ghats of Bindu Sagar

have changed in the past twenty-five years. There is little overt change. Most of the houses that abut the lanes look the same as they did in 1965–67 and are inhabited by portions of the same families. Although many of them are now hooked up to electricity, they still do not have such other modern amenities as piped water, flush latrines, gas stoves, or refrigerators. Open gutters on the sides of lanes continue to serve as the toilets for young children and the dumping ground for other household refuse. Their smells mix with those of cooking oils, spices, incense, thatch, and cow dung. The last-named is caked in large round patties on walls to dry and to be used later as cooking fuel. Cow dung is also used to plaster mud walls and dirt floors, which are less common now that most residents have covered their floors with cement. Some families, however, cannot afford to do so while others have rooms that must remain dirt floored to house cows at night. It is an advantage to have one's own milk supply. However, there are resident Cowherder families in the Old Town who still specialize in raising cows and selling their milk. Cows are let out to forage during the day and are part of the life of these lanes and neighborhoods.

Clustered between Bindu Sagar and Lingaraj Temple are numerous small shops that supply Old Town residents with the few packaged items and manufactured goods that they use: cooking oils, spices, flours, lentils, bottled soft drinks, fuel for lanterns, writing pads and pens for school children, soap, shampoo, and hair ornaments. There are also numerous tea stalls that sell locally prepared sweets to Old Town residents, pilgrims, and tourists. Old Town shops and tea stalls are small wooden sheds; there are no Western-style stores. However, a controversial new "shopping center" is under construction, and it will have stores with display windows, doors to enter, lights, and air conditioning.

In 1965–67, the boundaries of the Old Town were the Cuttack-Puri Road on the east, the railroad to the west, and rice fields to the north and south of town (Figure 2). The two roads entering the Old Town from the New Capital were unpaved, red arteries that during the wet season meandered through brilliant green rice fields. Beyond the railroad – Orissa's British-built link with the rest of India – were more open red and green fields and a small airport visited daily by two or three small propeller jets. By 1989, the airport has been expanded to accommodate larger and more frequently scheduled jet planes, the roads are paved, and the open fields between the railroad and the airport are rapidly being filled with houses and apartments.

Glimpses of the New Capital, 1989

In the New Capital the equivalent of the Old Town's sacred temple and water tank are the state capital buildings, which, together with the central bus station and marketplace, create a city center. In the 1960s this central market was the only shopping area for fresh produce and retail items. By 1989, however, smaller shopping areas have mushroomed throughout different parts of the city.

The New Capital represents Bhubaneswar's most recent transformation into a bureaucratic and cultural center. But this time it has become a state capital within a new nation-state, and its development in many respects symbolizes India's movement toward Western-style "modernity." For example, Otto Koenigsberger, a

Plate 5 (above and on facing page). New Capital under construction in 1964, with the Kandagiri Hills in the background

much sought-after European architect who emigrated to India in the 1930s, was hired to plan the new city. Koenigsberger envisioned Bhubaneswar as more than just a government town; it was to be a "lively nerve centre of provincial activities where workers and their representatives, manufacturers, businessmen, scientists, officials and last but not the least, politicians [would] meet and collaborate in the development of all aspects of provincial life."[17] In this, the town's latest "birth," commerce, science, and politics rather than temples, priests, and pilgrims were to predominate.

The New Capital was laid out along a Western-style grid pattern with major avenues and less major roads intersecting and creating a series of rectangular areas known as "units" (Figure 2). In 1965–67, there were eleven such units housing most government servants and their families. Imposing flowering trees and large houses set back from the road with fenced yards and Western-style gardens line the major avenues. These Type VII and VIII six-room houses are assigned to senior ministers and high-ranking government offi-

cials. Inside the residential units, houses are smaller and accommodate middle-level government servants. Both the large and the
small government houses are covered with white stucco, have
hook-ups to water and electricity, and, were it not for the presence
of cows and other livestock, resemble houses in American suburbia.

To a Western eye, the New Capital does not have the color of
the Old Town with its Byzantine streets and splendid medieval
temples. New Capital neighborhoods are, however, less congested
than Old Town ones, and most houses in them, with their modern
amenities, are from a Western perspective very comfortable. As the
city has grown it has incorporated and gradually surrounded five
small villages. These, with their mud-walled and thatched houses
and scattered rice fields, help to create a diverse and picturesque
urban landscape. Private housing areas have also blossomed since
the 1960s, adding to the architectural variety of the New Capital.
Squatter colonies and slums have cropped up in several areas and
house people who constitute some of the new city's service popu-

Plate 6. Orissa Legislative Assembly

lation: bicycle rickshaw wallas, washermen, cowherders, small shopkeepers, and day laborers. These are Bhubaneswar's "invisible" inhabitants – those that were not planned for but who are essential to any city's infrastructure.

One such group, however, – government-employed Sweepers – was planned for. A special area known as the Sweeper Colony, located near the railroad tracks and not far from where I resided in 1965–67, was set aside for members of this untouchable caste. The idea of interspersing government servants by varying housing in each New Capital unit did not extend to this outcaste group essential for cleaning government offices and houses. Sweepers were provided with their own housing, originally a row of connected cement one-room quarters. Each room is intended to house a family. Unlike other New Capital housing, these quarters do not have running water. Sweeper families must procure water for bathing, drinking, and cooking from a central public water pump. The colony also includes its own open-walled primary school, thus keeping these outcaste children separate from others.

In 1965–67, Sweeper Colony housing was already inadequate for

Plate 7. New Capital street scene, 1965

the number of Sweepers that had migrated to Bhubaneswar to find work. One Sweeper family, a part of my study for the last thirty years, responded by building themselves a two-room, mud-walled, thatched house on open land adjacent to the colony. This village-style house, more spacious than its cement counterpart and having some open land around it, always seemed to me to be more pleasant than the official government-provided houses. Today it stands huddled among the many dozens of similar mud-walled houses that have been built by newer immigrants, and the now densely packed Sweeper Colony looks like other urban squatter colonies and slums.

The changes in the New Capital's principal east-west artery, Raj Path, symbolize other ways in which the town has changed since the 1960s. Raj Path has grown from two lanes handling a modest amount of vehicular traffic to a divided road with heavy traffic and electric stoplights. The lights, which were installed in 1989, are staffed at busy times with police to encourage drivers to attend to them. Drivers also need to watch out for cows, which are a continual hazard. Despite increasingly heavy traffic, cows saunter along

25

Plate 8. Type IV officer quarter

or sleep in the middle of Raj Path, confident that vehicles will skirt them. Not only has the traffic on Raj Path and other major avenues increased in volume, but it has also changed in makeup. In 1965–67, men made up most of the pedestrians and drivers; women were rarely seen in such public areas, except for girls as they were carefully escorted to school in automobiles or rickshaws. The purchasing of food, for example, was entirely the responsibility of men – husbands, fathers, or male servants. In the evening, some women, in the company of men, came to the covered market area to buy saris, linens, and other household items. At that time I was the only woman to be seen in the open produce market, and, as a woman riding a small motorcycle, I was a total anomaly on the roads as well. By 1989, dramatic change had occurred: Women were a public presence along Raj Path and in the market areas, and women on bicycles and on the backs of motor scooters were a common sight. Some women even drove their own motor scooters and automobiles.

Raj Path has changed in other ways as well. Shops and produce are no longer restricted to the enclosed market areas but have spread (illegally) to most available sidewalks. There are many stalls

Plate 9. Type VIII senior officer's quarter

of beautifully arranged oranges, apples, mangoes, and bananas. Along the sidewalk, one can now purchase anything from handmade baskets, to sandals, shirts, brilliantly colored nylon lines, and armadillo shell (a medicinal item). Colored posters of Hindu deities and major historical figures such as Nehru, Gandhi, and John F. Kennedy are artistically arranged for sale on the sidewalk. And boxes of fresh eggs are piled high here and there, ready for purchase. Most egg vendors are also prepared with sidewalk burners and woks in which they can readily fry or scramble an egg on the spot for the hungry pedestrian. In the 1960s, by contrast, eggs were a rare commodity in Bhubaneswar.

Other kinds of commercial changes are also evident in the New Capital. A new electronics shopping area sells televisions and video players. Video tape rental stores, with supplies of Indian and American films, are abundant, as are copy centers and film-developing agencies. In 1965–67 all film had to be sent to Calcutta for processing; now it can be reliably done in Bhubaneswar. Interspersed with electronics shops are signs for other such up-to-date services as "computerized astrology." Five new hotels have been built, one of them a five-star Oberoi. Each hotel houses a restaurant, several of which are patronized by local residents as well as by out-of-town visitors. In 1965–67, other than the occasional small tea stall frequented only by men, there was only one restaurant in the New Capital. Local residents did not dine out. Now restaurants are more numerous and diverse, serving several different regional varieties of Indian cuisine as well as some Chinese food. What is most striking, however, is that families – men with their wives and children – dine out together, something unheard of in the 1960s and not yet realized in the Old Town.

There are many markers of change and modernity as one explores the New Capital. However, there are no dramatic skyscrapers, and there is only a small amount of industry. Contrary to Koenigsberger's vision, most planners of the New Capital desired an administrative town with a minimum of industry with its potential for noise, pollution, and labor problems.[18] Only in the late 1980s did the town planners begin to zone some areas of the city for light industry. What has principally transformed Bhubaneswar into a town that represents modernity, I would argue, is the access to Western-style secular schooling that it offers residents as well as the aspirations, occupations, and status system that such schooling implies.

Coincident with becoming an administrative center, Bhubaneswar also became a center of education. Between 1950 and 1965, for example, two universities, three colleges, and a special college of education serving the entire eastern region of India were opened. New primary and secondary schools were built throughout the New Capital, and schools in the Old Town and surrounding villages were expanded and upgraded. By 1965 all residents of Bhubaneswar had access to schools from the primary to the postgraduate level, and the establishment of colleges and specialized professional schools continues into the present. Among the schools that have been added are a training center for the restaurant business, a graduate school in education, and a women's college specializing in computer science.

This rapid expansion of public education is intricately linked with other forces for change. The proliferation of schools makes

Plate 10. New Capital Sweeper Colony and public water tap

possible new job opportunities, the concept of a "career" choice, first-time employment for middle- and upper-status women, and family social mobility. In this respect Bhubaneswar symbolizes well the new ideals of nationalism and democracy in post-Independence India. Formal education is no longer restricted either to the traditionally literate castes or to an elite set of civil servants trained to serve the British Raj, but has been opened to the general populace. Furthermore, the state of Orissa, with its history of economic neglect and stagnation under the British, has enthusiastically endorsed the goals of educational equality, economic development, and technological change.

The Bhubaneswar of today clearly represents a new incarnation, but one that is deeply rooted in the past. A serious problem with concepts of "modernity" and "modernization" is that they are frequently used in opposition to "tradition." Accordingly, a false dichotomy is built between the new and the old that obscures complex processes of integration and synthesis.[19] This is in part a result of Western-style thinking that tends to stress linear change – a movement *away* from one state of existence *toward* another, improved, state of existence – whereas in reality change is sporadic

29

and necessarily rooted in tradition. Over its many centuries Bhubaneswar has experienced periods of political and cultural up-
heaval as well as long periods of stability. It brings to this
contemporary period of transformation, therefore, a history of
change as well as long-established social structures and cultural
traditions that are salient to any analysis of family organization and
gender ideology.

Conclusion

Today, in both the United States and India, many questions are
being asked about the nature of family, of women's roles, and of
child care. Each nation however, comes to these questions from a
very different historical trajectory and set of cultural assumptions
and values. Longitudinal research among a cross section of families
in Bhubaneswar has provided me an opportunity to examine these
issues for one part of India. I shall try to give readers a qualitative
understanding of the inner dynamics of life in these families –
especially that of the women in them – as all members have confronted, adapted to, consolidated, rejected, or been excluded from
the forces of modernization and urbanization.

Chapter 2 will introduce readers to my fieldwork experiences in
Bhubaneswar and to the research strategies that I have used over
the past thirty years. In Chapter 3, on the Hindu patrifocal joint
family as it operated in the Old Town in the 1960s, I describe child-
rearing practices as I observed them in 1965–67 in an effort to
explicate how, from infancy, human behavior is molded to fit the
cultural expectations of joint family life existent at that time. I also
examine the gender differences embedded in this process to explain
how young girls are prepared for their lives as daughters-in-law,
wives, and mothers in their husbands' homes.

In Chapter 4 I compare family life in the Old Town with that in
the New Capital. Again, I use a developmental approach, analyzing
subtle differences in child-rearing practices that I observed in 1965–
67 and their implications for women's roles and interpersonal be-

havior. Chapter 5 focuses specifically on poor, low-status families for whom poverty, more than location in the old or new part of Bhubaneswar, determines the lives of women.

Chapters 6 and 7 address the changes in women's lives that I have been able to document over the past several decades. Dramatic new educational opportunities and girls' access to them for the first time are the subject of Chapter 6. I discuss the implications of such change for the patrifocal family system, which for centuries has depended upon the early arranged marriage of relatively uneducated daughters to older, more highly educated men. Chapter 7 presents the perspectives of three generations of women – mothers, daughters, and grandmothers – to the changes in education, family life, and gender roles that have occurred since my initial research in 1965–67. It is based upon the tape-recorded intergenerational interviews with women, and some men, that I conducted in 1989.

Finally, Chapter 8 addresses change in Hindu family and gender systems more broadly by comparing research from Bhubaneswar with studies of other parts of India and by situating the research theoretically. Theories of modernization in relationship to different cultural constructions of personhood are examined in an effort to understand not only how, in the broadest sense, the psychocultural development of women in Hindu India may differ from that of Western women but also how that developmental process may be changing. The implications of such change for India's patrifocal family system, as it is cross-cut by caste and class, are then considered.

Because my goal has been to write a book that is both accessible and carefully documented, I have mixed an informal narrative with numerous excerpts from field notes, parent-child behavior protocols, and interviews. Tables provide some quantitative information as well. My extensive use of excerpts from my field notes is intended to illustrate the kinds of information that I have used to forge more general points and to bring the reader closer to the people and situations I describe. Generally, I have selected excerpts because they are representative of numerous – sometimes hundreds – of similar events that I observed and recorded. Sometimes I have selected an excerpt because it represents for me a critical moment of insight into the family lives I have been trying to understand. All excerpts are dated so that the reader can know exactly what period—from the mid-1960s to the early 1990s – they represent. Finally, I use excerpts to make the text more compelling and to bring forth the "voices" of both the anthropologist and her Bhubaneswar "kin." My intent is to give readers a qualitative sense of people, place, and time as well as an enhanced appreciation of anthropological fieldwork in a complex society.

CHAPTER TWO

———

Field Methods and Longitudinal Research in Bhubaneswar

It takes a mixture of idealism, audacity, and naïveté to undertake one's first anthropological fieldwork in another society. One sets out expecting to enter a radically different sociocultural system as an empathic outsider, to learn in depth about it as a partial insider, and then to communicate to others with as much accuracy as possible what one has learned. And all of this involves moving back and forth between different languages and different sets of sociocultural assumptions, beliefs, and value systems. To begin such an endeavor takes, first of all, the conviction that it is possible to communicate across cultures.

I began my sojourn in India with just this idealism and also with, I suspect, some degree of audacity and naïveté. My journey began with a three-month stay in Poona, Maharashtra, at the Linguistic Institute of the Deccan College, where I was instructed in Oriya, the language that I needed to know in order to do fieldwork in the state of Orissa.[1] After mastering the rudiments of Oriya grammar and acquiring a modest vocabulary, I set off for Bhubaneswar. I was twenty-five years old and a recently married graduate student. As the third American to participate in the Harvard-Bhubaneswar Project, my initial transition to life in Bhubaneswar was reasonably smooth. My most critical challenge was to meet as quickly as possible a variety of Old Town and New Capital families with young children who would allow me to observe them regularly for the next twenty months. This required audacity on my part and an unusual degree of kindness and hospitality on theirs. Why, I have subsequently wondered, did these people allow a strange American woman to enter their homes and observe, month after month, some of the most intimate aspects of their daily lives? The answer is complex. It lies in part in the nature of family life and commitment to hospitality in India and, reciprocally, in my efforts to adapt to that family system by speaking Oriya and by dressing and eating in a culturally suitable manner. My efforts to offer a straightforward explanation of my research goals were, I believe, also critically important.

One cannot discount, however, the effects of India's colonial heritage and my position of privilege as a consequence: I was light skinned, Western, and educated. Although most Bhubaneswar residents had had little or no direct contact with the British, they undoubtedly had stereotypic views of their previous rulers. I experienced neither antagonism nor obsequiousness on this account; nevertheless, my light skin and education gave me status. My gender, however, was potentially problematic: Why was a young woman doing independent research? As an American woman, I was perceived both as distinct from the British and as something of a curiosity, and, as a married woman, I was more acceptable as a researcher than had I been unmarried. Whereas my privileged position may initially have gained me entrée to Indian homes, my "difference," as well as my commitment to learning from others rather than imposing my views upon them, made it possible in the end, I think, for me to do longitudinal research.

Sample of Families

My first research goal in Bhubaneswar was to identify the twenty-four households – that portion of a joint family residing together – that would represent the different systems of social stratification in each part of town. This meant finding families of different "caste" statuses in the Old Town and different "class" statuses in the New Capital. Because most Old Town residents identified themselves by their subcaste and lived largely in caste-based neighborhoods, it was not difficult to identify families of different social strata based upon the age-old criteria of caste, that is, birth into an extended patrilineal kin group, caste-associated occupation, and degree of ritual purity. India's caste system is vast and complex and has preoccupied numerous Western social scientists.[2] Very briefly, to summarize some of this extensive literature: One's caste status is based upon ties of kinship. Individuals inherit from their fathers their status within a localized kinship-based caste group known as a *jati* (the Hindi term for "caste"), or as a "subcaste" in the anthropological literature. *Jatis* are large, endogamous descent groups – groups within which one should marry – that are locally and regionally ranked by both ritual and socioeconomic criteria.

The basic Hindu paradigm used throughout India for ritually ranking groups of people is based upon the ancient emphatic hymn in which Brahmins (priests) emerge from the head of the primordial cosmic man, Kshatriyas (kings, warriors) from his arms, Vaishyas (merchants, traders) from his thighs, and Shudras (workers) from his feet. In this fourfold class (*varna*) system, dating back to Aryan society in ancient North India, those groups at the top (head) are considered inherently purer than those below them, with Shudras at the bottom (feet) being the least pure group. Below the Shudras are those people with no *varna* position who are commonly known as "Untouchables" and are considered inherently impure and ritually polluting to others. Within each of these five categories, however, are numerous subdivisions that have local and regional rankings; that is, there are different kinds of Brahmins, Kshatriyas, Vaishyas, Shudras, and Untouchables. Thus, throughout India there are literally thousands of different *jatis* or caste groups that vie with each other for position. The ritual status of the *jatis* is not monolithic and is believed to be affected by their members' behavior in this and in previous lifetimes. The Hindu principles of reincarnation, dharma (righteousness, moral actions), and karma (fate based upon one's past actions) underlie the caste system.

Jatis have an occupational as well as a ritual identity, and in many parts of India they are economically interdependent. Some have hereditary patron-client relationships: For example, Brahmin and Kshatriya landowners are often served by lower-status Shudras; some Shudras may work the land for them, and others provide such personal services as barbering, clothes washing, and house cleaning. Still other Shudras specialize in crafts such as carpentry, pottery making, weaving, and metalwork, and others are Cowherders who produce milk for their patrons. Hereditary occupations can also affect a caste's ritual status: Handling other peoples' dirty clothes, for example, makes Washermen ritually unclean, whereas pottery making has no such association for Potters. Therefore, communities often make a distinction between "clean" and "unclean" Shudras.

Once I had identified the local *jatis* of the Old Town and their status relative to one another, selecting a representative sample of families to study became a question of meeting families and gaining their acceptance (in anthropological parlance, "establishing rapport").[3] Expanding on a few initial introductions, I was able to use a network approach to become acquainted with numerous Old Town families that represented different *jatis*. Ultimately, my problem was not one of finding enough families willing to allow me to study them, but of meeting far too many, all of whom wanted to be visited on a regular basis. How could I explain sampling without insulting peoples' hospitality? My solution was to know privately that a particular family in a neighborhood was part of my sample, and on any given day to initiate a visit with that family, but then also to spend time with the other families who expected or had requested that I do so. In this manner, I came to know quite well entire Old Town neighborhoods and extended families, not just individual households.

To find representative families in the New Capital, I also used a network approach based upon a few initial introductions, but the families I came to know were scattered all over this rapidly urbanizing and expanding town. Unlike in the Old Town, there were no long-established neighborhoods of interconnected families in the New Capital; rather, people resided in newly built government "units" that had a mixture of houses ranging from Type I to Type VIII. These roman numerals designated houses of different sizes that were assigned to government servants according to their status in the civil service hierarchy. Top officials lived in large Type VI–VIII houses, whereas middle- and lower-level civil servants had smaller Type I–V houses. One's house was a marker of status in the government hierarchy, which in turn identified the individual's level of education and salary (the salary was public information). In 1965–67, the civil service hierarchy underlay an emerging class system that prevailed in the New Capital.[4] There, most men who were heads of households had attained their class status not simply by virtue of their birth into a particular caste, but by their educational and occupational achievements. Nonetheless, one cannot discount the effects of caste even in the New Capital. People of higher castes had generally had more educational opportunities than people of lower castes and thus outnumbered others in the higher ranks of government. As previously mentioned, at the bottom of the government system were the Sweepers (janitors by caste), who were assigned their own residential area.

After several months of meeting Bhubaneswar families I was able to select a set of twenty-four households that represented the systems of stratification in each part of town (Table 1). In the Old Town, my sample included four Brahmin (priestly) households at the top of the caste (localized *jati*) hierarchy, four ritually clean Shudra households (e.g., Carpenter) at the middle level, and four unclean (e.g., Washerman) or Untouchable (e.g., Bauri) households at the bottom of the caste system as it was represented in this region of India. These localized *jatis* were ranked by both ritual and socio-economic criteria, a system that was beginning to be affected by new educational and occupational opportunities in Bhubaneswar. Nonetheless, marriage was still within caste, with sons remaining in the natal family and *jati* and with daughters marrying out, sometimes into a family of slightly higher *jati* status. Hypergamy (marrying a girl upwards) is one means that the patrifocal family has of trying to improve its status; thus, daughters are an essential part of that process. To enhance their marriageability and the family's honor, daughters' purity had to be kept intact (see Chapters 3 and 8). Caste status and the sexual control of women in India are, therefore, inextricably interwoven.

My New Capital sample included four high-ranking government officials and their families at the top, four middle-level government families, and four low-level government families at the bottom. Whereas most Old Town families were formally joint in structure, the New Capital families were predominantly nuclear. As I will

Table 1. Old Town and New Capital Sample Households

Socio-economic status	Old Town		New Capital	
	Caste	Occupation of household head	Caste	Occupation of household head
Upper	Brahmin	Temple servant	Brahmin	Superintending engineer
	Brahmin	Temple servant	Karan	Deputy secretary, Revenue Dept.
	Brahmin	Contractor	Karan	Deputy secretary, Works & Transp. Dept.
	Brahmin	Elementary school teacher	Karan	Town planner
Middle	Barber	Barber	Brahmin	Asst. Sec., Finance Dept.
	Cowherder	Selling milk & govt. clerk	Bania	Sec., Construction Dept.
	Carpenter	Carpenter	Brahmin	Dept. Controller, Mining Corp.
	Bricklayer	Bricklayer	Karan	Community Develop. Dept.
Lower	Washerman	Washerman	Sweeper	Govt. Sweeper
	Washerman	Washerman	Sweeper	Govt. Sweeper
	Bauri	Laborer	Kayastha	Govt. Messenger
	Bauri	Laborer	Weaver	Govt. Nightwatchman

explain in Chapters 3 and 4, however, "nuclearity" of immediate household does not preclude psychological and socioeconomic "jointness."

Finally, for the purposes of my initial research, I selected families that had at least two children under the age of ten. Many of the families, especially the large joint ones in the Old Town, had older children as well. In Table 2 the sample of children upon which I focused are presented by their Old Town or New Capital residence, their caste/class status, and their sex. Not surprisingly, there were far more children (82) in my Old Town sample, where most of the households were structurally joint, than there were in the New Capital sample (48), where most of the households were structurally nuclear. There was also a significant imbalance between girls and boys: In the Old Town sample boys heavily outnumbered girls, in contrast to the New Capital sample. An unbalanced sex ratio, with boys outsurviving girls in infancy and early childhood, has

Table 2. *Number and Sex of Sample Children (1965–67)*

Status	Old Town		New Capital		Total
	M	F	M	F	
Upper	23	12	7	11	53
Middle	12	8	10	10	40
Lower	12	15	5	5	37
Total	47	35	22	26	130

been documented for parts of North India.[5] Whether the discrepancy between girls and boys in my Old Town sample was the result of a preference for sons and the neglect of infant daughters is not something for which I have evidence. Nonetheless, it is suggestive that in the New Capital, where the ideology with respect to sons and daughters has been changing, the girls in my sample actually outnumbered the boys.

These, then, are the families upon which I concentrated my initial research for the next twenty months and, subsequently, for the intervening years between 1967 and the present.

My 1965–67 Residence

Between 1965 and 1967 my husband and I lived in a transitional area located between the Old Town and the New Capital. To prevent my becoming identified with any single caste or class group, it was important that I not reside with a particular family. It also turned out to be serendipitous that the house we were able to rent was located in Gautam Nagar (see Figure 2), a newly developing area directly north of the Old Town and east of the railroad. This location gave me easy access to both parts of Bhubaneswar without identifying me with either one.

Not one of the planned "units" of the New Capital, Gautam Nagar was and remains a kaleidoscope of old and new elements. "Old" here is a relative term because the area includes several medieval temples, on the one hand, and a large monastic institution and school – the Ramakrishna Mission – established in 1919, on the other. "New" is also a relative term in that it refers to newly constructed buildings, some of which represent "modernity" (e.g., the state court house, the state travel lodge for tourists, and a movie theater) while others represent "tradition" (e.g., a medical clinic that specializes in traditional, non-Western *ayurvedic* techniques of healing). Gautam Nagar was transitional not only in the time periods and value orientations represented by its buildings but also in the mixture of residents who had moved to it from both the Old Town and the New Capital and in the range of castes and socioeconomic groups they represented. The nouveau riche who have purchased plots of land and constructed mansions for themselves in this area live side-by-side with the poor, some of whom reside in mud-walled, thatched huts. Most Gautam Nagar residents, however, are of the emerging middle class.

My home for two years epitomized many of these elements. It was a middle-class, "modern" home. Rectangular in shape, it had four cement-floored rooms, plus bathing and cooking areas. It was hooked up to electricity, which worked about half the time, and to the municipal water system, which brought water for about one hour each morning and each evening. A water storage tank was on the roof, but the piped water never arrived with sufficient pressure to fill it. Lacking a well, I soon learned to store water in oil drums to get through both the middle of the day and those days when no water came at all. (Much of Orissa is subject to droughts.) We kept buckets handy for "flushing" the floor-level toilet, for bathing, and for washing dishes. In the kitchen, a room with four walls and a water tap at floor level, I installed a two-burner, table-top gas cooking unit and a small electric refrigerator – the only one in the immediate neighborhood.

All four rooms of our house had shuttered windows, without screens or glass panes, which let in fresh air, sunshine, and a menagerie of wildlife that included toads in the bathroom, shrews in the kitchen, geckoes on every wall, and several species of bird, not to mention insects. One bird family actually nested for a season on top of the electric fan over our bed. I had persistent visions of cobras, a known danger in the area, entering through the open drains in the bathroom and kitchen – which, fortunately, they never did – and I took solace in the daily visit of a wild mongoose.

Unlike a more traditional Indian home whose rooms would be built around a central courtyard, our house was more Western in style. Its rooms were built in a block and were surrounded by an open walled yard in which, with the help of a gardener (Mali caste), I installed a vegetable garden and flowers. The yard was also home to our cook's cow and, later, to the cow's offspring. Our basil bush and marigolds, both used for purposes of worship by Hindus, were popular with neighbors. Abutting one side of the yard was a large, two-story home inhabited by a Brahmin family; on another side was the state travel lodge for tourists; on the third side was an open field extending up to the lovely, medieval Rameshwar Temple; and directly in front of the house was a small tea stall, a government office building, and a one-room mud hut that housed the night watchman for the office building and his wife and two children. Life immediately around me was, then, a confluence of the new and the old, the prosperous and the poor. Because of the open fields wildlife was still reasonably plentiful, but the only large animals left in this urbanizing area were jackals. My landlord told me that when he first built the house he occasionally saw tigers, but by 1965 those days were gone. Wild game had been pushed far to the outskirts of town, and by 1989 there were no longer any empty fields in Gautam Nagar that large animals could inhabit.

"Establishing Rapport"

In my initial efforts to explain to my sample families why I was in Bhubaneswar and why I wanted to spend time with them, I said that I was interested in child-rearing practices (using an Oriya expression that I had been taught, *poriba pila* – literally, "to bring up children") and that I wanted to come into their homes to watch how they took care of their children. In the Old Town, this explanation did little to help families understand my goals. The expression "to *rear* children" made little sense in a context in which children were expected simply to grow up. Most Old Town resi-

41

dents did not think of child rearing as a process, let alone as a process to watch and to reflect on. However, I came to understand that there were numerous cultural assumptions about what constituted good child care underlying what people considered a normal family life and that these could be inferred from adult interactions with children. Old Town residents were largely following unarticulated cultural scripts that probably had evolved over a long period of adaptation to an agricultural way of life.[6]

Some Old Town residents found my efforts to explicate the Oriya expression I had learned strange and amusing. I, too, must have seemed strange – a young, highly educated, recently married woman who wanted to watch other peoples' children rather than reside with her parents-in-law and produce children of her own. Nonetheless, people accepted me – in part because of the introductions I had used and in part because of my genuine interest in children and in everyday household activities. It was obvious that I had much to learn and that they had much to teach me. Thus I was welcomed into the inner courtyards – the bathing, cooking, and living quarters for women – of houses that were built to seclude women. Another of my attractions was that to women in purdah I represented the outside world; I was a novelty in their otherwise highly restricted and somewhat routinized lives. I even became a confidante for some of the women in their struggles to adjust to what at times must have been an onerous household hierarchy.

In the New Capital, by contrast, many residents did understand the somewhat abstract concept "child rearing." Particularly among upper- and middle-status families in which men were highly educated and wives had had some exposure to Western-style schooling, it was not such a foreign concept. More significant, however, was that these men and women were part of a new and increasingly competitive socioeconomic system, and they knew that their children's success in school would determine their future employment and marriage opportunities. Thus, they were beginning to focus on their children's development in a way that was familiar to Westerners but was clearly bizarre to Old Town residents at the time. My research goals were, therefore, more easily understood and accepted in the New Capital. For some parents I was even a possible source of information about "appropriate" child-rearing practices and effective techniques of family planning. For most New Capital mothers, however, I was a potential friend in their isolated residential communities. Unlike women in the Old Town, New Capital women did not reside in neighborhoods where they were surrounded by extended kin and long-term neighbors of similar caste and background.

Regardless of which side of town they lived in, life among low-status families was governed principally by poverty and by the need for everyone – men, women, and children – to work. Men and women worked outside the home at whatever jobs they could get, leaving their children behind to care for one another and to do a myriad of household tasks. In these families, children were perceived principally as household workers. The parents concern was not so much one of "rearing" children but of simply getting them to the stage at which they could take care of themselves, help out with younger siblings and cousins, and responsibly perform chores. The organization of daily life in these households was relatively informal and flexible, which made my comings and goings exceedingly easy. There were no pretensions about rules of caste purity, sex segregation, hospitality, and so on. These families simply seemed to take pleasure in my interest in them, welcomed me as an occasional diversion in a life of heavy work, and appreciated my small gifts in return.

For me, "establishing rapport" meant not only that Bhubaneswar families would welcome me into their homes but that they would not stop their usual activities on my account. It meant my being able to come and go with a minimum of disruption – just a greeting and, at some point, a cup of tea. My principal objective was to observe the interactions of parents and children in as natural a setting as possible – to sit in the corner of a courtyard and watch or to follow someone from room to room without seriously disrupting or affecting that person's behavior. In India, especially in large joint households with many family members and little privacy, this was an achievable goal. In nearly every case after a few months I could do just that – sit and watch – as long as I accepted the family's formal expression of hospitality at some point during a visit. This meant my sitting somewhere that they specified and accepting a cup of tea, usually accompanied by a sweet of some kind.

From the start of my research, adults taught children to address me as "Auntie," using either the Oriya term for mother's sister or father's sister. (These are separate categories of person in Orissa.) One child always called me "Scooter Auntie" because of my unusual mode of transportation – a small motorcycle. I was thus rapidly incorporated into the extended family system and to this day am addressed as "Auntie" by most of my "sample children," all of whom are now young adults. As time passed, I joined people during their meals – even eating out of the same dishes as other young women; attended all special family occasions, such as weddings and naming ceremonies for children; and participated in numerous religious rituals as well. For me, the ultimate expression of acceptance into Bhubaneswar family life was the day, sometime during my second year, when two Old Town girls told me that they knew why I had adjusted so well to life in Orissa. "You speak like us now; you dress like us; you even eat with us," they observed. "It's because you were an Oriya in your former life!" For young people who took seriously the Hindu belief in reincarnation this was, I think, *not* just an idle remark.

My Oriya was never fluent, but it became adequate enough for me to understand most parent-child conversations and to talk with people about the "domestic" world – women's daily activities, children and child care, family and kinship ties, gender roles, and schooling. In the Old Town, some of the fathers knew a little English, but none of the mothers and grandmothers did, so I was totally dependent upon speaking Oriya. In the New Capital, all middle- and upper-status fathers spoke fluent English, but only a few of their wives did. So again, I was largely dependent upon Oriya. And among low-status families, I was entirely dependent upon speaking Oriya; no member of these households had been to school for more than a year or two. As the years have passed, however, and as many of the young Oriya-speaking children I first knew have completed school, they have acquired a good mastery of English. Nowadays, I speak using a mix of English and Oriya.

Plate 11. Old Town Bauri women and children playing with my motorcycle

Research Techniques

From the beginning, I have used a variety of research techniques in my research in Bhubaneswar. In 1965–67, I combined informal participant observation with more formal, timed observations of caretaker-child interactions. The latter were designed to make possible systematic and comparative analysis of Old Town–New Capital child-rearing practices, but the former was essential to my gaining acceptance into family life in the first place, that is, to making people sufficiently comfortable with my presence so that I could then record their normal, everyday behavior. Of course, it was all the informal time that I spent just eating and chatting with family members that made my initial research so rewarding.

Sometimes accompanied by their husbands and/or their children, New Capital women who were not in strict purdah, would occasionally visit me. With them I could have some degree of reciprocity. However, Old Town women could not leave their homes and never came to see me, although many of their sons did. With one exception, only a few low-status families ever visited my home.

The principal exception was a family that lived next door and with whom I developed close, neighborly ties.

My more formal observations of children and their caretakers were based upon the techniques developed in the 1950s by Beatrice B. and John W. M. Whiting for the Six Cultures Study and for subsequent cross-cultural work in child development.[7] The Six Cultures Study was one of the first efforts to train teams of researchers to systematically collect the same kinds of data on children from a set of different societies during the same time period. The resulting data could then be compared, offering insights into similarities and differences between cultures in the development and care of children. As a graduate student, I had been trained by the Whitings in their observational and recording techniques, and I had also been given access to the behavior protocols that they had received from each research team for the Six Cultures Study and to some of their early analyses of those materials. The research done in a North India village by Leigh Minturn and John Hitchcock provided a particularly useful base for my work in Bhubaneswar.[8]

During a twenty-month period I collected sixteen hours of timed observations for each sample family. I alternated the times of the day at which I made these observations so as to cover major portions of each family's daily schedule: (1) Early morning, when children awakened and school children bathed, dressed, and ate before departing for school. This was a period when mothers were focused upon food preparation for school-age children and husbands. (2) Late morning, when mothers not employed outside of the home focused upon infants and young children – bathing, dressing, and feeding them – and then eating something themselves. (3) Midafternoon, when school-age children returned home. This tended to be a period of play, eating snacks, and studying. By early evening, women were once again engaged in food preparation for the evening meal. (4) The evening meal and bedtime for children. For each family I acquired four hours of behavior protocols for each of these four time periods.

The hundreds of behavioral protocols I collected for each of twenty-four families have enabled me to undertake significant quantitative analysis of parent-child interactions, including statistical comparisons of different families by caste and class status or by Old Town versus New Capital residence, of children by age and gender, and of different mothers and mother surrogates. Each protocol consists of a running documentary of the interactions of mothers and their surrogates with children for periods of fifteen to twenty minutes; each discrete interaction is subsequently coded, allowing analysis of 9,301 different actions by mothers and their surrogates as they took care of children or of children as they took care of themselves. Excerpts from these protocols, as well as from my more informal conversations with and observations of family members, will be used as illustrations throughout this book.

Such formal, timed observations not only permit quantitative analysis and the testing of hypotheses, but they also serve as a valuable corrective for inaccurate impressions that one can acquire while doing ethnographic research. Furthermore, they provide a basis to compare peoples' own reported perceptions of their care-taking behavior with their behavior as it has been systematically recorded. Such quantitative analysis requires the coding of behavior, however, which involves a complex set of decisions including, for example, deciding what constitutes "nurturance" and "self-reliance." Such models for coding, which grow out of Western social science, have certain cultural assumptions built into them, and they must be evaluated accordingly. I adapted the Six Cultures Study coding systems to my data, thus enhancing the possibility for cross-cultural comparison. Yet however useful the quantitative data are, I believe that it is essential to contextualize them with the rich ethnographic information that is acquired through many months and years of living with and talking to the people whose behavior one is trying to record, analyze, and understand. Quantitative and qualitative methodologies can enhance one another and help create as full and accurate a picture as possible of another society.

During my subsequent trips to Bhubaneswar in 1978, 1981, and 1987 I was less concerned with specific research methodologies than with maintaining my ties to Old Town and New Capital families and following the educational, occupational, and marital development of all their children. The trip in 1978, however, also involved my introducing a new husband to everyone, a somewhat delicate situation in a society in which high-status women are not expected to remarry. After my initial fieldwork in Bhubaneswar, my first husband and I separated, and then he tragically died. While people expressed regret at the loss of my first husband, they were very accepting of my new husband and were eager to meet my then two-year-old son, who was home with his maternal grandparents. In 1987 my mother, then seventy-eight years old, accompanied me to Bhubaneswar. Her presence stimulated certain kinds of conversations that might otherwise not have occurred. With a mother along, I suspect that I appeared more normal to many Bhubaneswar residents; I, too, had family ties. When they learned that my mother was recently widowed after fifty-three years of marriage to my father, many were astounded. Their stereotype of Americans was, of course, that we have all been divorced. My mother was graciously welcomed into all homes and became the stimulus for many conversations among different generations of women. In fact, it was those conversations that motivated my next trip to Bhubaneswar, in 1989.

Between trips to India I have maintained contact with families by exchanging letters regularly with those who are literate or who now have literate children. Their correspondence has included invitations to most of their children's weddings. In addition, I have always made a point of photographing families when I am in Bhubaneswar and then sending copies to each family. Although photographs are something that everyone appreciates and likes to have, most of the families have not invested in cameras. For poor families, the cost would be prohibitive, and yet, for special occasions, even these families go to photo studios at considerable cost. Thus, sending photos has been one small way in which I can express my gratitude for all the kindness and hospitality that I have received over the years.

In the winter and spring of 1989 I returned to Bhubaneswar with my husband and son specifically to interview women of different generations – mothers, daughters, and grandmothers – about their perceptions of women and changing gender roles in Bhubaneswar.

I used an informal, open-ended interview schedule designed to encourage the women to talk freely, and I tape-recorded their responses and conversations with one another. Sometimes these interviews were with a single woman, but more frequently they were with sets of women (and sometimes men) from one household who talked together and across generations. For example, on one occasion I sat on a double bed with four sisters, their mother, and their maternal grandmother, who all took turns discussing such subjects as age at marriage, moving to one's parents-in-law's house, dowry, menstrual practices, higher education, and careers. For me, such moments highlighted the wonderful intergenerational richness of the Indian extended family.

The 1989 trip was also the first time that my son, then twelve, accompanied me to Bhubaneswar. My husband, son, and I rented a house and for five months lived a middle-class Bhubaneswar life on the outskirts of the Old Town. Most New Capital families came to visit us on a regular basis, just as we visited them. However, from the Old Town only men visited; Old Town women still live highly restricted lives. Having a son with me at last made me seem more normal in the eyes of others: I too was a mother. Although my immediate family might be small, at least it was a family; and having met my mother two years earlier, people knew that I also had extended kin. Not surprisingly, my son was the center of attraction on this trip and in constant demand to be fed and fondled.

I mention these kinds of details for several reasons. Whereas I do not subscribe to postmodernist views that all social science is totally subjective and that the researcher is simply crafting a personal narrative out of a myriad of observations, conversations, and experiences in another culture, I do believe that the anthropologist, as the principal instrument of research, has an obligation to inform the reader of both her research methods and her qualitative relationships with the people from whom she learns. For me, those relationships have changed over time as my status has changed from that of a young graduate student to that of a middle-aged wife, mother, and professor, and as the girls and boys whom I first knew have grown into adulthood and assumed new roles while their parents and grandparents have aged. Such changes in roles and relationships have, in turn, stimulated different kinds of research questions and methods.

Some Reflections on Longitudinal Research

Longitudinal research implies change – changing conditions, changing relationships, and changing research methodologies. What has remained stable over the past thirty years is my interest in a set of families and their interest in me. What is perhaps remarkable is that, despite all the changes occurring in Bhubaneswar, some portion of twenty-three of my original sample of twenty-four families has remained in residence in the town. As the children whom I first studied have matured into adults, many have developed from being the subjects of my research into my research collaborators. They now reflect with me about the changes that they and their families have experienced and about their goals and dreams for the future. One New Capital unmarried daughter, with a master's degree in economics, became my research assistant in 1989 and helped me interview a few of the Old Town and low-status families for whom I had to rely on Oriya and wanted to make sure that the women understood my questions and that I understood their responses.

Among the goals of my original research in Bhubaneswar was that I remain as unobtrusive as possible and that my research techniques be unobtrusive so that I could observe caretaker-child behavior in their naturalistic settings. Sitting in a courtyard corner with a tiny notepad on which I would record only key actions in a sequence of actions became my modus operandi for formal observations. After an observational period, I would return home to type up in full the timed observation along with all the other things I had learned informally that day. I became proficient at memorizing long sequences of actions to be transcribed at home rather than in the presence of family members for whom my note taking might be distracting. Only when people wanted to teach me something and thought it appropriate for me to record it did I take fuller notes in their presence.

In my subsequent trips to Bhubaneswar, however, such nonobtrusiveness has not been necessary. For example, parents have wanted to tell me about their children's accomplishments; both parents and children have wanted to share information with me. My research techniques have become more overt and conversationally focused. I believe this has been possible because of the trust that has developed over time between the families and myself. For example, I felt comfortable tape-recording conversations only after many years of contact, and it worked best when I could do it in natural settings, allowing people to take the conversation in those directions they deemed suitable. Thus, my interview technique with mothers, daughters, and grandmothers in 1989 was to prepare questions about critical issues I wanted to explore with them and insert these into the conversation as opportunity arose. In this way, I could gather reasonably comparable information from different families but within a flow of conversation that was as natural as possible for them.

In subsequent chapters, I try to convey aspects of both the changing conditions in Bhubaneswar and my changing research techniques by including information from my dated field notes: for example, behavior protocols from timed observations of caretaker-child interactions, records of informal conversations and correspondence, and transcriptions of interviews. My hope is that these extracts from dated field notes will give readers not only a sense of the changes that have occurred but also an appreciation of the fieldwork experience and the nature of information upon which generalizations and insights are made.

CHAPTER THREE

The Patrifocal Family

Growing Up Female in the Old Town

A WEDDING

March 11, 1966

In the front of the house a large enclosure has been constructed out of corrugated tin. Within this enclosure on the righthand side facing the house there is an altar. When my husband and I arrive shortly after 8:00 p.m., a Hindu priest is preparing the altar for the wedding ceremony. Facing the altar are several rows of seats on which a few male guests are sitting. We are motioned over to take a seat there. Music is blaring out of several loudspeakers – music that we have heard from our house across the back fence announcing the week-long celebration.

I have been seated only a few minutes when a young man beckons me inside. I follow him up the front steps into the ground floor of the house, then up a staircase to the second floor and along a hallway to a back room where there are women seated on the floor. They motion me to be seated. I sit on the floor with three other women and a young girl who has her head bent toward the floor and her long black hair flowing down all around her. I cannot see her face. There are numerous children about – perhaps twenty or thirty. After a few minutes Mr. Das, our friend and neighbor and the head of the household, arrives and introduces me to the three women with whom I am sitting. They, too, are wedding guests of the Dases. After Mr. Das has left, I ask the women where Mrs. Das is. They point her out to me in an adjoining room, busily watching over wedding preparations. I ask about the bride, and they motion to the young girl seated across from me with her head bent toward the floor.

There are numerous children asleep everywhere around me on the floor, and across from me I can see into an adjoining room also filled with children, both awake and asleep. Apparently, we are all awaiting the arrival of the bridegroom. I ask the woman to my right what will happen when he comes. She responds, "They [the Das family] are Brahmin; I am Karan." [She cites their different caste statuses as an explanation for not knowing.] For two and one-half hours we sit like this, with women and children constantly coming and going from the room. The children are seemingly free to run around as they like, both inside and outside the house. When tired, they simply lie down with us on the floor and nap for a while. During the first hour the bride (the fifteen-year-old niece of Mr. Das) also occasionally rises from the floor and wanders from room to room. After about an hour she lies down on a large cot in the corner of the room and appears to fall asleep. No one pays any attention to her.

About 10:30 p.m. we women and children are motioned out into the open verandah-like hallway in front of the room where we have been seated. The wedding feast is about to be served. [Later I learn that the men have already been fed downstairs.] I am seated on the floor in one row, together with three other women and their children, all of whom are guests rather than family members. There are three other rows of children and adolescent girls belonging to the extended family. Mrs. Das and the other adult women of the family do not eat with us. Mrs. Das watches over the general serving of the meal while Mr. Das arrives and specifically directs the servants to make sure that each guest receives good pieces of fish. [In this part of India, fish is eaten on special occasions by high-caste Brahmin, otherwise vegetarian, families.] Food abounds – rice, lentils, several different vegetable curries, fish curry, and sweets – and is ladled from buckets onto banana leaves that serve as our plates. Seated on the floor with our food-laden leaves, we eat with the fingers of the right hand.

Just as we are completing our feast, there is much commotion outside. The bridegroom is arriving. The children, having heard the news, run downstairs without finishing their meal. The women descend a few minutes later and watch from just inside the doorway while the men await the bridegroom outside. The groom, wearing white and bedecked in flowers, arrives with a few male kin in a car that is led by a small group of musicians who are on foot. The groom and his male kin are greeted by the bride's father and taken to a neighbor's house to be fed. At this point the women return upstairs and some of the guests leave. While the groom is elsewhere, the bride, heavily veiled, is brought before the altar briefly and then returned upstairs.

The actual wedding ceremony does not get underway until past midnight.

(Excerpt from field notes)

I begin this chapter with an excerpt from my first observation of a Bhubaneswar wedding for several reasons. Weddings, like births and deaths, are a moment when a family is transformed and when a young woman, in particular, must make a major transition in life – from the role of daughter in her natal household to that of wife and daughter-in-law in her husband's household. In India, weddings are usually protracted events that mark the end of lengthy negotiations between two extended families. They are rarely the result of individual choice, love, or passion; rather, they are events that symbolize and affirm the collective nature of the family and the larger kinship units in which a family is embedded – the patrilineage and the subcaste (*jati*). In 1965–67, young brides and grooms in Bhubaneswar rarely saw one another before the momentous occasion of the wedding ceremony at the bride's home. For a young woman, the choice of the man with whom she would spend the rest of her life and whose children she would bear was made by her parents, persons she considered most capable of making a wise choice. She would have been reared to respect her parents' decision and to appreciate their efforts to provide her with an adequate dowry (gold jewelry for herself, household equipment, and a variety of gifts – often quite expensive – for the groom and his family).

The brief description I have cited – a small segment of a wedding as observed from inside the women's quarters of a traditional upper-caste Brahmin household – illustrates a number of the principles that characterize patrifocal family structure and ideology in this part of India. For example, the wedding takes place in a joint household that is structurally patrilineal and patrilocal. In this particular household two married brothers reside together with their wives and children. If their parents had still been alive, it would be a three-generational household. Because descent and inheritance in

54

India are usually traced through men, not women, it is sets of related males who ideally reside together and share property. Thus men are structurally central in this family and kinship system and women are peripheral: As daughters, their residence in their father's household is transitory; as wives, they are consanguineal outsiders – they are descended from some other patrilineal extended family and lineage and join their husband's extended family and lineage only through marriage.

The bride in this instance is fifteen years old and has completed ten years of schooling. (She has not "matriculated" – i.e., completed secondary school exams.) Although she is not a child bride, she is being married sufficiently young that there is every expectation she will adapt well to her father-in-law's household. Patrifocal family ideology stipulates that it is the bride's responsibility to make the major adjustments in marriage. Girls should, therefore, be reared to be obedient, self-sacrificing, modest, nurturant, hardworking, and home loving. They should always show self-restraint and contribute to family harmony. Such qualities are intended to enhance a girl's likelihood of adjusting well to her husband's family and minimize the potential disruption that an outsider might cause. Marriage at an early age, while a girl is still impressionable and has achieved little independence, is, therefore, one way to help ensure a successful transition. As one Indian gentleman expressed it during a 1966 conversation with me about my education and career goals, "American girls are given too much independence. A girl should marry young, before she has a chance to develop independent ideas."

Not only should a girl be young at the time of her marriage, but she should be sufficiently younger and less educated than the groom to preserve the male-based hierarchy and authority system of the patrifocal family. In the Das wedding, the groom was indeed older by five years and was more educated (B.A.) than the bride. Patrifocal family structure and ideology provide yet another incentive for marrying daughters young: An unmarried, chaste girl symbolizes family honor and purity and is considered a sacred gift to bestow upon another family.[1] By marrying their daughter at a relatively young age – often negotiations began at puberty if not

55

considerably earlier – the Das family was trying to protect her virginity and thus their honor. Delaying a girl's marriage much beyond fourteen or fifteen years of age was, in 1965–67, considered potentially risky by many Old Town families.

The Das wedding, as described, illustrates other principles of patrifocal family organization characteristic of life in the Old Town in 1965–67. For example, activities in the house were sexually segregated. Upon my arrival, I was immediately escorted upstairs to be with the women, while my husband remained downstairs with the men. Adult women and adolescent girls were relegated to the more secluded and private part of the house, whereas the men had access to the more public, out-of-doors, sphere where the groom and his male entourage would arrive.[2] For middle- and upper-status families, it was appropriate to keep adult women of child-bearing age secluded – in purdah – within the home where they would not have contact with strange men and where their contact even with the men of their own household was limited. Older women who were beyond their childbearing years and who were mothers-in-law and grandmothers, not young wives and mothers, were less rigidly secluded. However, on a ritual occasion such as this wedding, there was, with the exception of preadolescent children, a general separation of men and women. Young children had the run of the house and yard, although they tended to retreat to the women's quarters when they were tired, hungry, or in need of attention since this was where their principal caretakers were located.

Sexual segregation is further illustrated in the way that the wedding feast was handled and in the reception given the groom and his male entourage. The feasting demonstrates both the gender segregation and the gender hierarchy characteristic of Old Town households. The men were not only served separately from the women and young children, but they were served *before* the women and children. And when the groom's procession arrived, the men went outside to greet them and the women could only watch from the confines of the house.

Gender-differentiated roles and responsibilities constitute another principle of the patrifocal family. Women's roles, which ideally are confined to the private sphere, include child care and food preparation – a long and arduous task for large joint households in a society where there are few processed foods. Ordinarily, the adult women of a household would serve the food, first to the adult men and then to the children, and would eat something themselves only after all other members of the household had completed their meals. On this sacred occasion, however, food preparation was in the hands of Brahmin males, temple servants who specialized in cooking and serving food at such events. Furthermore, because it was such an important occasion, Mr. Das partially usurped the responsibility of his wife and entered the women's quarters to help supervise the distribution of food to female guests. Nonetheless, Mrs. Das was also in charge, and she and the other adult women of the family did not eat with the guests and children.

The subordination of the individual to the collective family is also demonstrated in the Das wedding and is reflected in the behavior of the bride during my period of observation. Although earlier in the day the bride was attended to by her female family members and friends and ritually prepared for the occasion, she is now left alone to await the bridegroom's arrival and the beginning of the religious ceremony. She fasts and for several hours interacts with no one, much of the time sitting on the floor with her head bowed and face invisible. She must patiently await the events – events over which she has no control – that will result in her transfer from one family to another and that will mark her formal transition from daughter to daughter-in-law. I specify the role of "daughter-in-law" over that of "wife" here to emphasize her entrance into another family where the husband-wife relationship will, ideally, be subordinated to the collective well-being of the extended family.

This period of waiting is for the bride one of great emotional strain and ambivalence. She is both excited and frightened – excited to be moving to the next stage of life and excited to see her bridegroom but frightened about all of the dramatic changes that will be entailed. She should, however, show no visible signs of emotion but should patiently await the events that will overtake her. In one Old Town wedding that I observed, the bride repeatedly fainted during the religious ceremony and had to be doused with cold water to continue. Other brides that I knew went to their new homes and became temporarily "frozen" – unable to eat, sleep, or have sexual relations with their husbands. There are numerous references in the ethnographic literature to the potentially traumatic nature of this event for many young Indian women.[3] Despite a daughter's training to trust her parents' choice of a bridegroom and parents-in-law, her transition to a new and often strange family can be difficult.

The atmosphere of the upstairs rooms during the two-hour wait I have described is characteristic of collective joint family life in other ways as well. Children of all ages are present for the long day and night of wedding preparations, feasting, and ceremony. However, they receive little supervision. They simply run around, entertaining themselves until they are so tired that they lie down on the floor and take a nap. No one directs them to do so. Children are expected to be present but not the focus of attention. Meanwhile, the women of the household are engaged in various preparations for the wedding. In the morning they decorate the bride's feet and hands with elaborate designs in red henna, a process that might take several hours. They lay out the bride's extensive wardrobe for the day so that she can change quickly from one sari to another for different parts of the ceremony. And they pack the bride's trousseau – the personal clothing, jewelry, and other effects that she will take with her to her new home.

Finally, there are references to caste in the narrative. The marriage had been arranged between families of the same subcaste of Brahmins, the priestly caste that is the top-ranked group in India's fourfold *varna* system of social stratification (see Chapter 2). The categories of Brahmins resident in the Old Town have different ranks. In the Das wedding, a specific category of Brahmin priests was in charge of the food and another in charge of the ritual preparations. A Das family friend, who belonged to a different high caste, could not tell me just what would be happening because wedding protocol and ceremony can vary by caste status.

In this chapter I explore how these principles of patrifocal family structure and ideology are inculcated and expressed in Old Town upper- and middle-caste women's behavior. A conversation that I had nearly a year later with two Old Town adolescents illustrates some of the values that underlie these principles and the ways in which two young, articulate women think about them.

A CONVERSATION ABOUT MARRIAGE: MAHAPATRA HOUSEHOLD

March 2, 1967

Today Mita (eighteen-year-old girl) and her sister, Sita (sixteen years), and I discussed marriage patterns in India and the United States. They initiated the conversation by asking about divorce in the United States – a phenomenon they had heard of but could not imagine. "Why," they asked, "would anyone want to leave one's husband or wife?" I tried to explain that husbands and wives are sometimes unhappy with one another. They responded, "But you are part of a joint family." [The idea that the husband-wife relationship could be central to one's happiness made little sense to them. In their conception of family it was the patrifocal joint household that was central.] As a woman, they went on to explain, one's relationships are primarily with other women, and the source of one's unhappiness is more likely to be other women than one's husband.

"What," they asked, "becomes of children in the case of divorce?" I explained that they usually stay with the mother, but not always. "Could the mother remarry?" "Yes," I said. [This was an idea they did not like.] "How," they asked, "could children get along with a man who was not their own father? And how could a father love a child that was not his own?" I explained that in the United States people could and often did learn to love others in such circumstances, but the girls found this idea difficult to accept. Finally, Mita burst out, "Of course, we Hindus believe that everyone loves everyone else, but . . ." She went on to explain that love is not so much something that grows with or is inspired by another individual but is an expected part of certain relationships and *not* a part of other relationships.

Despite these attitudes and contrary to tradition, the girls went on to explain that they were proponents of remarriage for women in the case of the death of a husband, especially where there were no children. They favored widow remarriage under such circumstances because they considered it to be a tragedy for a woman to be without

59

children. [Hindu men have always had the prerogative to remarry. Higher-caste widows, however, have not.]

Next Mita asked, "Could a man have more than one wife? Was that allowed in the United States?" I said, "No, it is not allowed." "Wasn't it even allowed when there were no children?" they asked. "No, under no circumstances was marriage to more than one woman at the same time legal in the United States," I replied. This they could not understand. "Aren't children sacred in your country?" Mita then asked. [By this she seemed to mean, wasn't the most important thing in life to have children? If a man could not have children by one wife, then shouldn't he be allowed to take another wife?] "What happens when a man has no son?" they then asked. "What did he do with his property?"

(Excerpt from field notes)

An Old Town Neighborhood

Mita and Sita belong to a large, joint Brahmin family that resides in Harachandi Sahi, one of the oldest neighborhoods of the Old Town. In 1965–67, there were twenty-five members of this family living together: three brothers, their wives, and ten children; their widowed mother; an older sister, her husband, and three children; and a younger married sister and her baby. It was a somewhat unusual arrangement because married sisters do not normally remain with the natal family. In this case, however, because the brothers' father had died when they were too young to run the family, their brother-in-law (Older Sister's husband) assumed responsibility. The younger sister and her baby were residing with them only temporarily. She had given birth to the baby in her husband's household outside of Bhubaneswar and had come home for a visit when the baby was six months old. She remained for a year.

In 1965–67, Mita and Sita's family was one of sixty-two households in Harachandi Sahi, one of the neighborhoods that spiral out from Bindu Sagar, the sacred water tank in the center of the Old Town. Harachandi Sahi is inhabited largely by Brahmin families that are descended from ancient priestly and temple servant families whose traditional occupations have been to take care of visiting Hindu pilgrims, to attend the temples and their deities, and to perform sacred rituals. There are several different categories of temple servants that have a hierarchical relationship to one another: Those who serve as priests and perform rituals for others have the highest status, whereas those who are temple cooks have the lowest status. In addition to Brahmin families, Harachandi Sahi is also home to a small number of clean Shudra families, such as Carpenters (Badhie) and Milkmen (Gauda). On one lane, separate from the other caste households, reside a set of Barber (Bhaudari) families, somewhat lower in caste status than the other Shudras but, nonetheless, "clean" Shudras. There are no unclean Shudras or Untouchable families in Harachandi Sahi.

Not all of Harachandi Sahi's families rely entirely on their caste occupations. For example, Mita and Sita's father and two uncles have private businesses in the Old Town, and a third uncle is a low-level government servant. In this particular Brahmin family, the men had received enough formal schooling to have occupational alternatives to priestly and temple services. Three had matriculated, and one had completed a B.A. and an LL.B. (law degree). By contrast, none of their wives had received any formal education (Table 3). In other Brahmin families, however, temple services continued to be in 1965–67 the principal occupation for many men, although a number of Brahmin families owned agricultural land and were self-sufficient in rice and vegetables – an economically important consideration. Not having to purchase staple foods significantly lowers a family's expenses. Furthermore, with the influx of new residents to Bhubaneswar, building and renting houses had become another source of income for some Brahmin families.

Most of the Carpenter and Barber families in Harachandi Sahi continued to practice their caste occupations. In one Milkman family, however, the father broke away from his brothers and the joint family after the death of their father. He, too, had matriculated, and, after serving in the army, he joined the government service. Meanwhile, he reduced the number of cows he owned to a half dozen and left his wife in charge of them. She fed and milked them

Table 3. *Mean Number of Years of School Completed:*
Old Town Parents

Status	Fathers (N = 26)	Mothers (N = 26)
Upper/Middle	7.0 (Range: 0–17)	1.4 (Range: 0–7)
Lower	2.0 (Range: 0–7)	0.5 (Range: 0–5)

daily and sold the milk to neighbor families, thus contributing to the family income.

Those Old Town families that have found ways to supplement their traditional caste earnings are clearly prospering more than others. This is evidenced in numerous small ways, from the acquisition of bicycles and motor scooters to home improvement. Because space in Harachandi Sahi is scarce and all homes are built physically contiguous to one another, the only way to expand is upward. Larger and more prosperous families may have homes that are two or three stories high with stucco walls and cement floors rather than mud walls and dirt floors. Their homes also have reinforced cement ceilings rather than thatch roofs. With regard to interior decor, however, there is little difference between homes. In all homes furniture is scarce – most eating, sleeping, and working is done on the floor – and there are few decorations of any kind. The only area of the house that may be highly adorned is the *puja* room – the room or the part of the house set aside for daily prayer by family members. Here the walls are often covered with brightly colored, pictorial representations of Hindu deities, and there are shelves that hold other religious icons representing the deities worshipped by members of the household. On special ritual occasions women sometimes decorate the entranceways and outside walls of their homes with elaborate designs made with white rice paste.

In 1965–67, no home in Harachandi Sahi, regardless of the family's caste or socioeconomic status, had electricity or running water. Families depended on kerosene lanterns for light in the evenings and on wells for their water. Most had a well in the backyard, although some families were dependent upon public wells.

Portrait of a Joint Family

The Mahapatras – Mita and Sita's family – reside in a typical Harachandi Sahi house. It is long and narrow, with a series of rooms, verandahs, and courtyards extending back from the street (Figure 3). It has one cooking area, a cowshed, a well, a small vegetable garden, and a sizable backyard with a latrine. The yard contains some fruit trees but is otherwise uncultivated. The house is one story but is supplemented by a small two-story addition with a storeroom and a cook area downstairs and a bedroom and an open-roof verandah upstairs. This verandah, together with the courtyards of the main house, provide play areas for children as well as work areas for women.

The main house has four small rooms, one for each brother and his wife, and children, and one for the brothers' widowed mother. Each subunit of the joint family stores its personal belongings in its room and sleeps in the room at night. While visiting, Younger Sister and her baby sleep with Grandmother, whereas Older Sister and her husband and three children sleep in the small house across the street. Because the four "bedrooms" are windowless, they are dark and not much used during the day. The life of the house goes on in the interior courtyards and verandahs and is totally invisible to the outside world.

The women who have married into the family (First, Second, and Third Daughter-in-law) observe purdah: They do not leave the house except for very special occasions, not even in the company of a husband. Grandmother, by contrast, a widow with grown children, is not as restricted. If she desires, she can go out in the public lanes of Harachandi Sahi or visit one of the nearby temples. Not only do the three daughters-in-law of the family observe purdah, but they also exhibit formal respect in a variety of ways for their mother-in-law (Grandmother), their older brothers-in-law, and their husbands. For example, in the presence of respected elders they keep their saris draped over their heads and their heads bowed so that their faces are not visible and there can be no eye contact. They also lower themselves to the ground and kiss the feet of their respected elders, including their husbands, as if they were

63

deities. If their father-in-law were alive, they would have to avoid eye contact with him altogether, a rule that also holds for the younger two sisters-in-law with respect to Oldest Brother. They should have no direct contact with him, and in the presence of others, they can interact only in a modest fashion with their own husbands. By contrast, for them to have contact with Youngest Brother not only is acceptable but can be openly friendly and famil-iar.[4] Built upon principles of age, gender, and consanguineal versus affinal ties, such rules help to regulate relationships within these very large, patrifocal joint households.

In the early weeks of visiting the Mahapatra household, I had difficulty identifying one daughter-in-law from another because I could not see their faces. At first, they kept their heads bowed and covered in my presence. Although I was a woman, I was still a stranger. (Had I been a man, they would not have appeared in front of me at all.) Until they overcame their initial shyness and modesty and allowed me to see their faces, I learned to identify them by their bracelets and toe rings. In this part of India a woman's mar-ried status is indicated in several overt ways: She wears an iron bracelet (along with glass and gold bangles) on the wrists of each arm; a silver ring put by her husband during the wedding cere-mony on the center toe of each foot; and red ochre in the part of her hair and in the middle of her forehead, also first applied by her husband during the wedding ceremony. Although I could not see these marks, I learned that each woman's jewelry was distinctive and could be used to identify her. Once the three daughters-in-law grew accustomed to my visits, however, they no longer kept their heads bowed in my presence. In fact, I became a confidante to Second and Third Daughter-in-law, both of whom periodically complained to me about First Daughter-in-law.

An upper-status Old Town joint family like this one is organized hierarchically. While a father is alive and well, he is the head of the household, and everyone else is expected to be subservient to him. However, the operation of affairs *inside* the house – food prepara-tion, cooking, cleaning, child care, and so on – is under the aegis of his wife. She is the top-ranking woman of the family, and all daughters-in-law are under her authority. She directs their work

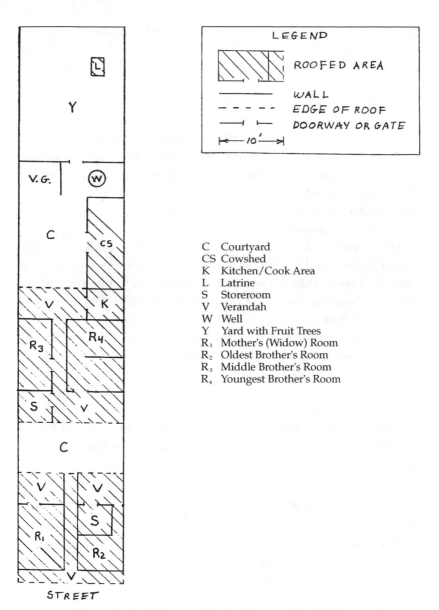

LEGEND

ROOFED AREA

———— WALL

- - - - - EDGE OF ROOF

⊢——⊣ ⊢— DOORWAY OR GATE

⊢—10'—⊣

C   Courtyard
CS Cowshed
K   Kitchen/Cook Area
L   Latrine
S   Storeroom
V   Verandah
W   Well
Y   Yard with Fruit Trees
R_1 Mother's (Widow) Room
R_2 Oldest Brother's Room
R_3 Middle Brother's Room
R_4 Youngest Brother's Room

Figure 3. The Mahapatra Family House in the Old Town

and may even control the time they can spend with their husbands. In the case of the Mahapatras, however, the father of the family had died, leaving his wife a widow. While her three sons were young, her son-in-law headed the family, and she and her married daughter did the household work. Once her oldest son was grown and married, he assumed the position of household head, and his wife gradually became the top-ranking woman, directing her two younger sisters-in-law. Grandmother slowly retired from mundane affairs and spent more and more time visiting temples, performing rituals, and attending to grandchildren when it suited her. Her married daughter and son-in-law also spent more time across the lane in their separate quarters.

The division of labor within the house that had evolved by 1965 placed Third Daughter-in-law, the wife of the youngest brother and thus the lowest-ranking woman in the household, in charge of the most burdensome task – the preparation of meals for a family of twenty-five. Sita called her the "ICS officer" ("Indian Cooking Service," a play on the term Indian Civil Service). Whereas Second Daughter-in-law assisted her younger sister-in-law much of the time, First Daughter-in-law rarely did. She was nominally in charge of the children, but in reality each mother attended to her own children, with extensive help from Grandmother, older siblings, and cousins. First Daughter-in-law was, therefore, resented by her two younger sisters-in-law, who could complain safely to me – an outsider.

DAUGHTER-IN-LAW RELATIONSHIPS: THE MAHAPATRA RESIDENCE

April 5, 1967

Third Daughter-in-law worked and talked with me while I sipped tea. She was cleaning the cowshed. First, she used a broom to sweep some of the dirt away. Then she gathered up all the cow dung with her right hand and made a pile of it. While Third Daughter-in-law was busy working, First Daughter-in-law walked by with Rabi (her one-and-a-half-year-old son) trailing behind her. Rabi was crying, but First Daughter-in-law ignored him. Third Daughter-in-law leaned toward me and whispered, "The Bad One" (*dusta*). She repeated this phrase several times. At first I thought she was speaking of Rabi but then realized she meant First Daughter-in-law. She went on to say, "I do not like First Daughter-in-law. She is not nice. She does not do any work."

(Excerpt from field notes)

The Daily Schedule

The day begins early for the women in a large family such as this one. Adult women rise between 5:00 and 6:00 a.m. to cleanse and purify themselves before beginning to prepare food. The men and children of the house must be given an early morning snack (e.g., cold rice and rice water from the night before or a roasted, crispy rice cereal) and then a full hot meal before they leave for work or school. The latter usually includes hot rice, one or two vegetable curries, lentils, and perhaps an omelet. (As Brahmins, the only meat the Mahaptras eat is fish and this only on special occasions.) After the men and school-aged children leave, the women tend to the infants and preschool children of the household, bathing and hand-feeding them. And only after all of these morning chores are completed do the women themselves bathe and have something to eat. By this time it is nearly noon.

For adult women the early afternoon may be spent either on other household tasks or in resting and visiting with one another while looking after the preschool children of the family. Between 3:00 and 4:00 p.m. school-age children begin to return home and require a snack, after which the evening's hot meal must be prepared. Food preparation and cooking is very time consuming in these homes in which there is no refrigeration – fresh foods are purchased daily by men as women cannot go out of the house to the public market – and few processed foods are available. For example, before rice or lentils can be cooked, they must be carefully sorted through for stones and other foreign objects. All spices and condiments must be hand ground with stone mortars and pestles; there are no prepared "curry" powders and pastes. Mango pickles and chutneys that accompany meals must also be prepared periodically. And several times a year rice paddy from the fields must be transformed into rice through an elaborate drying, husking, and polishing process. For young adult and middle-aged women, the day begins early and ends late: Bedtime is not until 10:00–11:00 p.m.

As the daily schedule makes clear, adult women in Old Town upper-status joint households are preoccupied with household chores, food preparation, and child care from morning to night. Their service to others always comes first. As shall become clear in subsequent sections, as in food preparation, many aspects of child care are highly labor intensive.

The Mahapatra household exemplifies the ideal patrifocal joint family in many respects, although, like other households, it also exhibits important variations. Not all families in Harachandi Sahi were structurally joint in 1965–67. There was some variability in size and structure depending upon such factors as the number of surviving brothers in a given family and their desire to remain together, especially after the death of their father. Under traditional Hindu family law, property may be divided among grown brothers at any time, but it is most commonly divided after a father's death.[5] Among the families that I knew there was, and continues to be, a remarkable degree of joint living. Nonetheless, in 1965–67 some households were small and nuclear in structure: They have become joint only with the growth and marriage of sons. The term "nuclear," however, is really applicable only to household structure, *not* to ideology. Even members of nuclear households had close relatives living next door, down the road, or in an adjoining *sahi*, and might be sharing agricultural and income-producing property. Although in physical structure the household might look like a nuclear family, it was likely to be economically joined to other households.

Most households were also joint psychologically in that their residents thought of themselves as intimately connected with other branches of the family, even if they did not all reside together under the same roof. This intimacy extended to shared child care and even to the adoption of one another's children. A childless, especially a sonless, branch of the family might be given a child by a branch of the family that was more fortunate. In 1965–67, just in

68

Plate 12. Mother and two sons playing on rooftop of house

my small sample of middle- and upper-status families in Hara-chandi Sahi alone, I was aware of three such arrangements, one that involved the transfer of a girl to a childless couple and two that involved the transfer of boys to branches of the family that had no sons and heirs. In all instances the children knew who their "natural" parents were and, in fact, moved back and forth between the households of their biological and adoptive parents, all perfectly ordinary behavior within the context of joint family living.

The conversation with Mita and Sita, reported earlier, offers several clues to understanding adoptions such as these and, more importantly, to understanding the roles and attitudes of women in patrifocal joint families. The sisters stressed, for example, the centrality of having children, both as the defining event ("sacred") of a woman's identity and as a necessary legacy in order for a man to carry on his patrilineal descent line and to pass on his property. Intrafamilial adoption helps to reinforce and to realize these central values that have both sociocultural and psychological significance in joint family life. Mita and Sita also alluded to two other issues that are critical to understanding joint family life – especially from the perspective of women. One is the idea that a woman's relationships are primarily with other women.[6] The other is a concept of love tied more to specific kinds of relationships than to specific individuals.

To understand how women learn to adapt to and find fulfillment in a life that entails marriage to a stranger, the subordination of the husband-wife relationship to the collective interests of the joint household, and the sacrifice of personal interests and desires – even to the point of giving one's child to another relative – it is important to examine early childhood when these values are first inculcated. An examination of early childhood is also pertinent to an understanding of "relational" love, which is closely connected with how young women approach their arranged marriages and the move to their husband's household.

Early Childhood: Socialization for Interdependence

As has already been made clear, having children is greatly desired in Old Town families. As Mita and Sita indicated, for a woman to be childless is a tragedy. To bear children not only is personally rewarding for a woman, but it also helps cement her position in her husband's family for it is she who produces the next generation of patrilineal heirs – sons. Nonetheless, all the women I have known have welcomed their daughters as well as their sons.

Although a child's gender is marked at birth and may lead to a special celebration in the case of a son, in the early years of life a child's gender is less critical than is learning to be a cooperative member of a corporate group, where group coherence and harmony are valued over individuality.[7] This lesson must be learned regardless of the child's gender. Of course, how this sense of group identity – of mutuality, interdependence, and interpersonal responsibility – is ultimately played out will be deeply affected by gender. Gender-differentiated roles are continually being modeled by adults and will gradually be acquired by children. In the first few years of life, however, it is not so much gender that is emphasized as the child's membership in a group. There is, for example, no

70

symbolic pink or blue blanket to publicly signal whether a new baby is a girl or a boy. Nor is color-coded clothing used; infants and toddlers, if dressed at all, tend to wear similar clothes. What is stressed is that the newborn child is just one more member of a group in which collective family interests outweigh individual interests.

The principal value that Old Town children must learn is *interdependence* – the understanding that they are one of many, are *not* unique individuals, and that their survival rests on learning how to live closely with others, and how to cooperate with and take care of one another. This learning of interdependence begins shortly after birth, following a brief period of ritual pollution during which mother and child are isolated from others.[8] For a brief time – twenty-one days among high-caste Brahmin families and often a shorter period among lower-status families – mother and child are kept separate, after which they are ritually bathed and purified and the new infant is introduced to the rest of the immediate family and to the extended kin. At this moment, the new child may be given a name, but in most families that I observed, name giving was reserved for the first birthday. This aspect of potential individuation is, therefore, postponed.

Old Town families use a variety of techniques – often unconsciously, I believe – to achieve their goal of trying to produce children who will be interdependent in both identity and behavior, who will identify with the family as a whole, and who will seek to behave in ways that are compatible with extended family interests. The common American middle-class objective of producing relatively autonomous, independence-oriented individuals who can make their own decisions and who will eventually live on their own, pursue their own interests, select their own spouses, and establish their own separate households is anathema to most Old Town families. When children do behave in such independent ways it is generally regarded as a family tragedy.[9] How, then, do Old Town families instill in their children a deep sense of interdependence and commitment to the *collective* well-being of their families, which, in turn, is built upon clearly differentiated gender roles?

The following description and analysis of early childhood in Old

Town families is based upon my initial two years of systematic observation of parent-child interactions as well as upon my conversations with mothers and mother surrogates in the course of their care-taking activities. Although most Old Town residents could not articulate in the abstract a description of their child-rearing practices, they could respond easily to explicit questions about behaviors that I observed. It is from my observations and their explications of child care practices that I, the ethnographer, then construct a cultural model of early child care – a synthesis of the underlying beliefs, assumptions, and conventional scripts that guide peoples' "child-rearing practices" as they try to produce young women and men who will fit into the sociocultural system in which their family is enmeshed.[10]

During the first two years of life the child is nursed on demand, ritually bathed, and, during most of its waking moments, carried about on someone's hip or held in someone's lap. She is never isolated in a separate room or even in a separate sleeping space, such as a cradle, but is made a part of all household activities all of the time. When the child is tired, either she falls asleep in someone's lap and then is carefully placed on a mat on the floor or her mother lies down with her until she falls asleep. At night infants always sleep with their mothers, which makes nighttime feedings easier and also provides the child with much physical contact and, presumably, emotional security. Older children also sleep with other people – with mothers, fathers, grandmothers, or older siblings— throughout childhood, adolescence, and up to marriage.

Contrary to some theorists who have argued that infancy in India is a time of total indulgence, my research in the Old Town indicates that this is *not* the case.[11] By Western standards, young Indian children are very much present in all aspects of everyday life and receive considerable physical contact; nevertheless, they also learn that they are *not* in control of the critical events of daily life and that they must submit to the authority of others. An obvious example is the highly ritualized daily bath throughout which infants commonly cry. Their crying suggests that they do not find the bath a pleasurable experience, but the lack of maternal responsiveness to their crying teaches them that they are not in control of the situation. Rather, the daily massage and bath is something to which they must submit and a time during which they cannot expect to receive any overt affection or reassurance. It is a time during which they are held and manipulated by the firm hands of others – their mother's or another caretaker's. It is a protracted affair that lasts anywhere from twenty minutes to an hour.[12]

THE DAILY BATH: THE MAHAPATRA RESIDENCE
March 6, 1967

Third Daughter-in-law helped Younger Sister with her baby, Rajan (boy, seven months). Younger Sister brought two bowls in and set them next to Third Daughter-in-law, who was seated on the courtyard floor. One bowl contained mustard oil and the other turmeric paste. Third Daughter-in-law lay Rajan on her outstretched legs with his stomach down. She rubbed mustard oil all over the back of his body and then massaged him for five minutes. Then she applied the turmeric paste to his back and let it remain for another five minutes. Then she turned him over and applied mustard oil to the front of his body, again massaging him. This took another five minutes. Rajan, who had remained quiet for the first ten minutes of the "bath," now began to cry. He cried lightly but steadily for the next period of oiling and massaging. Third Daughter-in-law ignored his crying and just continued the bath. Younger Sister, who was sitting nearby, also ignored Rajan's crying. After finishing another five minutes of massaging, Third Daughter-in-law rubbed turmeric paste all over the front of Rajan's body and let it sit for another five minutes. She even put a little turmeric paste in his mouth.

When the oiling and massaging process was completed, Younger Sister took Rajan to the middle of the courtyard, squatted down next to him, and removed the turmeric paste with a towel. Rajan continued to cry. Now Younger Sister set him in a bowl of water that contained some turmeric and special leaves. She gently poured water all over him as he continued to cry. After bathing him in one bowl of water, she rinsed him in another bowl of plain water. Rajan did not stop crying until the bath was over. After rinsing him, Younger Sister dried him with a cloth and put a shirt on him. Then she applied kajola (a black paste) around his eyes and put a large black dot on his forehead and smaller ones on the soles of his feet [to protect him from evil spirits].

(Except from field notes)

Similarly, although she nurses on demand – in response to an infant's cries – by not responding immediately, a mother again makes it clear that *she*, not the child, is in control. Old Town mothers respond anywhere from several seconds to several minutes after an infant begins to cry and then rarely nurses it to satisfaction. Typically, they pick up a child and nurse it on one breast for a few minutes and then deliberately remove it before it is satisfied. When the child begins to cry again, it is given the other breast, which is again removed before the child has reached satisfaction. A complex sequence of infant crying and delayed maternal response is thus set in motion in which the mother retains control and the child has to keep "asking" for more.[13]

NURSING: A BRAHMIN HOUSEHOLD
October 8, 1966

It was morning, and Mrs. Senapati was busy cooking in the kitchen. She came out of the kitchen for a moment, and Giti (nine-month-old girl) saw her. Giti put her arms up toward her mother, and Mrs. Senapati took her and held her for a moment. Giti immediately stopped crying. Then she started crying again. Mrs. Senapati carried Giti into the small room next to the kitchen and sat with her on a mat. She held Giti on her lap and nursed her for three minutes on her left breast. Then she abruptly removed Giti from the breast, sat her down on the floor, and returned to the kitchen. Giti stood up and remained in the center of the room crying. No one paid any attention to her. Ten minutes later, after Mrs. Senapati had served the older children their morning meal, she picked Giti up and held her for ten minutes. Mrs. Senapati tried to feed her some cake, but Giti flung it onto the floor. Mrs. Senapati tried some curried vegetables with the same result. Finally, Mrs. Senapati set Giti down on the floor and returned to the kitchen. Giti lay crying on the floor. Ten minutes later Giti was still crying. Mrs. Senapati again picked her up and sat down on the

Plate 13. Servant massaging infant

back steps with her, nursing her. She gave Giti her right breast. After three minutes Mrs. Senapati rose, still holding Giti. Giti hung loosely at her mother's side and continued to suck on her mother's breast for a few more minutes. Then Mrs. Senapati set Giti down and went to get some more rice for Giti's six-year-old brother, who was requesting it. Giti again stood alone, crying. Five minutes later Mrs. Senapati returned and picked up Giti. She again took Giti to the back verandah and nursed her for one minute. Then she stopped Giti from suckling and made her sit on her lap. Giti smiled momentarily but again began fussing and crying. Mrs. Senapati laughed and tried to get Giti to smile. Finally, Giti broke into a smile. A few minutes later Mrs. Senapati pulled back her sari and let Giti nurse some more. [This intermittent nursing of Giti occurred over a period of one and one-half hours.] *(Excerpt from field notes)*

This pattern of infant request and maternal intermittent response is strikingly discrepant from contemporary American middle-class

Plate 14. Servant and mother bathing infant

concepts of what constitutes "maternal indulgence." In the Western literature "indulgence" implies an emotional focus on the child, not a pattern such as this one of a mother's reluctant and interrupted physical response to her infant and minimal overt emotional involvement in the activities of nursing, bathing, and other forms of caretaking.[14]

As young children develop physically and can follow their mothers and other caretakers around, they become more active "seekers" of food and attention, but it is still up to their mothers and other caretakers to decide whether or not to respond positively. Later, with the introduction of solid foods, a mother may retain full control by insisting upon hand-feeding her child. She will most likely insist upon bathing her child as well. In these respects Old Town children are kept physically dependent for an extended period, commonly from birth until about ten years, although the exact amount of time depends upon a child's position in the sibling

Plate 15. Mother bathing six-year-old son

hierarchy as well as upon the presence or absence of potential
caretakers who can assist the mother.

Most Old Town children learn at an early age that they are one
among many and that although their mother is their principal caretaker, she is not their only source of care and attention. There are
fathers, grandmothers, aunts, older siblings, and even neighbor
children who will participate in taking care of them. They learn to
regard a variety of persons as potential caretakers, thus reducing
the overall amount of mother-child interaction that takes place.
Table 4 demonstrates with quantified data from my timed behavior
protocols (see Chapter 2) the distribution of caretaking activities

Table 4. *Proportion of Nurturant Acts[1] Performed by Mothers and Other Caretakers[2]*

Mother/mother surrogate	Old Town (N = 100)	New Capital (N = 55)
Mother	53	58
Father	5	11
Grandmother	10	12
Older sibling, female	17	5
Older sibling, male	4	3
Mother's sister	1	2
Father's sister	4	0
Father's brother's wife	2	0
Neighbor or servant	4	9
Total	100	100

[1] "Nurturant acts" were defined as those actions instigated by mothers and other caretakers to respond to children's needs: e.g., offering comfort to crying or distressed children, nursing and/or hand-feeding them, bathing and dressing them, carrying them, and offering other kinds of instrumental care and help.
[2] These figures are based upon 16 hours of systematically collected, timed observations of caretaker-child interactions for each household.

among different household members in Old Town and New Capital families. "Nurturant acts" include caretaking activities such as holding, carrying, feeding, bathing, and dressing infants and young children.

The presence of numerous potential caretakers in Old Town households does not intensify the nurturance infants and young children receive so much as it disperses such care among a variety of people.[15] The nurturing and indulging of Old Town children is constrained by the belief that children's basic needs should be tended to but otherwise children should not be the focus of attention. In fact, to give too much attention to an infant or young child is considered dangerous for the child. It might attract the Evil Eye or some other undesirable force, resulting in the child's illness or death. I was warned, for example, not to make flattering remarks about any Old Town babies because if anything were to happen to it, I could be held responsible. My attention to the child might be construed as having brought the evil force. Thus children were rarely praised. The operative philosophy with respect to "child rearing" was that children should be allowed to grow up at their own pace in a setting densely packed with relatives and friends, all of whom were potential caretakers and/or play-mates.

The practice of not giving a child a personal name right at birth is yet another way to emphasize the child's status as one more household member who is expected to develop a sense of identity based on interdependence with others. By contrast, the predominant cultural model of child care among contemporary middle-class Americans emphasizes the child's individuality and preparation for less interdependence with and more independence from others.[16] During their early years Old Town children are addressed either by kin terms, by a variety of nicknames, or even simply as "baby." Furthermore, their being called "first," "second," or "third son" or "daughter" undoubtedly helps to communicate to these young children the importance of kinship, gender, and birth order (sibling hierarchy) and to de-emphasize any special identity that comes with a personal name. It is also another means of protecting young children from dangerous forces. Thus, in my experience, most children do not receive their "real" name until their first birthday and often do not use that name until they are adults. Meanwhile, however, children are carefully inducted into the system of kinship: They are addressed by kin terms and are taught how to address others by appropriate reciprocal kin terms. A high proportion of adults' verbal interaction with infants and young children consists of teaching them kin terms and getting them to recite the terms accurately and then to use them appropriately.[17] Caretakers repeat over and over to infants and young toddlers the terms for different family members such as "mother," "father"; "older sister," "younger sister"; "older brother," "younger brother"; "father's sister," "father's brother"; "mother's sister," "mother's brother"; "grandmother," "grandfather." Whereas in the United States we might begin by teaching a preverbal child the names for things, Old Town caretakers of preverbal children emphasize the words for people and relationships.

LEARNING KIN TERMS: A BRAHMIN HOUSEHOLD
January 2, 1967

For a full half hour Grandmother, Older Sister, Second Brother, and Rabi (one-and-a-half-year-old boy) sat in the front room of the Mahapatras' house. Grandmother and Second Brother took turns holding Rabi. They, together with Older Sister, told Rabi to greet me. They repeated the command over and over again, also asking Rabi who I was. Rabi finally looked at Older Sister, then at me, and said, "Nani" (father's older sister). Everyone laughed with pleasure. [Rabi had addressed me in an appropriate fashion, making an association between his aunt and myself, which pleased everyone.] Then, to everyone's delight, Rabi began reciting over and over again the term for "father's younger brother" (the appropriate term of address for Second Brother).
(Excerpt from field notes)

Old Town children thus learn early in their lives that they have many important relatives whom they must know how to address with appropriate kin terms and that they can extend these terms to other persons like myself. Later, they will learn that the nature of relationships with a father's extended kin is different from that of a mother's kin (e.g., patrilateral first cousins are "brothers" and "sisters"), that gender and age are significant factors in how one deals with others, and that different categories of kin bring with them different sets of responsibilities and obligations.

An early sense of interdependence is also reinforced by group sleeping and eating patterns. As previously indicated, in all Old Town homes children between infancy and adulthood sleep together with others.[18] Even as infants they do not have a separate space such as a crib or cradle in which to sleep but sleep on floor mats or wooden platforms together with their mothers and siblings. Mothers and young children characteristically sleep together, separate from fathers, although sometimes older children sleep with a father, grandparent, or some other relative. For example, in the Mahapatra household Rabi slept with either his father or his grandmother for a long time after his younger brother was born, allowing his mother to focus on her newborn infant.

Children in the Old Town also eat together, separate from adults.

Whereas gender structures adult dining, gender segregation is generally not implemented for preadolescent children. At mealtimes children line up to be served; they usually squat on the floor and then eat in unison or are hand-fed. In some families children sit very close to one another and eat out of the same bowls.

In infancy and early childhood, therefore, one learns to depend upon a variety of other persons. If your mother is not free to hold and carry you, someone else will be. If you have been displaced by a new sibling, then your grandmother or aunt might become your principal source of care and attention. She might become the person who, for example, sleeps with you at night or bathes you in the morning. Although all of your basic needs will be tended to, much of the time this will be done by someone other than your mother or father (see Table 4). Multiple-caretaking is the rule rather than the exception. A good example of shared caretaking in action follows.

MULTIPLE-CARETAKING: A BRAHMIN HOUSEHOLD
December 16, 1966

Older Sister (father's older sister) left the room and returned carrying Bapu (Rabi's one-month-old brother). Two neighbor girls (sixteen and eighteen years old) came in and sat down. Older Sister lay Bapu on his back on the wooden platform on which she was seated. Bapu urinated and began to cry. Older Sister ignored him. One of the neighbor girls picked him up and held him for a moment. Then she passed him to the other neighbor girl. They took turns bouncing him on their laps. Bapu's mother came in and took Bapu and held him for several minutes. Then she handed him back to one of the neighbor girls and left the room. Grandmother then came in with Rabi, who was half asleep. She told him to greet me, which he did. She smiled and took him out of the room. Several minutes later she returned with him and asked him where his brother was. Rabi pointed to Bapu. Grandmother then picked up Rabi and carried him out of the room.
(Excerpt from field notes)

Young children learn that the central activities of their day are being fed and bathed and being either carried about or allowed to

81

crawl or toddle around the interior courtyards of the house, watching others. They are provided with no toys but do have numerous playmates. Little or no attention is given to their motor and verbal development: Their first words and first steps may go unnoticed. With the exception of feeding and bathing, a rather laissez-faire atmosphere reigns in the house. One is simply allowed to grow up at one's own pace. Self-conscious "child rearing" is not a relevant concept.

Consistent with this approach to child care, both the toilet training and the weaning of children also are handled casually. In fact, Oriya has no words for "to toilet train" or "to wean." Old Town infants are not diapered. Whoever is holding or carrying an infant tries to sense when it is about to urinate or defecate and hold it away from her or his clothing so that it can eliminate directly onto the earthen or the cement courtyard floor, which can be easily washed. Accidental wetting of clothing is taken in stride. As a child develops its crawling and walking skills, it is encouraged to eliminate in a corner of the courtyard or into the open drains in front of the house. Similarly, "weaning" is a gradual process that often begins when a mother finds herself pregnant again; however, the process can last most of the nine months of her pregnancy. If a mother does not become pregnant again, she will allow her child to nurse until it loses interest – up to four or five years of age.

A number of techniques, then, are used to inculcate in young Old Town children a sense of interdependence – the need to rely on a variety of persons for care and attention, an incipient identification with the extended family as a whole, and the knowledge that elders are in control. As Stanley Kurtz (1992, p. 77) has cogently argued in his synthesis of Indian child-rearing studies, even nursing behavior is organized to subtly push the infant away from exclusive dependence on its mother toward membership in the larger group. While nursing, a mother responds physically to her child but withholds empathic attention, thus encouraging the child to seek emotional satisfaction in relationships with others, not in an exclusive relationship with her. Meanwhile, other household members participate in child care and help to attract the child away from an exclusive focus on its mother. The child is, accordingly, encouraged to sacrifice his or her early emotional attachment to the mother for a more generalized attachment to the whole family and acceptance by that group. The more intimate dyadic relationship between mother and child, which is often assumed in contemporary American psychological literature and is part of middle-class cultural models of child care, is controlled and muted in this joint family context. Here the child must learn early to value the pleasures of group membership over those of intense dyadic relationships. Attention and affection, he learns, will come more consistently from the joint family than from specific individuals. He also learns that some degree of emotional control and personal sacrifice are required of him to sustain such group membership. A sense of individuation and personal autonomy, the expected outcomes of middle-class American caretaking practices, are *not* the intended outcomes of Indian child rearing. A very different cultural model is operative.

The child in an Indian household also learns that she must relate to a hierarchy of others. In early childhood, her mother is usually in control of nursing, feeding, and bathing, and the child must submit to her in these contexts. But many other persons will participate in her care and will implement the same kinds of intermittent asking and response sequences of behavior that were established in infant nursing behavior. Several observers of Indian children have noted the teasing games of repeated asking and receiving, such as the offering and denying of food and comfort, in which both children and their caretakers participate.[19] With me, for example, mothers would often hold out an infant and say, "Take her. Take her home to America with you." When the young child responded by crying in fear, the mother and others present would laugh hilariously and repeat the action. Over time, young children came to find these teasing threats amusing as well and would pretend to come with me. Such practices probably keep young children actively engaged in dependent seeking–type activities with others until they are old enough to reverse roles and become the teasers/givers. In this manner an active form of interdependence among family members is again inculcated.

There are limits to these "games," however. Just as infants learn to submit to the rigors of the daily bath, older children learn that they must submit to being hand-fed. The authority figure in this instance would be a mother, grandmother, or older sister, but in other contexts it might be a father, grandfather, or older brother.

HAND-FEEDING CHILDREN: THE MAHAPATRA RESIDENCE

March 28, 1967

It was 9:50 a.m. in the Mahapatras' courtyard. Second Daughter-in-law placed about six cups of rice on a brass plate, some lentils in one bowl, and some fried vegetables in another bowl. She carried these things to the verandah in front of her room. She set the dishes of food, which were for Lili (girl, eight years) and Dipu (boy, six years), on the verandah floor. She then sat down on the verandah with the two children and began to hand-feed them. She mixed lentils with rice, forming it into balls, and popped the balls alternately into each child's mouth. Lili cried and resisted being fed. Second Daughter-in-law slapped her lightly and went on feeding her. For half an hour she proceeded to hand-feed the two children until they refused more vehemently by shaking their heads and keeping their mouths closed. Second Daughter-in-law reprimanded them, shoved their heads back with her left hand, and pushed food in their mouths with her right hand [the pure hand for handling food]. Once Dipu stood up and walked away. His mother shouted at him repeatedly until he returned. Later she left the children for a moment to go get a bowl of yogurt. When she returned, the children had disappeared. She went after them, physically dragging them back to their positions on the verandah floor and then forcing more rice balls mixed with yogurt into their mouths until all the food was gone. When she stopped, the children jumped up and ran off. At 10:25 a.m. they rinsed their mouths with a cup of water, gathered up their books, and left for school. Meanwhile, with a bucket of water and a broom, Second Daughter-in-law cleaned the verandah floor, now strewn with bits of food.

(Excerpt from field notes)

Socialization for interdependence and submission to authority has implied emotional effects. Affect is intentionally controlled and diffused among family members. Just as it is believed that intimacy and affect between husband and wife should be controlled so as not to jeopardize the collective well-being of the family, so too must the mother-child relationship be controlled. "Love" as it is found in the Western romantic tradition that assumes an emotionally laden pair-bond that is intense, exclusive, and highly individualized is not what is inculcated. In fact, the Indian cultural model views such love as a dangerous individualistic emotion.[20] Instead, a concept of love that is based upon familial interdependence and a sense of duty (dharma) to one's relatives is encouraged. Initially, it is communicated to the child by various persons through constant physical contact – holding, feeding, carrying, and co-sleeping. Later, it will be communicated in other ways, but always with set limits. "Love" and concepts of dominance and submission are inextricably connected. As Mita and Sita tried to explain in their conversation reported earlier, "love" is not so much an emotion generated by a specific individual as it is a deep sense of emotional connectedness associated with the members of one's extended family.[21]

Such feelings of what I shall call "relational love" are extended to nonfamily members as well – to friends, spouses, and other affinal kin. Mita and Sita, for example, frequently spoke to me of their affection for and friendship with me and their fear that I would one day go away and forget them. They wanted to build into our relationship some sense of dharma – some agreement that I would take the friendship seriously and, after leaving India, would continue to communicate with them.

Later Childhood: The Development of Gender-Differentiated Roles and Behaviors

An old Oriya proverb states: "When a boy is seven years old, he will be given a sacred thread; when a girl is nine years old, she will be given in marriage." The Sacred Thread ceremony is a Brahmin prerogative in the Old Town and symbolically marks the end of early childhood for boys. It is a kind of initiation rite for high-status Hindu males when, traditionally, they acquire the insignia of full status in their caste – the sacred thread that is worn across the chest and over the right shoulder – and move from childhood into the first of four recognized stages of life.[22] During the Sacred Thread, or "Twice-Born," ceremony, they are symbolically "reborn" as students and sent off to study sacred texts (the Vedas) with a guru (Brahmin teacher). In theory, only later will they return to their parental homes, marry, and become responsible members of their families (the "householder" stage of life).

In 1965–67 in Harachandi Sahi all Brahmin boys between the ages of seven and ten went through the Sacred Thread ceremony. Instead of going to live with a guru, however, they remained at home and attended a secular school, receiving their religious training outside of school. Old Town upper-status girls, by contrast, had no similar initiation rite. For them, the principal marker of development was marriage. In fact, in 1965–67 there were two categories for Old Town girls: "married" and "unmarried." The Oriya term for unmarried girls (*bheNdia*) also included uninitiated boys; both were considered to be immature persons.

Traditionally, these girls were expected to have a short childhood. In early childhood (from birth to about five or six years old) they, like boys, were primarily socialized into joint family life. Not until later childhood (from about six to ten years old) did gender-based training begin to be seriously implemented and preparations for marriage made. Ideally, a girl's marriage was arranged during this period of her life and consummated when she reached puberty. In response to my questions about when they were married, Old Town mothers and grandmothers usually spoke of "going to their in-laws" (*not* to their husband's home) at anywhere from twelve to fifteen years of age. Several, however, referred to "being married" at ages from seven to nine – depending upon the age at which their marriage was first arranged and when they made the move to their in-laws' home. Because girls of their generation were rarely sent to school, they spent this period of older childhood until puberty preparing for marriage.

Today, as in the past, girls experience a gradual transition at about age six or seven from being the recipients of care to assisting in the care of others – especially, of younger siblings and cousins.

My 1965–67 parent-child observations indicate that girls of this age are rarely directed to assume child care and other household responsibilities. They simply begin to do so, modeling their behavior on that of adult women in the family. In the process they learn not only to nurture others but also to express authority over the younger members of the household, both males and females, who are in their charge. They experience firsthand an authority structure that is based upon age as well as on gender.

The only clear developmental marker for girls in later childhood is the onset of menstruation. Although this is still a highly ritualized occasion in some rural parts of Orissa, it is not in the Old Town. A girl in the Old Town is not suddenly secluded for days and then brought out of isolation and publicly celebrated as she would be in parts of South India and in the coastal villages of Orissa.[23] Nonetheless, with menstruation a girl is subject to restrictions that will continue throughout her childbearing years: She should remain separate from other family members; she should rest from all work; she should not touch others or touch food; she should not bathe, comb her hair, or tend to other parts of her body; and she should avoid certain foods. While menstruating, a woman is considered to be in an untouchable state – quite literally an untouched and wild state in which she is temporarily unbathed and wears her hair uncombed and unbound.[24] At the end of her menses she is brought back into a normal state by ritually bathing, by preparing her hair, and by putting on fresh clothing. Menstrual restrictions set a woman apart and remind the family of her reproductive powers, which must be controlled until she is properly married. Once married, she is separated from her husband during her menses but should be sexually reunited with him afterward.

Frederique Apffel-Marglin (1994) has documented both menstrual practices and a four-day festival of the menses held annually in an Orissan coastal village. Citing villagers' explanations, Marglin finds symbolic parallels between these two kinds of events that suggest their agricultural origins. The festival of the menses, she suggests, is a celebration of the earth that takes place at the end of the hot, dry, fallow season just as the monsoon rains are about to arrive to bring life back to the land. The land has rested and, with the onset of rain, will be planted and thus regenerated. During the festival, men and women stop their work and rest, just as women rest during their monthly menstrual periods. And just as women bathe and are sexually reunited with their husbands following menstruation, following the festival the land will be rained upon and sowed. In Hindu cosmology the earth is considered female and the rain, male. Thus, in village life, where the agricultural cycle is paramount, associations are made between that cycle and women's cycles of menstruation, pregnancy, and childbirth.

According to one of Marglin's male informants, people come to worship the Mother Goddess during the festival so that she will bring forth good crops. Villagers believe that the Mother Goddess is bleeding during the four-day festival, just as she bleeds through women during the rest of the year. "The Mother, the earth and women are the same thing in different forms," the villager said (Marglin 1994, p. 28). In such a village, a girl's first menstruation will be publicly celebrated and her new status affirmed. Associations are made between the onset of her reproductive powers and the goddess who created the world and has the power to regenerate it.

In the Old Town, most of these agricultural associations have been lost, although many of the restrictions on a woman during her menstruation have been retained. In addition to the restrictions already mentioned, Old Town women told me that they should not enter a temple or the family *puja* room during their menses because they are in a temporary state of ritual impurity and untouchability, which would offend the deities. (States of ritual impurity are associated with all life crises, including childbirth and a relative's death.) For an Old Town girl experiencing her first menstruation, however, to have to refrain from touching others and sleep separately from others is highly symbolic in households where co-sleeping is customary and physical contact is used to express emotional connectedness among family members.

As a female who has reached sexual maturity but is not yet safely married, a girl is considered highly vulnerable and must learn that her behavior can have adverse effects upon her family. In Hindu cosmology all bodily substances except mother's milk are considered powerful and potentially polluting. Although both men and women can ritually pollute as well as be ritually vulnerable, such attributes are more frequently associated with women. Menstruation is particularly significant in a patrifocal society where it is believed that a girl's sexuality must be carefully controlled and channeled so that reproduction occurs within the right context – in a family of the right *jati* and socioeconomic status. A virgin daughter's marriage into an appropriate family brings honor upon her natal family; a girl's sexual relations and pregnancy outside of marriage brings serious dishonor. The control of female sexuality is, therefore, critical to the maintenance of the patrifocal family system and to the caste system of which it is a part. Since it is girls who move between families, enabling interfamilial ties to be created, and who produce the next generation for their in-laws, it is they who can potentially disrupt the whole status system. By imposing restrictions upon their behavior, beginning with their first menstruation, society teaches girls to guard their sexuality and their family's honor.[25]

MENSTRUAL TABOOS: MAHAPATRA HOUSEHOLD
February 8, 1967

Tonight Sita (sixteen-year-old girl) told me that she could not say her prayers because she was menstruating. [Usually, she, her mother, her sister Mita, and her aunt (Younger Sister) perform early morning and evening *puja* together.]

(Excerpt from field notes)

MENSTRUAL TABOOS: ANOTHER BRAHMIN HOUSEHOLD
March 9, 1967

Today Older Sister (twenty-three years old) and Daughter-in-law (nineteen years old) were whispering and laughing together. Daughter-in-law wanted Older Sister to ask me something, but Older Sister shook her head no. They continued to whisper and giggle, so I asked what was on their minds. Daughter-in-law finally got the courage to ask me how often I menstruate. They had heard, she explained, that American women menstruate only every six months. When I explained that American women, like Indian women, usually menstruate once a month, they seemed greatly relieved. I asked if they practiced menstrual seclusion. They said, yes, that when they are menstruating, they cannot cook or touch others. At such times, Grandmother does the cooking.

(Excerpt from field notes)

Given the cultural ideology that a sexually mature but unmarried girl can bring serious dishonor upon her family, the once common practice of early marriage for girls becomes understandable. To arrange a daughter's marriage before puberty and to send her to her in-laws at the time of puberty were reasonable safeguards for an upper-status family to take. All Bhubaneswar grandmothers, as well as many mothers whom I have known since 1965–67, experienced marriage according to these beliefs and practices. How they, their daughters, and their granddaughters talk about it will be the subject of a subsequent chapter on changing attitudes and practices with respect to marriage and gender roles (Chapter 7).

Once a girl has reached puberty it is believed not only that she must be carefully protected but that she should begin to practice the decorum of an adult female. This is when, for example, the rules of female seclusion and sexual segregation begin to be enforced. An adolescent girl should no longer wander as young children do about the neighborhood where she might be seen by strange men. She should begin to wear mature clothes – a sari that covers her legs and, when appropriate, her head and face and that symbolizes modesty and adulthood. She should observe other signs of respect and modesty as well. For example, Old Town adolescent girls bowed their heads in respect when greeting me. At first, I did not understand the respect hierarchy in Old Town upper-status families and bowed my head in response. Young children, who understood the rules well, found my inappropriate behavior highly amusing and enjoyed teasing me by bowing their heads in imitation of me and then laughing. What I had to learn as a young adult woman was that adolescent girls should bow before me but that I should bow before their mothers and grandmothers. I also discovered that adolescent girls, unlike their younger kin, became very conscious of not touching me with their feet – the most polluting part of the body according to Hindu ideology. When they inadvertently did, out of respect they would reach down and symbolically "kiss" my feet. They were practicing the kinds of behavior they would have to exhibit in the homes of their in-laws.

Not all of these rules were learned and expressed smoothly, however. For example, a number of adolescent girls whom I knew in 1965–67 actively resisted having to wear a sari. They found that it was cumbersome and impeded their activities, especially at school. There were instances of teachers actually sending messages home to girls' parents, asking them to enforce the girls' wearing of saris to school. The principal alternative to the sari at the time was a short Western-style dress that was worn by young girls and that revealed their legs up to and above the knees. This was not considered suitably modest clothing for postpubescent girls. Subsequently, Punjabi-style pants and tunics (*salwar-kameez*) have entered Bhubaneswar, giving school-going adolescent girls an alternative to the sari.

Old Town girls, as they approached puberty, became more and more engaged in the preparation of food. Those who were not attending school regularly assisted the adult women of the household in the preparation, cooking, and serving of food to other members of the family. Those in school had less time for cooking but were often highly engaged in food preparation for ritual occasions when many special dishes were made. They took pride in these events and often invited me to come watch them and participate in eating the special foods they made.

By 1965–67, however, schooling was having a dramatic effect upon the development of Old Town girls (see Chapter 6). Although it did not change fundamental attitudes toward marriage and the expectation that marriage constituted adult status for girls, it did result in the postponement of marriage and in the extension of older childhood. In fact, schooling was largely responsible for the introduction of a new stage of postpubertal adolescence for Old Town girls during which they still had to be protected. Accordingly, there was among Old Town families a strong preference for all-girls' schools. Even if a daughter did not continue her schooling after she reached puberty, it was becoming less acceptable for her to marry at a young age. In my sample of Old Town upper- and middle-status families, for example, only one girl married at a relatively young age (twelve years). Most girls married between ages sixteen and twenty, after completing secondary school and perhaps some college. The 1960s were a time of transition when many families were conflicted about how long to delay their daughters' marriage and allow them to attend school (see Chapter 6).

MARRIAGE ARRANGEMENTS: MAHAPATRA HOUSEHOLD

February 22, 1967

A few days ago a neighborhood friend (a sixteen-year-old girl) told me that Mita (eighteen years old) was going to be married soon. Today I asked Mita about it. She denied it, although she admitted that her mother had brought an astrologer to the house to read her stars. The astrologer had announced that she would marry within three or four months to a rich man. Her sister, Sita (sixteen years old), and the other girlfriends present teased her about this. They all agreed that astrologers tell the truth – "at least 90 percent of the time!"
(Excerpt from field notes)

On the occasion just described Mita acted unusually shy and modest, suitable behavior for a young bride-to-be. She did not want to discuss the implications of the astrologer's visit. However, it was only a week later that at her initiative we had the conversation about marriage reported earlier in this chapter. By then she was ready to admit that when astrologers are involved, marriage negotiations are well underway. A girl's father, she explained, is in charge of early negotiations. Once arrangements have been worked out with the groom's family, the father tells the girl's mother, who in turn tells other members of the family. Gradually, the news reaches the girl's friends, who begin to ask her about it. "Only then," Mita asserted, "should a girl speak about her up-coming marriage, and then she should speak frankly."

Plate 16. Young girl (seven years) ready for school

During our conversation I asked Mita whether she would have any say about her father's choice of groom. She said that she could object to him when they had an "interview" but that she trusted her father's judgment in such matters. "One believes what one's father says about the groom and does what one's father says to do," she added. The interview, a relatively new phenomenon then in Bhubaneswar, was a visit by the potential groom and some of his relatives to the girl's home to see her, what Mita described as "having to stand up and be examined." I asked her on what grounds she might object to a groom; she could not think of any. The other girls present intervened and told me of a Sanskrit saying about what different people look for in a groom: "The girl wants

93

Plate 17. Girls (twelve years) in their first saris

him to be handsome. The mother wants him to be rich. The father wants him to be intelligent. Other family members want him to be of the right caste. And friends want him to put on a good feast.''

The arrangement of Mita's marriage represented both change and continuity in the Old Town – change with respect to her age and schooling but continuity with respect to parental authority and the significance of marriage. The notion that Mita might have some kind of veto over the choice of groom was also new but not something she was likely to implement. At the time both she and her parents were feeling conflicted. Mita wanted to attend medical school before getting married. Her parents were sympathetic but knew that by Old Town standards her marriage had already been delayed and that at eighteen she constituted a risk to the family and community. Further education and increased age would only make marriage negotiations more difficult, and not to marry a daughter would bring dishonor on the family. Accordingly, Mita's marriage was arranged and consummated soon after I left India in 1967.

The Transition to Wife and Daughter-in-law

The advantage of growing up in multigenerational Old Town households, or in nuclear households surrounded by extended kin, is that from their early childhood girls are provided an intimate view of the roles and statuses that women must assume. As young children girls may be as carefree as boys. Nonetheless, they regularly observe how adult women behave in different contexts and at different stages of life. They see that mothers are in control of events critical to early childhood, such as feeding, bathing, and sleeping. Yet mothers also are restricted to the house and must avoid contact with most adult men, whereas men can come and go freely from the house. A mother's contact even with her own husband might not be very frequent. With women, mothers are respectful of older sisters-in-law and of their mothers-in-law and yet may have openly friendly relationships with younger women in the household. Girls, then, learn first-hand that a woman has control in some contexts and is highly constrained in other contexts and that a woman's behavior changes with her age and with each role that she assumes.[26]

In 1965–67, Old Town girls were gradually socialized into this hierarchy of relationships and behaviors. Daily they observed both the powers that women exhibited and the restrictions that women lived under. These extremes were represented by new sisters-in-law, on the one hand, and by grandmothers, on the other. Sisters-in-law arrived in their new households as strangers who were generally fearful and modest in their decorum and had to adapt to their new lives. During the first few days after their arrival, they were put on display for friends and neighbors to see – an apt symbol of their initial status.

DISPLAY OF A NEW BRIDE: A BRAHMIN HOUSEHOLD
June 15, 1967

The new bride was in one room of the house surrounded by strange women and children. She sat huddled in the middle of the floor, her head bowed and her eyes closed. I was brought in to see her. The women forcibly moved her head up from its bowed position so that I could take a look at her. Her eyes were red from crying. The women then pointed out to me each piece of jewelry she was wearing. The young bride, they said, would not talk or eat.

(Excerpt from field notes)

The presence of grandmothers in a household, by contrast, gave girls a very different perception of women's roles and behaviors. A grandmother could tell a girl's mother what to do and might even treat her father like a boy. And grandmothers did not have to do daily chores but could leave the house to visit neighbors or to worship at temples.

Old Town girls could learn by direct observation what the expected stages of a woman's life would be like. As caretakers of younger children and assistants to their mothers, they could practice many requisite behaviors. As members of joint families, they, together with their brothers, learned from infancy the significance of interdependence and self-sacrifice. However, unlike their brothers, they also learned that they would one day have to transfer these feelings to another family, that of their husband. Nonetheless, they could see that their brothers too had little autonomy in decision making: Boys' marriages were also arranged, and their schooling and careers were likely to be managed by elders concerned more with the long-term economic well-being of the family than with their sons' personal interests and desires.

Distinct for girls, however, was the gradually acquired knowledge that their sexuality outside of marriage was potentially dangerous to themselves and to others. It was the transmission of this belief system that provided the rationale for imposing on girls menstrual taboos, restricting their movements outside of the home, limiting their education, and arranging their marriages at relatively early ages. The positive and, I believe, powerfully attractive side of this belief system was the girls' knowledge that through appropriately arranged marriages they would achieve adulthood and the very highly valued status of motherhood.

In 1989 I also systematically asked mothers and grandmothers about their transition in status from daughters to daughters-in-law, and they regularly responded: "I was a child in my parents' home; here I am a daughter-in-law. Here I have responsibilities. I take care of the entire family. I make the household decisions." Their responses made it clear that they had become the domestic managers of a large and complex hierarchy of interdependent relationships and responsibilities – the joint family. They made such comments with pride and also, it must be noted, from the perspective of mature women who had adapted successfully to their husbands' families and had born and reared children.

Motherhood

Whereas marriage marks a Hinda woman's adulthood, motherhood, it is often said, symbolizes her fulfillment. In a society that stresses patrilineal descent, to bear children – especially sons – is critical, and girls learn from an early age that this is their responsibility. By channeling their sexuality to this end, not only do they bring honor to their natal family, but they also produce heirs for their husband's family. From a structural perspective, then, motherhood increases a woman's security in her in-laws' home and represents the beginning of her transformation from the potentially lowly status of new daughter-in-law to the highly respected statuses of mother, mother-in-law, and grandmother. As Mita and Sita pointed out in our conversation about marriage, to be barren is considered a tragedy and is sufficient cause for a man to take another wife.

This concern with bearing children was something that I experienced firsthand. Because I arrived in Bhubaneswar for my first two years of fieldwork as a young recently married woman, Old Town women regularly monitored me for signs of pregnancy. They were sure that over a two-year period I would become pregnant. When I did not, they expressed concern and wanted me to take measures, such as bathing in the special water tank of an Old Town temple, to enhance my chances of pregnancy. They did not find persuasive my explanation that I wanted to postpone childbearing in order to do research and complete my Ph.D.

Motherhood is clearly central to patrifocal family structure and ideology and is highly elaborated in Hindu myth and cosmology.[27] Indian girls are reared to consider themselves preeminently mothers, and Old Town women are no exception. "Wifehood," which is also culturally elaborated in Hindu doctrine, is in reality deemphasized in the everyday life of a joint family. Husband-wife conjugal bonds, especially in the early stages of a marriage, are controlled to preserve the well-being of the joint family. Interpersonal respect and distance are part of the cultural ideology that defines such relationships. Just as intense and exclusive ties between a mother and child are believed to jeopardize the collective family unit, so might too intimate a relationship between a husband and wife. Accordingly, young married couples are given private sleeping spaces at night, but they are allowed little contact with one another during the day. Whereas physical intimacy begins at once, emotional intimacy between husband and wife develops only gradually – especially with the bearing of successive children – and should not be openly expressed. For example, husbands and wives should not speak directly to one another, address one another by name, or touch one another in front of others, and, in the Old Town, they should not be seen together publicly. The control of conjugal intimacy is so pervasive that my husband and I find that, largely unconsciously, we accommodate to it when residing in Bhubaneswar: We refrain from having any physical contact with one another or from speaking to each other openly or intimately in the presence of others.

In the early years of marriage, then, the role of daughter-in-law takes precedence over that of wife in a joint family setting; motherhood does not suddenly change these expectations and patterns of behavior. In her husband's household a young bride is inducted into a world of women where she must negotiate new relationships and responsibilities. Ideally, motherhood helps her to cement these relationships as the women share in the care of a new baby and family member. The young mother's identity is not, however, suddenly transformed. When I asked mothers and grandmothers to reflect back upon those years, a few referred to becoming a mother as "fulfilling," but the majority saw "motherhood" in far more complex terms. Some pointed out that they were themselves just children when they had their first babies and that they had to rely on their mothers-in-law for everything. Others were allowed to go "home" to have their first child and could return to the status of daughter and be cared for by their own mothers and kin. In the Mahapatra household, for instance, Younger Sister remained with her natal family for a full year after bearing her first child. The transition to the new status of mother was, then, often a gradual one.

Most Old Town women, in reminiscing, focused upon the responsibilities and obligations associated with their change in status. As they successfully bore children for their husband's family, they were increasingly enmeshed in it. They spoke of the on-going responsibilities and sacrifices required of them in taking care of their children, grandchildren, husbands, and daughters-in-law, referring rarely to motherhood per se but rather to the dharma of motherhood. Again, when I asked what had given them the most satisfaction in life, they did not single out motherhood but spoke with satisfaction of being household managers and nurturers. As the son of one woman put it, his mother was in charge of the "growing of the family."

INTERVIEW: CARPENTER HOUSEHOLD
March 19, 1989

When I asked Mrs. Badhei what in life had brought her the most satisfaction, she hesitated and at first found it difficult to respond. I queried her about motherhood. She said, "No, it was all good – the moving from one role to another: from daughter to wife, wife to mother, and mother to mother-in-law." [Her oldest son has not yet married, so she is not yet a mother-in-law.] I asked what it would be like when she had a daughter-in-law. She said, "It will make me happy. The next generation will come."

(Excerpt from tape-recorded interview)

Conclusion

The response of Mrs. Badhei – a Carpenter wife and mother – is illuminating in at least two respects: first, her inclination to reflect upon her life as a sequence of roles that together brought her satisfaction; and, second, her anticipation of the next stage, the one that will ensure continuity of her husband's family and patriline. In the United States, a society that tends to emphasize the present and de-emphasize descent and lineality, it can be difficult to understand the satisfaction associated with reproductive and familial continuity. Similarly, in a society that stresses individual rights over family cohesion and parental authority, it can be difficult to appreciate the satisfaction to be derived from participating in a more communal system that constrains the behavior of individuals, especially of women.

In this chapter, I have tried to identify the underlying cultural and structural principles of the patrifocal family system as they were exhibited by upper-status Old Town households in 1965–67 and discussed by mothers, daughters, and grandmothers in my subsequent visits to Bhubaneswar. My specific concern has been to examine how such principles are first inculcated in children and then used to shape women's lives and interpersonal relations. Again, for Western women it can be difficult to appreciate the degree of fulfillment that women in a society that is more formally patriarchal than ours can achieve. To do so, we need to understand something about the value of interdependence – the commitment to others that grows out of the different socialization experience and set of familial expectations in India that motivate most young women and men to fulfill their roles within the joint family system. We must also try to appreciate the sense of personal security that comes from a system that clearly designates roles and expectations for each family member and restricts choices. In such a system young people have to contend with fewer ambiguities than they do in the contemporary United States. Furthermore, prior to this Indian generation there was no period for schooling and adolescence during which a young woman might reflect upon her designated roles and consider options, let alone rebel.[28] Marriage occurred early and moved women abruptly into the next stage of life. Even now things have changed only slightly. As Sita (age thirty-eight) remarked in a 1989 interview about the transition from daughter to wife and mother, "There is no choice." The story behind this comment will be explored more fully in Chapter 7.

Finally, two additional aspects of the patrifocal joint family system as it operated in the Old Town in the 1960s should be emphasized. One is the degree to which women formed support networks among their friends and kin. This is not to suggest that women's relationships were uniformly friendly and supportive, for like all relationships, they were cross-cut by hierarchies of age and authority that could engender tension and conflict as well as mutuality and good will. Nonetheless, the potential for intimacy and support was present in a way that many middle- and upper-status Western women, who have grown up in nuclear households, have had to discover for themselves. Second, within India's gender-segregated, hierarchical family context, women had clear spheres of responsibility and influence. They believed that their roles as household managers and caretakers complemented the roles and responsibilities of men. To view Indian women simply as subservient and "oppressed" – as much Western literature has tended to do – is a serious misrepresentation of these women's lives, feelings, and personal attitudes.

CHAPTER FOUR

Variations and Transitions

Being a Wife, Mother, and Daughter in the New Capital

"Old Town people are like villagers. They send their daughters to school for only five to seven years. Then they make them stay at home until they marry. Girls marry from fourteen to seventeen years of age, whereas boys marry from twenty-one to twenty-two years. In contrast, in the New Capital girls don't marry until they are twenty-one or twenty-two and boys until they are twenty-seven or twenty-eight."

Mrs. Das, an upper-status mother in the New Capital, made this comment one day while I was observing her two young children, participants in my 1965–67 socialization study. Mrs. Das belonged to the New Capital's educated elite, and her statement could be viewed simply as an effort to negatively stereotype Old Town residents. This was not, I believe, her intent. Rather, she was trying to convey to me some of what she saw as important differences between the old and new parts of Bhubaneswar. What is most interesting about her statement is its focus upon gender – specifically, her perception that there were significant differences in years of schooling and age of marriage between Old Town and New Capital girls. Her statement is important not so much for its accuracy as for the changing ideology about daughters that it implies.

The 1960s in Bhubaneswar was a period of fomentation and change. Many new schools had been established in the New Capital, making higher education accessible to Bhubaneswar residents for the first time. For all families it was a time of decision making, especially for the more conservative old town families: How much schooling should they invest in? Should sons be directed away from traditional caste occupations and trained for new opportunities, especially for those represented by government service in the New Capital? What about daughters – how much education should they have, and for what purpose? As Mrs. Das's statement makes clear, however, marriage was the critical issue in both the Old Town and the New Capital. For girls, the question was simply one of how long their marriage could be safely postponed and how much education would enhance their marriageability.

Mrs. Das's statement implies that girls' education had become more desirable among New Capital residents than among Old Town residents. At the ideological level, this was probably true. Middle- and upper-status families had moved to Bhubaneswar's New Capital because the household head (father) was an officer in the state government. This meant that he was highly educated in the relatively new Western-style school system that the British had introduced to India – that he had earned at least a bachelor's degree and probably a master's degree (see Table 5). Many of these government officers belonged to the first generation in their families to achieve such an education. Most such men came from rural parts of Orissa where there had been no educated elite and, in particular, no tradition of sending girls to school. Families who invested in education did so to enhance the occupational opportunities for their sons – the family heirs and the next generation responsible for the extended family's welfare. Thus most girls suitable for marriage to such men did not have a comparable education. Families began to invest in their daughters' education only as they learned that a pool of young educated men was being produced who had some preference for educated brides.[1] As one New Capital father explained to me:

"Today husbands need literate wives. For instance, a wife should be able to answer the telephone and take messages, and she should be able to receive telegrams. In the past, a boy married at sixteen years and a girl at eight or nine years. Nowadays, a boy waits to marry until he has finished his schooling and has a job. Then he [his family] looks

for a girl who is also educated. In order to marry a daughter nowadays it is important that she be educated."
(Except from November 11, 1966, field notes)

Mr. Behera, a middle-level government officer with a bachelor's degree, had married a woman eleven years younger than himself who had attended school for ten years. Her marriage had been arranged when she was only fourteen years old. Mr. Behera, however, intended to give his two daughters more education than his wife had received. He planned to send them to college and to encourage them to study medicine. "Medicine," he said, "would be useful in the house and would also enable a girl to be an 'earning partner' if necessary."

Clearly, in the 1960s attitudes regarding women's education and age of marriage were in transition in Bhubaneswar, and Mrs. Das was correct in that New Capital middle- and upper-status residents were generally one generation ahead of Old Town ones in thinking about these issues. They – at least the men – came from families that had already invested in Western-style schooling and new occupations. Many had left natal villages to pursue a higher education, traveling to other parts of Orissa and elsewhere in India and, in one case, to an Ivy League university in the United States. As a group, they were far more educated, traveled, and "worldly" than their Old Town counterparts. Their wives, however, were far less educated and cosmopolitan than their husbands (Table 5).

Both Mrs. Behera and Mrs. Das represent this period of transition. Although the former was married at the age of fourteen – the age of marriage characteristic of Old Town mothers – she had been sent to school for some years first. In fact, she had hoped to continue her education but was removed from school and married "to ameliorate my elderly and ailing [paternal] grandmother who wanted to see at least one grandchild married before she died." Similarly, Mrs. Das's education was halted at age nineteen in order for her to marry when her parents received an offer from a highly eligible groom and his family from the right subcaste. She had completed the intermediate year between secondary school and

Table 5. *Mean Number of Years of School Completed:*
New Capital Parents

Status	Fathers (N = 12)	Mothers (N = 12)
Upper/Middle	16.75 (Range: 14–19)	9.7 (Range: 0–15)
Lower	5.25 (Range: 4–7)	0.0

college (twelve years of schooling) and had hoped to continue on to medical school.

"I was young compared with most of my friends who are just marrying now [four years later]. My brother was married only two years ago at the age of twenty-eight. Girls have to marry sooner than boys, however. They have to marry when a good match is found. If a girl is a good student, she may be unhappy about being married. But if she is a bad student, she is just marking time until her marriage. Some girls even go on to graduate school because no husband is found. Some parents, especially Brahmins, still marry their daughters very young. They do not like having the responsibility of an unmarried daughter." *(Excerpt from August 26, 1966, field notes)*

Mrs. Das had dreamed of going to college to study medicine but seemed resigned to her parents' decision to arrange her marriage when a desirable bridegroom became known. She explained that she came from a small caste community in southern Orissa where "there were not many men to go around." Due to the limited choice of appropriate men, parents of daughters "had to take advantage of a good marriage prospect when it came along." Mr. Das, with his American master's degree and his excellent job potential, was considered such a prospect.

   Mrs. Behera and Mrs. Das represent the range of ages at which mothers in my New Capital middle- and upper-status sample had married. Half had married at 19, and the other half at 14–15 years. Their mean age of marriage was 16.9 years, which was considerably higher than that of their Old Town counterparts, whose mean age of marriage was 14.2 years. Nonetheless, it was not as high as Mrs.

Das's statement at the beginning of this chapter indicated. Differences in education, however, were far more dramatic. The mean years of schooling for New Capital mothers was 8.9, whereas for Old Town mothers it was only 1.5 – almost negligible. The level of education of Mrs. Behera and Mrs. Das was much higher than that of women of comparable age and status in the Old Town, although considerably lower than that of their husbands (Table 5).

The range of years that New Capital mothers had attended school is, however, more telling. The oldest mother in my sample had had no formal schooling whereas the youngest one had completed a bachelor's degree (fifteen years of school) and in 1966–67 was enrolled in a master's program. Clearly, at this time, women's education and marriage were in a state of flux in Bhubaneswar.

From Caste to Class

Middle- and upper-status New Capital residents like the Das family constituted a new educated elite in Bhubaneswar. From their perspective, life in the Old Town did resemble the past – a rural, village-type existence. For many of these New Capital families, however, it was a very recent past: A high proportion of them were first-generation urban residents. Six of eight fathers in my sample, for example, had village origins. What differentiated them from their rural kin and from Old Town residents was their extensive Western-style education and their status as officers in the state government.

Differences between Old Town and New Capital fathers, and to some degree, mothers, in patterns of Western-style schooling are indicative of another important change occurring in Bhubaneswar in the 1960s – a transition in the criteria for social stratification. Whereas in the Old Town *ascribed* status according to caste was still predominant, in the New Capital *achieved* status in the civil service hierarchy prevailed. Status in the government determined what neighborhood one lived in, how large a house one was assigned, and with what non-kin families one associated. Furthermore, to achieve a middle- or high-level government position required aca-

Plate 18. Mother braiding daughter's hair with two-year-old son nearby

demic success, high scores on the Indian Civil Service examination, and competence on the job.

In these respects, life in the New Capital encapsulated what had happened elsewhere in India during the previous century of British colonialism. The British had introduced Western-style education to India during the early nineteenth century to train government bureaucrats and by midcentury had put in place a limited, although nationwide, educational system.[2] Although the spread of such schooling was uneven and at first tended to reach primarily high-caste urban males, it did provide the beginning of a new social order. Western-style education went hand-in-hand with the intro-

Plate 19. Mother serving breakfast to five daughters

duction of wage-based occupations and a more commercialized and industrialized economy. A middle class of government officials, moneylenders/bankers, industrialists, and professionals such as doctors and teachers emerged during the late nineteenth and early twentieth centuries in India in response to British imperialism. This movement, from a rigidly caste-based system of social stratification to a somewhat more open class-based one, was slower to reach some parts of the country than others. British centers of trade such as Bombay, Calcutta, and Madras were affected first, whereas more remote and rural areas like much of Orissa were brought more slowly into the new socioeconomic order. For example, my 1965–67 landlord was the first person from Orissa to receive a Western-style college education, including a sojourn at Oxford, and to join the British Indian Administration Service.

The transition from caste to class is, therefore, a relatively recent phenomenon in Orissa and one that has been in process during my years of research in Bhubaneswar. Construction of the New Capital,

Plate 20. Girls going off to school

with its schools and new job opportunities, has presented Old Town families who reside in caste-based neighborhoods with educational and occupational alternatives. It has also presented them with status criteria that are non-Hindu in origin. Meanwhile, New Capital families have become intensely concerned with these criteria, focusing on their children's education and subsequent occupational and marital prospects. In the process, ironically, concerns with dowry seem to have become heightened rather than dissipated (see Chapters 6 and 7).

Caste, however, has not become irrelevant during this process any more than race has become irrelevant in the United States. Members of different caste groups have tended to move laterally into the new socioeconomic system: Families from high castes, for example, with a heritage of literacy, move more easily into the new educational and occupational structure than do others.[3] Thus the families in my middle- and upper-status New Capital sample are principally high-caste Brahmins and Karans (a high-ranking scribe caste). Members of low-status Shudra castes and stigmatized Untouchables are not represented in these upper-status groups (see Chapter 5). Arranged marriage as an institution, which thus far has

109

remained strong in Bhubaneswar, also serves to affirm caste identity. Nonetheless, the concept of social mobility based upon achieved educational and occupational status has been introduced to residents of Bhubaneswar. As I shall try to demonstrate, this idea is having a significant effect both upon family decision making and upon individual choice and opportunity. Importantly, it is having an impact upon the next generation of women as well as of men.

Transitions in Patrifocal Family Structure and Ideology

In the mid-1960s, growing up in the New Capital was very different from growing up in the Old Town. Because families had moved only recently to the New Capital and were not long-term residents, they were not enmeshed within neighborhoods of extended kin and caste ties. Nor did most of these households constitute the ideal joint family: Sets of brothers had dispersed to pursue different professions, and most parents lived elsewhere – often in their home town or village. From the perspective of Western modernization and urbanization theory, it looked as if the nuclear family were emerging as predicted. On the surface it appeared that extended families had had to break into smaller units to be more mobile and to take advantage of new occupational opportunities. In reality, however, families were in many respects still ideologically joint as well as structurally joint. The largely autonomous Western-style nuclear family was *not* what had emerged, which I only gradually appreciated as I spent months observing the comings and goings in peoples' homes and as I spoke about family with New Capital parents.

In the Das household, for example, I gradually became aware that a younger brother and a nephew of Mr. Das were residing with the family on a permanent basis while they attended high school and college, respectively, in Bhubaneswar. Several other families also had nieces and nephews semipermanently residing with them so that they could attend school in Bhubaneswar because New Capital schools were considered superior to schools elsewhere in the state. But joint family ties and responsibilities also went much further than this.

A CONVERSATION ABOUT EXTENDED FAMILY: THE MISRA HOUSEHOLD

June 7, 1967

While I was observing the Misras' three young children today, Mrs. Misra explained that her husband's paternal uncle lives permanently with them, something I had not realized. "He is not well. By living in Bhubaneswar he can be near doctors. Although he is married, he has not lived with his wife for many years and has no children." Mrs. Misra then spoke of having guests all of the time. Today, for example, her brother and her husband's brother-in-law are staying with them. "This is the way the Indian family works: One must always be ready to take care of and live with the other members of one's family. And one [as a woman] must obey one's parents-in-law."

(Excerpt from field notes)

June 21, 1967

Today Mrs. Misra explained to me that because her husband (a high-ranking government official) is the eldest son in his family, he has many duties and responsibilities. "He has had to give gold and cash for his sister's marriage even though he is opposed to dowry. His father, uncle, and other relatives come and live with us whenever they like, and we must pay the bills. For example, we pay all of Mr. Misra's uncle's doctors' bills. We have also been supporting one of Mr. Misra's sisters and her children for eight years since her husband died."

(Excerpt from field notes)

Mrs. Misra's remarks, made in an effort to educate me about the Indian family, were principally explanatory. Mrs. Misra was trying to indicate the degree to which joint family obligations, especially economic ones, prevail even if the whole family is not residing together under one roof. A man such as her husband, a successful eldest son, is particularly obligated to care for his extended kin. I have never heard Mrs. Misra complain about these extended family obligations, although she has indicated that her husband's brother does not assume the same degree of responsibility even though he could afford to do so. There is, however, a dilemma for families

111

like this as members enter the wage economy and try to share their resources with the extended family. Not all men and their wives assume these responsibilities with as much good will as have the Misras.

Mrs. Misra refers here to her husband by his surname. Married couples in Bhubaneswar generally do not use one another's first names and often practice teknonymy: They address one another as "the mother" or "the father" of one of their children. This is just one of the many ways that the husband-wife relationship is marked as respectful rather than intimate. It is also noteworthy that Mrs. Misra speaks of "obey[ing] one's parents-in-law." This tenet of patrifocal family life had been instilled in her even though she had not had to reside with her parents-in-law as a young bride. After marriage, she had continued to live with her own parents for several years while her husband was transferred from one government post to another. The decision that she should remain with her parents rather than reside with her in-laws was justified on the grounds that she had grown up in a town and would find it difficult to adjust to life in her parents-in-law's village.

Several New Capital households also had aging parents residing within them, sometimes on an occasional basis and sometimes permanently. In one such household I had assumed that an elderly grandfather was just visiting when I first met him but was quickly corrected.

A CONVERSATION ABOUT JOINT FAMILIES: THE MOHANTY HOUSEHOLD

July 7, 1966

It was evening and Mrs. Mohanty and I were sitting on the front verandah of her home together with three of the Mohanty children. Mr. Mohanty arrived home. He drove up to the verandah, got out of the car, and disappeared into the house. A little later he came out and sat down on the verandah with us. Mr. Mohanty's father, whom I had not met, also came out and sat down. Mr. Mohanty introduced him to me. His elderly father smiled in response. [Mrs. Mohanty continued to sit with us but was careful never to make eye contact with her father-in-law.] I asked Mr. Mohanty how long his father was staying with them. He found this question startling. "We have always lived as a joint [his term] family," he said. We then began to discuss different kinds of family systems, comparing India and the United States. Mr. Mohanty emphasized how important it was in the Indian system for daughters-in-law to live with their husband's family "so that they can learn the ways of that family and so that they can be near their mother-in-law."

(Excerpt from field notes)

In this instance I had naïvely assumed that because the Mohantys resided in a house that had been assigned to them based upon Mr. Mohanty's position in the government, Mr. Mohanty's father was a visitor rather than an integral member of the household. Again, it is interesting to note that Mr. Mohanty, in trying to explain the Indian family system to me, selected the parents-in-law–daughter-in-law relationship to discuss. This was not because it was an issue in his household. He and his wife had been married for many years. At that time, he was fifty-three and his wife forty-four. They had been married when she was fifteen years old and had produced twelve children, the oldest of whom was thirty. Thus, theirs was a long, stable, and highly productive marriage, and Mr. Mohanty undoubtedly knew first-hand how critical the mother-in-law–daughter-in-law relationship was to the maintenance of the patrifocal joint family.

In 1965–67, six of the eight middle- and upper-status New Capital families in my sample were structurally extended, and all eight were ideologically and economically joint.[4] All relied on village property and kin for a substantial portion of their food, particularly rice, each year, and all were enmeshed in joint family obligations and responsibilities. For one of the two "nonextended" households, the father's paternal first cousin ("cousin brother") and his wife and children lived nearby, enabling the two families to be together regularly. That family also received lengthy visits from a maternal grandmother who had been widowed and took turns residing with her various children.

One family in 1965–67 was extended in an unusual manner. Rather than the traditional father-son household, it was a father-

113

daughter household. A married daughter and her three children resided with her parents and younger unmarried sister in the New Capital. This living arrangement had been created to enable the married daughter to pursue a master's degree at one of the universities in Bhubaneswar. Both her father and her husband were government officers, but at the time her husband was posted outside of Bhubaneswar, whereas her father resided in the New Capital. By living with her parents in their assigned house, the daughter was able to continue her education. During this period, her husband visited on weekends, and her mother helped with child care. In this instance, a woman's aspiration for higher education and a career had prevailed over the ordinary constraints of patrifocal family structure and ideology. It represented a radical break with tradition in this part of India.

Even when patrifocal family traditions were maintained as much as possible, there were, nonetheless, significant qualitative differences in family life between the New Capital and the Old Town that affected both gender roles and socialization practices. For example, no New Capital mother resided with her mother-in-law. Several had lived patrilocally with their parents-in-law in the early stages of marriage but not after they had moved to the New Capital. Although several elderly widowed fathers-in-law lived in the New Capital homes of their children, they were no longer in positions of authority. This meant that New Capital husbands and wives were freed from the supervision of elders most of the time. From a woman's perspective this was critical: As wife and mother the woman was in control of household affairs; she did not have to submit daily to the authority of a mother-in-law or an older sister-in-law. Although she did have to tender respect and subservience when her in-laws visited, most of the time she was free from any such constraints.

In the absence of mothers-in-law and sisters-in-law, the organization of work within New Capital homes was very different from that in Old Town households. Women, freed from the hierarchy of female relationships, often found themselves quite alone. They turned to neighbors and friends, including myself, for companionship, but the household work could be a lonely and heavy burden.

114

Most New Capital middle- and upper-status women did, however, have the assistance of part-time or full-time servants. Such servants, who were almost always young village men, did much of the food shopping, helped with food preparation and sometimes with cooking, and assisted with house cleaning and child care. Upper-status households might have several servants, plus a driver, whereas middle-status households often struggled to retain just one part-time servant. Regardless of the circumstances, wives were in charge of all household affairs and, in the absence of other assistance, were sometimes helped out by their husbands and/or older children.

Independence from one's parents-in-law could be a mixed blessing. For example, the Mahapatras, a middle-status family, could not afford a servant when I first knew them. Mr. Mahapatra worried about his wife's workload because she was "weak." (She had had some difficulties with pregnancy and childbirth.) Mrs. Mahapatra found the care of three young boys, aged three to nine, and an eight-year-old niece who also lived with them, burdensome. Even though she would have liked to have had a daughter, she would sometimes remark: "Three children are enough. They are a lot of trouble, and I have no time. I have to do everything myself." The Mahapatras had been a joint family until shortly before I met them in 1966. Mr. Mahapatra's parents had lived with them but had recently moved back to their village to look after their property there. Mr. Mahapatra assisted his wife by doing the daily food shopping and by occasionally sending home a peon from his office to help her. Nonetheless, most of the time Mrs. Mahapatra was alone to cook, care for the four children, and run the household. "In many ways," she said, "it was easier to have my mother-in-law here to help out and take care of the children. Now Mr. Mahapatra and I cannot go out visiting because there is no one to look after the children." In addition, Mrs. Mahapatra felt isolated in her neighborhood where she had found no compatible women with whom to associate.

In the absence of patrilocal residence and the regular supervision of in-laws, patrifocal family structure and ideology were beginning to change in the 1960s.[5] There was, for example, little or no sexual segregation in the home. How could there be when much of the

115

time there was only a single adult woman in residence? Sexual segregation, if it occurred, was reserved for those times when extended kin were visiting and there would be sets of women who could work and socialize together, separate from the men. Or it might occur when a husband was entertaining his male friends and colleagues. At such times, his wife would retreat to the back of the house and supervise the preparation and serving of food. Dining under such circumstances was usually sexually segregated: The men would eat first and separately from the women. But on a daily basis many New Capital husbands and wives ate at least one meal together. For example, the Mahapatras always dined together in the evenings after the children had been fed. They also addressed one another by their first names, another sign of increasing intimacy between husband and wife.

Other kinds of constraints on women characteristic of Old Town patrifocal family life were also disappearing. For example, most New Capital women did not observe stringent restrictions at the time of menstruation. This seemed to be the result of both practical considerations and changing ideology. With only one woman in charge of cooking in a household, to observe prohibitions on the handling of food would have been a major inconvenience, especially for the men of the household. More importantly, however, these more educated New Capital husbands and wives no longer believed that a menstruating woman was dangerous and polluting and should be avoided. The one restriction that some New Capital women did say they continued to observe, out of respect for the deities, was to not enter a temple or perform *puja* during the first few days of menstruation.

Similarly, by the 1960s birth pollution restrictions were not being observed. Although some New Capital women gave birth at home, most were beginning to go to hospitals for the births of their children. In this new and different setting, restrictions on touching women after childbirth were no longer deemed relevant, and most women asserted that such prohibitions were not observed when they came home from the hospital either.

CHILDBIRTH POLLUTION: CHANGING PRACTICES AND ATTITUDES
December 11, 1966

In response to my inquiry, Mrs. Mahapatra said that during her three pregnancies her husband and the doctor had watched her carefully because she was weak. All three of the children were born in hospitals. For the last birth, when they were living in a rural area, a specialist came from the city to attend to her. "Births in the hospital are easier because there are no restrictions. I did not have to be isolated or observe any ritual pollution. By the time I came home from the hospital the period of ritual pollution was over."
(Excerpt from field notes)

Most significantly, perhaps, the observance of purdah – the seclusion of young married women within the home – was also disappearing. Although New Capital women did not move freely outside the home, they did visit friends in their neighborhoods, and they did accompany their husbands to retail markets in the evening, to the homes of friends, and occasionally to the theater or cinema. Thus, unlike married women in the Old Town, they were not rigidly restricted to the house, and the strict division between private and public spheres of life was beginning to crack. Here again the absence of in-laws – particularly, mothers-in-law – to enforce rules of female seclusion was undoubtedly critical, as was their husbands' Western-style education and exposure to other parts of the country. Most New Capital men wanted to have a more companionate relationship with their wives and did not want them restricted to home, let alone restricted to only certain parts of the house.

In Bhubaneswar during the 1960s beliefs and practices about husband-wife relationships were very much in transition. For older couples, where there were large discrepancies in age and education, husband-wife relationships tended to be more formal and constrained than for younger more educated couples. This is perhaps best reflected in sleeping practices. On the one hand, Old Town women usually slept with their children and separate from their husbands, symbolizing the priority of the mother-child relationship

117

over the husband-wife relationship. (This is in dramatic contrast to the American ideal in which the centrality of the husband-wife relationship is symbolized by the "master" bedroom – separate from the children's bedrooms – which may be furnished with a "king-size" bed.) On the other hand, New Capital couples were experimenting with a variety of sleeping arrangements. These were to some extent dependent upon available space and the number of extended kin in residence. Nonetheless, in the homes of two of the younger and most educated couples in my sample, the husband and wife slept together in a room separate from their children. In contrast, each of the two oldest, and least-educated, mothers in the sample slept with her children in a room separate from that of her husband. The most striking example was Mrs. Mohanty, who still had eight of her twelve children living at home. All eight children slept with her on beds pushed together in the center of a large room, while their father and grandfather each had a separate room to himself.

Two Family Portraits from 1965–67

The Dases reside near the center of the New Capital in a Type VIII house, the largest of the houses available to government officers. Their house is surrounded by other Type VII and VIII houses assigned to high-level officials in the Indian Administrative Service (IAS) and Orissan Administrative Service (OAS). Unlike houses in the Old Town, these houses are spacious and are surrounded by large Western-style fenced yards. Instead of turning inward, toward interior courtyards and verandahs where women can remain secluded from the public world, New Capital houses tend to face outward, toward their front yards and the tree-lined streets (Figure 4). To visit one another in the New Capital women must cross these relatively public spaces, whereas in the Old Town they can often use a back access to each other's courtyard.

The Das home has five large rooms plus two bathrooms, a kitchen, a storeroom, servants' quarters, and a garage. The house is equipped with running water, electricity, ceiling fans, and a tele-

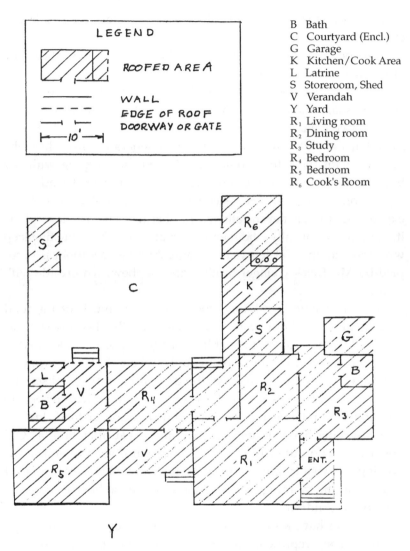

LEGEND

ROOFED AREA

———— WALL
— — — EDGE OF ROOF
DOORWAY OR GATE
|—10'—|

B   Bath
C   Courtyard (Encl.)
G   Garage
K   Kitchen/Cook Area
L   Latrine
S   Storeroom, Shed
V   Verandah
Y   Yard
R_1 Living room
R_2 Dining room
R_3 Study
R_4 Bedroom
R_5 Bedroom
R_6 Cook's Room

Figure 4. The Das Family House in the New Capital

phone. The room that one enters first is a living room with Western-style furniture – eight chairs, two tables covered by matching tablecloths, a central rug, a large built-in bookcase – and walls decorated with framed pictures of Hindu deities, as well as one of John F. Kennedy, a much-admired figure in India. Off of the living room is a dining area, also furnished with a Western-style table and chairs.

One room of the house serves as Mr. Das's home office. The others are bedrooms. Although the Dases have enough space to sleep in separate rooms, Mr. and Mrs. Das and their two young children share one room. Mr. and Mrs. Das sleep together on a bed, and the two children sleep on separate mats on the floor. Mrs. Das says that the children have always slept separately from her. She did not want them to become "habituated" to sleeping with her because then they would not want to stop. Her friends, she says, wonder how she can sleep without her children, but she explains that it has never bothered her because she has never done it. Somewhat critically, she mentions that some children still sleep with their mothers at ten years of age. Another bedroom is occupied by Mr. Das's younger brother and nephew, who reside with them.

The Dases have a full-time cook who does much of the food shopping and food preparation. Mrs. Das says that because she was in school right up to the time of her marriage, she never learned to cook. Now she does the cooking only when the cook is away, although she supervises much of the daily preparation and serving of food. Mrs. Das says that traditions have changed with respect to husband-wife relationships and the consumption of food. Instead of her serving her husband and waiting to eat after him, as Old Town wives do out of respect, she dines with her husband in the evening. They sit together at the dining room table. They would eat together in the morning as well if she were not so busy feeding her two young children.

The Dases have a son and a daughter and plan to stop with two children. They represent "modernity" not only in their levels of education and professional status but also in their ideas about what is a desirable family size and their knowledge of how to implement those ideas. By contrast, Mr. Das was one of thirteen children. The Dases' prosperity and modernity is also symbolized by some of their more costly acquisitions: an automobile, a gas stove, a telephone, a sewing machine, a radio, a tricycle, and a baby car-

riage. (Such items as gas stoves and telephon
in short supply in Bhubaneswar and are diffic
alone to afford.) In addition, Mr. Das is assign
jeep.

In one respect the Dases were strikingly di
other New Capital families in the 1960s. Mr. Das had observed that
in the United States women did most of the grocery shopping, and
so he encouraged his wife to go alone to the central market in
Bhubaneswar in an era when middle- and upper-status women
rarely did this. Mrs. Das went about once a month to stock up on
staples. The degree to which such a seemingly small issue was
considered a critical change is captured in the following conversation between Mr. Das and his father-in-law.

A MEN'S CONVERSATION ABOUT WOMEN'S ROLES: THE DAS HOUSEHOLD

April 20, 1989

FATHER-IN-LAW: The woman is the queen of the house. She has to
look to the domestic affairs, and the male has to do with the outside.

MR. DAS: That is the stark argument to beguile women, to cheat
women. I feel strongly that they should come out. Economic independence, education, these are the two things. Originally, you
treated them as second-class citizens, mostly.

FATHER-IN-LAW: Of course, [some] women should be educated, [but]
not all. But the thing is this: Their jurisdiction is mainly the house.

MR. DAS: This is the generation gap!

FATHER-IN-LAW: I am not taking care of the house. She [referring to
his wife, Mrs. Das's mother] does everything. But she does not go
near the market. She cannot go. I go.

MR. DAS: That's the generation gap. In our house I have trained her
[referring to Mrs. Das] so that she will take care of marketing.
She'll take care of any emergency. But for something serious, she
takes care of the situation in a much more competent way. She
can do anything.

(Excerpt from tape-recorded conversation)

121

Mr. Das, in fact, often refers affectionately to his wife as "the boss." It was she, he says, who made the decision on what parcel of land they should select for building a retirement home in Bhubaneswar. And it was his wife's decision that, in midlife, they become strict vegetarians.

In contrast to the Dases, the Tripathys appear to be a much more "traditional" family. Mr. Tripathy is a middle-level government servant with a bachelor's degree. His wife, whom he married when she was fourteen, is fourteen years his junior and has had ten years of schooling. They have ten children – three sons and seven daughters. Because of their family size, instead of living in the three-room Type V government house they would have been eligible for in the 1960s, they rent a private home in a neighborhood not too far from mine. This house has four main rooms, a kitchen, a bathroom, and a small servants' quarter (Figure 5). The Tripathy house, unlike the Das home, has no room set aside exclusively as a "living room." The room that one enters first is a gathering room by day and a bedroom at night. It contains a small table, two chairs, and three beds. Some of the children sleep here. Another room has no furniture but contains many trunks with the children's clothing. Mr. and Mrs. Tripathy sleep on mats on the floor of this room with their three youngest children, daughters aged six months, two years, and three and one-half years. A third room is principally a storage area and sewing room. It contains many sacks of rice and Mrs. Tripathy's sewing machine. It also serves as Mr. Tripathy's "study." He secludes himself here in the early morning and evening, and his two younger sons are tutored here as well. The fourth room is a combination *puja* room and study area for the older school-going girls. It contains one small table, mats on the floor for sitting and sleeping, some books and musical instruments, and pictures of Hindu deities on the walls. The oldest girls of the family sleep here as well.

The Tripathys' house is equipped with such modern amenities as running water, electricity, and ceiling fans but no telephone or gas stove. The "kitchen" is really just an open food preparation area where, as in the Old Town, Mrs. Tripathy cooks on a floor-

122

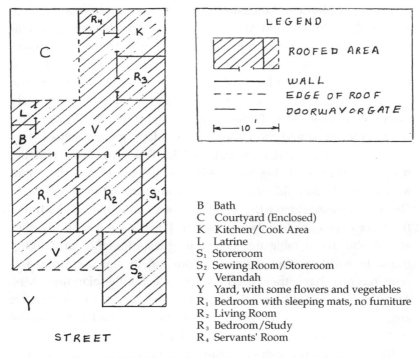

LEGEND

///// ROOFED AREA

——— WALL

- - - - - EDGE OF ROOF

—— — DOORWAY OR GATE

|←—10'—→|

B Bath
C Courtyard (Enclosed)
K Kitchen/Cook Area
L Latrine
S_1 Storeroom
S_2 Sewing Room/Storeroom
V Verandah
Y Yard, with some flowers and vegetables
R_1 Bedroom with sleeping mats, no furniture
R_2 Living Room
R_3 Bedroom/Study
R_4 Servants' Room

Figure 5. The Tripathy Family House in the New Capital

level dirt *chula* (stove that burns coal or cow dung). Mrs. Tripathy complains that there is only one bathroom for a family of eleven (one son is away at college) to use every morning.

In village fashion, the Tripathys kept in the 1960s and continue to keep several cows, their calves, and some chickens in the back and side yards of their house. In this way they have their own supply of milk and eggs. Unlike the Dases, the Tripathys have few material possessions. Their 1960s house had very little Western-style furniture. For transportation there was one bicycle and no automobile. The extent of the family's observable material wealth consisted of a sewing machine and two sitars (large musical instruments). However, they did have two servants who helped out with child care and household chores, although Mrs. Tripathy did all the cooking.

The overt physical dimensions of their more traditional lifestyle are paralleled by Mr. and Mrs. Tripathy's observable conjugal relationship. They never dine together, for example. In the early morning, Mrs. Tripathy rises, feeds the children snacks, and then prepares a hot meal for her husband and school-going children. She takes food into a private room for her husband, who eats separately from the children. Mrs. Tripathy never eats until her husband has left for the office and the children have departed for school. Her schedule is very similar to that of Old Town women, with the principal difference being that she has no sisters-in-law with whom to share the household work and no mother-in-law to supervise it. She does, however, have the assistance of a young man and woman from her village. Unlike the Dases, the Tripathys never sit together at a dining room table nor entertain guests together in a living room. In addition, they do not go out together as a couple, and only recently have they tried to practice family planning. Mrs. Tripathy is one of thirteen children, but she does not want to have any more children of her own. She is one of several New Capital mothers who sought birth control advice from me.

Mrs. Tripathy represents an interesting mixture of old and new behaviors for a married woman. On the one hand, she is deferential toward her husband. She would never address him by name, for example. One day she heard me call my husband by his first name and expressed surprise. She said that she cannot use her husband's name "because it would be disrespectful." On the other hand, Mrs. Tripathy behaves in some remarkably independent ways. For instance, in 1965–67 she frequently came to visit me, wanting to learn as much as she could about American practices – in particular, how to bake Western-style cakes and cookies. And for one period she rose at 5:00 a.m. every morning in order to walk into town and take early-morning sewing classes. She did this alone, returning in time to prepare the family's morning meal. In recent years, she has assumed practically all responsibility for the family as her elderly husband has grown senile. Her once distanced and respectful relationship with him has, by necessity, been transformed.

The Next Generation: Implications for Child Care and the Socialization of Gender Roles

Among New Capital middle- and upper-status families in the 1960s the Dases and Tripathys probably represent two extremes in the family settings they provided their children. One household was very small and the other very large. There were also disparities in material wealth and social status. Nonetheless, both families were high caste – Karan and Brahmin, respectively. Both resided in neighborhoods where they were surrounded by nonkin. And although both families were periodically extended, as relatives came to visit or to stay for prolonged periods, neither was formally patrilocal nor patrilineal in structure. In both households, mothers were not supervised by in-laws in the care of children and the management of the household. They were strikingly autonomous by comparison with Old Town mothers.

How, then, did these more autonomous household settings, with their more Western-educated parents and professional fathers, affect the care of children and the subsequent development of gender roles and gender ideologies?

Early and Middle Childhood

New Capital children were *not* born into large, multigenerational, hierarchical, and sexually segregated households where they were just one member among many and where the principal lesson to be learned in early childhood was interpersonal mutuality and interdependence. It is not that New Capital parents did not value this constellation of behavior, but they did not have the same personal resources to make it happen. Furthermore, they had come to value other, sometimes conflicting, behaviors. For example, in the absence of mothers-in-law, sisters-in-law, and most other extended kin in New Capital households, multiple-caretaking of children could not be as extensive as it was in the Old Town. The holding, carrying, bathing, and feeding of young children had to rest more in the hands of mothers, with some help from fathers, than be spread among a variety of extended kin. Thus New Capital mothers and

125

fathers together accounted for 73 percent of all nurturing acts that I observed directed toward infants (birth to two years), whereas the comparable figure in the Old Town was 64 percent. More striking, however, was the difference in participation of other relatives. In the Old Town, the care of infants was provided by extended kin and neighbors – principally grandmothers, aunts, and older sister – more than one-third (36 percent) of the time. By contrast, in the New Capital, extended kin participated in the care of very young children only 12 percent of the time. There, servants frequently substituted for extended kin. New Capital children were not, therefore, learning to the same degree as Old Town ones that they had a variety of "mothers." In New Capital homes, with only one exception, there was a single adult woman in residence; additional child care had to come from fathers and from relatives and servants who were generally males. In only two households with large numbers of children were older sisters available to help out.

These patterns of caretaking are even more striking if one considers the concerted efforts made by adults to teach young children specific skills or to give them information or to entertain them in some special way – what I have called "stimulating acts." In the New Capital, the principal agents of such stimulation were mothers, whereas in the Old Town, predictably, such behavior was well dispersed among extended kin and neighbors. Not only was the New Capital child's biological mother more actively engaged in efforts to stimulate him, but stimulating acts occurred more frequently in the New Capital than in the Old Town. Table 6, which is based upon analyses of my 1965–67 timed observations of parent-child interactions, demonstrates that mothers in the New Capital played with their children, taught words and motor skills to them, sometimes tutored them, and encouraged them in their activities with significantly greater frequency than did the mothers and extended kin of children in the Old Town.[6] They had begun to adopt what LeVine et al. (1994) have called a "pedagogical model" of child care rather than a "pediatric model." The pediatric model focuses upon the survival and health of the infant, whereas the pedagogical model characterizes caretakers whose principal concern has become preparation for schooling – that is, stimulation of

126

Table 6. *Rates[1] of Maternal Stimulation of Old Town and New Capital Children[2]*

Act	Old Town (N = 100)	New Capital (N = 55)
Smiles at	.03	.03
Plays with	.4	.9
Offers object	.3	.3
Offers information	.06	.06
Teaches words	.3	1.1
Teaches motor skill	.06	.7
Teaches handiwork	.01	.03
Tutors	.2	.4
Encourages in some activity	.1	.4
Total	1.5	3.9

[1] "Rate" refers to the number of acts performed per child over a period of 16 hours during which timed parent-child protocols were collected.
[2] With $d.f.=8$, x^2 of 23.81 is associated with $p < .005$.

behavioral development and acquisition of skills, protoconversation, and active engagement in social exchanges.

The philosophy in Old Town families that children should be allowed just to grow up meant that intentional efforts to teach and to entertain children, with the exception of teaching them kin terms, were unusual. By contrast, the Western concept of "child development" had begun to enter New Capital households: Children were no longer allowed just to grow up but required nurturing and molding in particular directions. For example, the Dases purchased a walker in Calcutta for their one-and-a-half-year-old daughter because they were concerned about her "slow" motor development. They were also worried about the social and cognitive development of their two-and-one-half-year-old son. Like many New Capital parents, they wanted to make sure that he began life with a suitably stimulating and educational environment.

NURSERY SCHOOL: THE DAS HOUSEHOLD
July 25, 1966

Several times recently Mrs. Das has expressed concern about Adrash's (two-and-a-half-year-old son) social and cognitive development. Today she said that she wants to send him to the Stewart Nursery School

(a prestigious private school) so that he will learn to talk, play, and be "smarter" [her term]. She contrasted Adrash with her sister-in-law's children who, she says, at his age talked a lot more and were "very smart."
(Excerpt from field notes)

Soon thereafter Adrash was admitted to a nursery school where, according to Mrs. Das, "the children are very young but very smart. They can do the English alphabet, read and write some, and they play together."

Another New Capital mother was concerned about her five-year-old son's learning and placed him in a prestigious English-language kindergarten. In addition, she regularly tried to teach all three of her young children both the Oriya and English names for things. She would give them the terms for items in the house and, while taking walks, for outdoors items, and then she would encourage them to repeat the words after her, something I never observed Old Town caretakers doing except when they were teaching children kin terms.

INTENTIONAL TEACHING: THE PANDA HOUSEHOLD
August 31, 1966

It was evening, and Mrs. Panda and her three children were together in the front sitting room of the house. Binoda (one-and-a-half-year-old boy) and Laxmi (two-and-one-half-year-old girl) were occupying themselves by climbing up and down on a chair. Bijan (five-year-old boy) began pointing out items in the room and reciting their names in English. Mrs. Panda praised and encouraged him. She told him to recite the ABCs for me, which he did. He also counted in English up to 100. When he reached 100 and began over again, his mother told him to stop. Then she recited the English terms for different parts of the body to Binoda who does not yet speak, encouraging him to point to the right part of his body. If Binoda hesitated or pointed incorrectly, Mrs. Panda would repeat the term over and over again in both Oriya and English until he pointed correctly. Twice she took Binoda's hand and pointed it to the correct part of his body. Meanwhile, Bijan, who knew all of these terms, occasionally chimed in.
(Excerpt from field notes)

Although toys for children were rare in Bhubaneswar households, New Capital middle- and upper-status families tended to have a few that they purchased in more cosmopolitan cities like Calcutta and New Delhi. New Capital parents had begun to take an interest in how their children "occupied" themselves and were appreciative of the toys that I occasionally brought their children.

JIGSAW PUZZLES: THE PANDA HOUSEHOLD

August 22, 1966

I gave Mrs. Panda the jigsaw puzzle that I had brought for Bijan (five-year-old son). Neither she nor her mother had ever seen anything like it. I tried to explain to them how it worked, but they did not understand. Finally, I took off the plastic wrapper and demonstrated. Mrs. Misra decided that it must be "a psychological test," some sort of "IQ test." I tried to explain that it was just a toy.
(Excerpt from field notes)

August 31, 1966

Today Bijan came in with the jigsaw puzzle that I had recently given him. He took all the pieces out of their wooden frame and then began putting them back in. He asked me to watch. He had no difficulty fitting the pieces together and finished very quickly. Mrs. Panda said in a pleased manner that the puzzle kept him busy much of the day. [She is always trying to find activities to occupy him and to keep him from disturbing his younger siblings and his grandmother.] For the next twenty minutes Bijan, working alone, continued to take the puzzle apart and put it back together.
(Excerpt from field notes)

Their own experience with Western-style schooling had influenced New Capital parents' attitudes toward child rearing. Not only were they concerned with stimulating their children physically and cognitively, but they also exhibited other kinds of changed attitudes. For example, most New Capital mothers considered it inappropriate to breast-feed their children for the first several years of life as Old Town mothers did. In fact, they introduced bottle-feeding during the first few months of infancy, usually justifying it on the grounds that they "did not have enough milk" to breast-feed, and they spoke of "weaning" as moving the child from a bottle to a cup rather than as curtailing nursing.

Such changes in parental attitudes and behavior have all kinds of implications for the next generation of New Capital residents. Fewer extended kin – especially, female kin – implies not only less sharing of child care but less diffusion of affect among children and adults.[7] Under such circumstances, children are less likely to become emotionally attached to the extended family as a collective unit. At the same time, they begin to receive attention that focuses on them more as individuals – on their *personal* physical, social, and cognitive development. They learn to identify themselves as more than just one among many, and they gradually learn that their parents have ambitions for them, especially if they are boys.

Showing off skills by children was not only tolerated but also sometimes encouraged in New Capital households, something that I never witnessed in the Old Town and that was not restricted to boys. Furthermore, children were encouraged to acquire skills. Several of the Tripathy girls, for instance, were musically inclined and would perform for me and others. One day they performed a song-dance-drama on the roof of their house where they had created a stage with a curtain and had put out chairs for an audience. They wore costumes that they had created and played music, danced, and acted in a short play that they had written. Their brothers were members of the audience, along with their mother, little sisters, grandmother, myself, and some neighbor women.

Other child care practices also served to differentiate Old Town and New Capital families. New Capital mothers, for example, relied more on verbal commands than on physical restraint to control their children than did Old Town caretakers.[8] Prolonged physical care of children was also less common in the New Capital, where the lengthy massage and bath of infants was a rare phenomenon, and children were encouraged to begin to feed and bathe themselves at an earlier age than in the Old Town. For instance, the Tripathys' three-and-a-half-year-old daughter regularly bathed and dressed herself.

SELF-RELIANCE: THE TRIPATHY HOUSEHOLD

October 1, 1966

This morning while her mother was cooking and her older siblings were getting ready for school, Maya (three-and-a-half-year-old girl) took off her dress and ran around the house naked. Then she went to the water tap in the courtyard, turned it on, and played and bathed under it. She splashed her body all over with the water. After about five minutes she went into the bedroom/clothes room and got a pair of underpants and put them on. Then she opened one of the trunks, took out a dress, and put it on.

(Excerpt from field notes)

Even for much younger children who were not yet capable of bathing themselves, New Capital mothers were by Old Town standards unusually tolerant of their children's efforts to help.

A NEW CAPITAL BATH: THE BEHERA HOUSEHOLD

August 29, 1966

At 9:25 a.m. Mrs. Behera began to prepare for her morning bath by rubbing coconut oil on her hair. Then she rubbed some on Bapu's (two-and-a-half-year-old son) hair and began to bathe him as he stood under a water tap in the courtyard. Bapu, however, wanted to wash himself. He took the cup from his mother and poured cups of water over his head and down his body, calling to me to come watch. When his mother tried to soap him, Bapu took the bar of soap from her and soaped himself. Then allowing his mother to complete the soaping process, he took a cloth and began rubbing his body with it. Again, when it was time to rinse off the soap, Bapu wanted to do it himself and his mother complied with his wishes. Bapu rinsed himself with water. His mother did insist upon washing his face, however, something Bapu was reluctant to do. He made unhappy faces in my direction while this was going on. Then Mrs. Behera began to dry him with a towel. Bapu grabbed a corner of it and tried to dry himself. He also tried to use the end of his mother's sari to which she did not object. At 9:30 a.m. the bath was completed. Mrs. Behera then led Bapu by the arm into the bedroom to get him dressed. She and Bapu discussed what he would wear. Bapu decided on a

particular pair of pants and a shirt, which his mother then helped him put on.
(Excerpt from field notes)

This description of a morning bath typifies much mother-child interaction in the Behera and other New Capital households. Although such behavior might be familiar to many middle-class Americans, it was, from an Old Town perspective, unusual. What was strikingly different about it was the amount of subtle give-and-take exhibited between mother and child. Although Mrs. Behera was physically in control, much of the time she allowed Bapu to take charge of his bath. The same kind of mother-child interaction characterized getting Bapu dressed and fed each morning. It strongly resembled those middle-class Anglo-American patterns of mother-child behavior that Margaret Mead once described as "giving the child the illusion of independence."[9] In the Old Town, by contrast, middle- and upper-status children were not being given the illusion of independence. There, mothers and their surrogates remained overtly in control of such basic caretaking tasks as bathing, dressing, and feeding children throughout their early childhood and often well into late childhood.

Table 7, based upon my timed observations of parent-child behavior, indicates how Old Town caretakers extended their physical care of children – holding, bathing, feeding, dressing, and so on – into later childhood to a significantly greater degree than did New Capital caretakers. If one examines all caretaker acts that I observed over a two-year period, in the New Capital, 93 percent of them were focused on infants and children under five years of age compared with 88 percent in the Old Town, where 11 percent of such nurturance was directed to six to ten year olds. If one compares rates of such caretaking, New Capital children by the age of six had almost ceased to receive such care. In the Old Town, however, a relationship of dominance-submission was being cultivated and the child's physical, as well as emotional, dependence on others was both encouraged and prolonged.

In a complementary fashion, Table 8 substantiates differences in Old Town versus New Capital children's efforts to be self-reliant –

132

Table 7. *Proportion and Rates[1] of Nurturance[2] Directed to Different Age-Grades of Children in the Old Town and the New Capital[3]*

	Old Town (N = 100)		New Capital (N = 55)	
Age of child	%	Rate	%	Rate
0–2	68.7	33.9	72.3	47.4
3–5	20.3	10.7	21.0	15.1
6–10	11.0	3.1	6.7	.003
Total	100.0	12.5	100.0	18.0

[1] "Rate" refers to the number of acts performed per child over a period of 16 hours during which timed parent-child protocols were collected.
[2] "Nurturance" was defined as those actions instigated by mothers and other caretakers to respond to children's needs: e.g., offering comfort to crying or distressed children, nursing and/or hand-feeding them, bathing and dressing them, carrying them, and offering other kinds of instrumental care and help.
[3] $x^2 = 8.72, p < .01$.

Table 8. *Proportion and Rates[1] of Old Town and New Capital Children's Self-Reliant Acts[2] (Birth–10 Years of Age)[3]*

	Old Town (N = 63)		New Capital (N = 55)	
Act	%	Rate	%	Rate
Self-care	34.2	4.3	39.0	10.7
Self-entertainment	65.8	8.3	61.0	16.8
Total	100.0	6.3	100.0	13.8

[1] "Rate" refers to the number of acts performed per child over a period of 16 hours during which timed parent-child protocols were collected.
[2] "Self-reliant acts" were defined as children's efforts to take care of themselves by bathing, dressing, and/or feeding themselves or performing other such actions that made them independent of the nurturant assistance of a caretaker.
[3] $x^2 = 4.35, p < .05$.

to bathe, dress, and feed themselves (self-care) or to entertain themselves by playing alone rather than seeking attention from an adult. New Capital children's rates of self-care and self-entertainment are more than twice those of Old Town children. Also, the overall proportions of these two kinds of behaviors are significantly different on the two sides of town. Extended caretaker nurturance of children in the Old Town was associated with the reduced amounts of self-reliant behavior that Old Town children exhibited. By contrast, in the New Capital, where mothers were more tolerant of their children's self-care efforts and where they ceased giving older children physical care, children became more actively engaged in taking care of and entertaining themselves.

What are some implications of these differences in mothers' and children's behavior? The prolonged physical dependence of Old Town children, together with the inhibition of many of their efforts to be more self-reliant, is consistent with the Old Town family goal of cultivating interdependence. Familial interdependence requires that children not think of themselves as self-reliant and potentially independent individuals. They must grow up believing that they need one another and that such interdependence involves some degree of subservience to others while they are children, youths, and even young adults. They must learn to trust and to obey the decisions of elders, knowing that someday they will become the elders, with authority over and responsibility for others. Furthermore, for children, receiving care and attention from a variety of caretakers helps to establish the necessary affect and trust among extended kin that makes joint family life possible.

Familial interdependence was also highly valued in the New Capital, but children there were being allowed – often encouraged – to help take care of themselves. A certain degree of self-reliance was also valued, and in some homes was necessary, because of the paucity of potential caretakers. Mothers who are alone to care for children and to manage the household simply cannot do everything for their children; they must allow them, and even encourage them, to be more on their own. When such attitudes and behaviors are combined with a self-conscious awareness of children's capacities to develop and learn, significant change can result. New Capital parents, in both conscious and unconscious ways, were doing things early that would promote their children's personal aspirations. Their model of child care was adaptive to a society that was increasingly oriented toward formal schooling and competition for higher education and jobs.

Were there any significant gender differences in the handling of

New Capital infants and young children? None that were discernible. In small households, both sons and daughters were getting more focused attention from their mothers and fathers than were children in the Old Town. In households with numerous children, however, parental care and attention varied, principally by the age of the child. Regardless of their gender, children up to the ages of four or five were the recipients of much nurturance and attention, whereas older children were expected to be reasonably self-reliant. New Capital girls, just like their brothers, learned to entertain themselves with toys when these were available.

SELF-ENTERTAINMENT: THE PANDA HOUSEHOLD
November 30, 1966

For forty minutes this evening Laxmi (three-year-old girl) sat in a corner of the sitting room playing quietly with a set of plastic blocks. She piled one on top of another to form towers, and she arranged them in neat, straight lines. After piling up the blocks, she would knock them down and begin again. She kept this up until 9:00 p.m. when dinner was served.

(Excerpt from field notes)

SELF-ENTERTAINMENT: THE TRIPATHY HOUSEHOLD
October 12, 1966

When Mrs. Tripathy and five of her daughters were visiting me today, I brought out a reasonably large and complex jigsaw puzzle for them to play with. [They had never seen one before.] They all immediately grabbed for it. Kalika (eleven-year-old girl) got it from the others (her three-and-a-half-, ten-, twelve-, and thirteen-year-old sisters). She sat down on the floor with it and began to take the pieces out while the others gathered around to watch. I brought out another puzzle, which the other girls then grabbed for. Amalu (thirteen year old) got it, but Giti (ten year old) managed to take it away from her. Amalu hit her, and Giti hit back. After several bouts of reciprocal hitting, Giti sat down to do the puzzle while the others gathered around her. Maya (three year old) moved back and forth between the two puzzles and sets of older sisters. At one point she took some of the puzzle pieces from Kalika and piled them on top of one another. Kalika pushed her away several times and continued to work on the puzzle until it was about two-thirds finished. Then she called to the others to look, but they were absorbed in their own puzzle and ignored her. Kalika continued working on the puzzle until she had finished it. She smiled in a seemingly pleased fashion and held it up for the others to see. This time they looked but did not say anything. Meanwhile, Maya climbed up on a chair, waved her hands, and mimicked what Kalika had just said. Kalika gave her an annoyed glance and began doing the puzzle over again. For an hour and a half they and their mother, who had joined the group of girls, worked intensively on the puzzles. *(Excerpt from field notes)*

It is interesting that Mrs. Tripathy worked on the puzzle *with* her daughters. She, too, was a novice at doing jigsaw puzzles and found such a toy intensely involving. Also worth noting is her tolerance for her daughters' aggressive interactions with one another. It was not uncommon for them to push, shove, and hit one another as well as their younger brothers. They were not being socialized at this stage to be polite, demure, and unassertive girls – at least, not in such situations.

Later childhood and adolescence

Gender became a somewhat more salient category in later childhood when older children (six to ten years) began to assist their mothers in child care and household chores. Just as in the Old Town, New Capital girls were more likely to help out than boys, but the critical factor was really birth order. Who of the right age and maturity was available to help? Middle-status mothers needed more assistance from their children than did upper-status mothers who had several servants. Even in the Tripathy household, where there were two servants, there were so many children and so much child care was required that the older children routinely helped out.

SIBLING CHILD CARE: THE TRIPATHY HOUSEHOLD
October 1, 1966

Padmini (twelve-year-old girl) went to the front verandah and picked up Rukmini (six-month-old girl) and brought her into the bedroom and set her down on one of the trunks. She held Rukmini in a standing position and asked Maya (three-and-a-half-year-old girl) to bring a dress for Rukmini. Maya handed her one. Padmini put this on Rukmini, but it was much too big for her. Padmini took the dress off and asked Maya to bring another one. Meanwhile, she held Rukmini with one arm and patted her affectionately on the bottom with her other hand. Maya held out another dress. Padmini shook her head no. Maya held out another one, but Padmini said, "No. It's dirty." Finally, Padmini sat Rukmini down on the trunk and, supporting her with one hand, reached into the other trunk and found a suitable dress. Then she stood Rukmini up, put the dress on her, and carried her to the kitchen where Mrs. Tripathy was preparing the morning meal.
(Excerpt from field notes)

In the Tripathy household with so many older girls, little was asked of the two boys, who were only five and six at the time. Subsequently, as young adults, they have assumed many household responsibilities. In other households, however, where a boy was the eldest child he might assist with child care but more rarely with other household chores, such as house cleaning and the serving of food. These were considered girls' chores.

By comparison with low-status children, however, middle- and upper-status children were performing few chores (see Chapter 5). This was particularly true in the New Capital where a tremendous emphasis was placed upon education. These children's principal responsibility in the home was to study and to try to do well on highly competitive exams. Doing schoolwork and being tutored daily were major activities for them in the afternoons and evenings.

STUDYING: THE BEHERA HOUSEHOLD
August 22, 1966

At 6:20 this evening Sanju (nine-year-old girl), Manju (seven-year-old girl), and their cousin, Rana (ten-year-old girl), were sitting with a

137

neighbor boy (twelve years) on the verandah steps. They were talking about school and comparing their marks on various exams. Mostly, the girls were interrogating their neighbor. At 6:30 p.m. the Behera girls went inside. Sanju and Rana took books out of their school bags and sat down on opposite sides of a table and began to study. Sanju wrote and Rana read. When I entered the room, Rabi (five-year-old boy) and Manju took out their schoolbooks to show me. Rabi began to read out loud to me. Then Mrs. Behera entered the room and began to look through all of Manju's notebooks. As she opened each one she announced to me what it was.

(Excerpt from field notes)

BEING TUTORED: THE MOHANTY HOUSEHOLD
July 21, 1966

At 6:05 p.m. Menaka's (eight-year-old girl) and Kamala's (six-year-old girl) tutor arrived. [He comes every evening from 6:00–8:00 p.m. to tutor the girls in history, geography, and arithmetic.] The girls stopped playing immediately and went inside. They did not go directly to their tutor, however, and at 6:15 p.m. I overheard the tutor reprimanding them for being late. The tutor worked with one girl at a time. He began with Kamala, asking her a lot of questions about her reading. Meanwhile, Menaka sat reading a book out loud to herself. When the tutor finished questioning Kamala, she began writing out some lessons. The tutor then turned to Menaka and began asking her questions.

(Excerpt from field notes)

Many New Capital girls and boys received special tutoring. Even though parents' educational ambitions were higher for their sons than for their daughters, they wanted both girls and boys to succeed in school. Who received special tutoring depended, therefore, more upon academic need than upon gender. For example, after having observed the Tripathy boys but not the girls being tutored at home, I suspected that there was a gender bias and asked Mrs. Tripathy about it. Her response was that the girls studied on their own whereas the boys did not; therefore, the boys needed the special supervision of a tutor. At the time I continued to be suspicious but have had to conclude that Mrs. Tripathy's assessment was correct. In that particular family, the girls have all outperformed their brothers scholastically and have completed more schooling than their brothers (see Chapter 6).

The tremendous emphasis that middle- and upper-status New Capital parents put on education tended to override any concerns they may have had about female sexuality. Parents sent both their sons and their daughters to the best schools that they could – often to private, coeducational schools where the instruction was in English. Unlike Old Town girls, most New Capital girls were not in all-girls' schools. Girls (as well as many boys) were, however, carefully escorted back and forth to school, and school classrooms were physically divided by sex: the girls sat on one side of the room and the boys on the other. In addition, conversation between girls and boys was discouraged, and in a variety of ways, girl-boy contact was minimized. For example, in 1978 Mrs. Panda told me that when her son Bijan was about thirteen years old, his headmaster called home to report that he had been seen talking with a girl several times and neglecting his studies. "We quickly put an end to that!" she said.

Although New Capital girls were being encouraged to do well in primary and secondary school, in the 1960s the expectation was that they would ultimately marry whereas their brothers would have careers. Thus, there was not the same concern with what field a girl might enter should she attend college. In fact, at that time some parents were unsure whether they would even send their daughters to college.

EDUCATIONAL GOALS FOR DAUGHTERS

August 1, 1967

Mrs. Panda announced today that all of her children would go to college. Then she qualified her statement and said that at least the boys would go and that they would decide upon their own fields of study.

(Excerpt from field notes)

August, 3, 1967

Today Mrs. Tripathy said that her two sons would definitely go to college. After that they would do some kind of government service. "Perhaps the girls will also go to college if they pass their matriculation exams. They might go for a while anyway."
(Excerpts from field notes)

In the 1960s, New Capital parents' educational goals for their sons were clear: They should receive the best and highest education possible and then enter some professional service. Sons, after all, have the responsibility to help support their extended families. The question of a college education for daughters was less certain. Attitudes were in transition with respect to years of schooling and age of marriage for girls. A delicate balance between a girl's level of education and her marriageability was required, and parents did not know at the time just what that balance would entail. Meanwhile, however, girls were being sent to good schools and were developing their own aspirations for a higher education and perhaps even a career.

Discrepancies in the ages at which daughters in the same families were married attest to this being a transitional period for many New Capital families. For example, Mrs. Panda was married at age nineteen, whereas her younger sister was twenty-six when her marriage was arranged and consummated. Similarly, in the Tripathy household the eldest daughter was married at age twenty and the next sister not until age thirty-three. In the Mohanty household one daughter, Kalpana, "came of age" in 1967 while I was still in Bhubaneswar. She was twenty and in her third and final year of college. She would be getting a bachelor of science degree soon and wanted to continue on for a master's in mathematics, but her parents considered it time for her to get married. One day I asked Kalpana if she would try to persuade her parents otherwise, and she said, "No. It will just be luck if I get to continue in school. That's the way it is in India."

A CONVERSATION ABOUT MARRIAGE: THE
MOHANTY HOUSEHOLD

August 21, 1966

Two friends of Kalpana's (twenty-year-old girl) were visiting today. They began discussing marriage practices in India. [They are all of marriageable age, and Kalpana's marriage is, I believe, currently being arranged.] Both girls were adamant that the traditional system of marriage and dowry is a bad one. One asserted, "Parents are only interested in getting their daughters married. Girls are not supposed to be educated. They are just supposed to get married, cook, and have children." The other joined in, saying, "The dowry system is bad. The boy's family demands all kinds of expensive things from the girl's family, such as a watch, motorcycle, and Rs. 10,000 in cash. If the boy has a good position, he can demand even more." In addition, they added, the boy's family wants the girl to be beautiful. "This is very hard on the girl's family." Kalpana kept lowering her head and blushing throughout this conversation.

(Excerpt from field notes)

Kalpana's wedding took place eight months later to a young man with a master's degree who was in his mid-twenties and who had a promising career in government service. Kalpana did not meet him until the day of the wedding. When he visited the Mohantys' house for the final marriage settlement some months before the wedding, he met her siblings but was only shown a photograph of Kalpana. The recently emerging practice of allowing the prospective bride and groom to meet during the marriage negotiations was not observed in this instance. Tradition prevailed.

The wedding itself was large and elaborate, with about five hundred guests in attendance. Unlike the first wedding that I attended in Bhubaneswar, men and women were not segregated. They wandered freely throughout the large house and yard, where a series of tents had been erected. When I arrived at 7:00 p.m., Kalpana was seated on the floor of one room in the house and was surrounded by college girlfriends. They sat and joked with her, trying to make her laugh. She did giggle and laugh some but kept her head bowed so that her face was not visible. Later the groom,

141

his father, and male friends arrived with much fanfare and were welcomed at the gate by both Mr. and Mrs. Mohanty, along with Mrs. Mohanty's sisters. The women each took turns holding betel leaves to the groom's cheek. Then they threw rice at him, after which he and his male entourage were led into the house. Only later, when the feasting took place, was sexual segregation imposed: The men were fed first in one of the tents, then the women. Meanwhile, the children were served separately in a different tent.

This New Capital wedding occurred a year and a half after the wedding described in Chapter 3, and their differences symbolize some of the transitions occurring in patrifocal family structure in Bhubaneswar in the 1960s. For example, in this New Capital wedding with the exception of when they dined, men and women were not spatially segregated. Furthermore, instead of only the men of the household going outside to greet the groom and his entourage, Mrs. Mohanty and other women of the family participated. And, unlike the young bride described in Chapter 3 who sat alone for hours awaiting the arrival of the groom and the beginning of the wedding ceremony, Kalpana was surrounded by college friends who kept her entertained. Although the bride and groom had not met before, they knew that they were relatively close in age and education. A more companionate relationship would be possible and, indeed, has occurred, as is evidenced in the following exchange that took place twenty years later.

HUSBAND-WIFE EXCHANGE: MOHANTY/MAHAPATRA HOUSEHOLD

February 1, 1987

Today my mother and I were having lunch with Kalpana, her husband, and two of their three teenage daughters. We all sat together in their small living room. Kalpana's husband explained that she was the last child in her family to have an arranged marriage. "We did not even meet beforehand," he said. Then he continued teasingly, "If I had seen her, I would not have married her." Kalpana interrupted and said laughingly, "Yes, I am too dark!" [She refers here to her skin color. Light skin is preferred in India and is especially prized in brides.] They sat side by side during this conversation, and Kalpana's

142

husband pressed her hand affectionately after making the above remark. They were openly affectionate and expressive with one another
– a striking contrast with Kalpana's parents' more formal and respectful relationship.

(Excerpt from field notes)

Conclusion

In the 1960s, patrifocal family structure and gender roles were in
transition in the New Capital. Middle- and upper-status children
were growing up in truncated joint families where mothers had to
be the principal caretakers. The mothers had no extended female
kin with whom to share child care and housework. This situation
had two important consequences for New Capital children: They
could not experience the same degree of emotional bonding with a
variety of female caretakers that Old Town children did, and they
were encouraged from an early age to be more self-reliant. These
subtle, but nontrivial, differences in early childhood socialization
helped prepare the next generation of New Capital residents to be
more independent and mobile – characteristics that were compatible with their parents' educational and occupational aspirations for
them.

Parents' aspirations for their daughters, however, were less clear
than for the sons who would be their patrilineal descendants and
inheritors. This generation of New Capital girls was growing up
with mixed signals about their future roles and about what were
suitable aspirations, not unlike the generation of middle-class
American women in the 1950s. They were being intellectually stimulated at home and encouraged to do well in school but were
simultaneously taught that their appropriate roles would be those
of wife, daughter-in-law, and mother. Unlike Old Town girls, however, they could not witness firsthand and on a daily basis women
occupying the roles of daughter-in-law, mother-in-law, and grandmother. In addition, the husband-wife relationships that they could
observe were themselves in transition.

Furthermore, this generation of New Capital girls was being kept at home far longer than girls of their mothers' generation. Unlike their mothers, who married anywhere from fourteen to nineteen years of age, these girls were not marrying before they reached eighteen and most were in their twenties – some even in their thirties – before getting married and leaving home. This meant that they experienced an adolescence and early adulthood as daughters rather than as daughters-in-law, wives, and mothers. Remaining in their natal homes with their siblings meant that they could develop long-term attachments to their brothers and sisters, as well as to their parents – again, something that was more difficult for women who married at puberty. It also meant that they could pursue a higher education, an opportunity that had not been available to most of their mothers but that many of their mothers had desired. And, in the course of pursuing their extended education, many New Capital girls developed career aspirations (see Chapter 6).

Another aspect of New Capital girls' prolonged "daughterhood" was that they entered marriage as more mature, more educated, and potentially more assertive and independent young women. Accordingly, meeting the patrifocal expectations of modesty, obedience, and self-sacrifice in daughters-in-law and wives has become increasingly complicated (see Chapter 7). Nonetheless, most New Capital girls (the remark of Kalpana's husband notwithstanding) have continued to accept their parents' authority in the arranging of marriage.

CHAPTER FIVE

——————

Caste/Class and Gender

To Be Poor and Female

If one is poor in Bhubaneswar, it is very difficult to fulfill certain patrifocal family ideals. Most low-status, poor women work outside of the home and contribute to the family's economic welfare. Because of this, they cannot observe purdah – an important symbol and practice of higher-status families – and, accordingly, their sexual purity can always be questioned. However, low-status families do try to protect prepubescent girls by assigning them chores either within or close to home and by arranging their marriages as soon as they reach puberty – or, as they would say, "as soon as a girl is big."

A poor, low-status married woman is oriented much more toward economic survival than toward the continuity of a husband's patriline. Whereas middle- and upper-status women usually responded "being a wife and mother" when asked what brought them the most satisfaction in life, lower-status women responded "surviving." As Mrs. Patro, one Old Town Bauri woman, put it, "I am always concerned with survival – that's my objective. I like working in the fields. What is most important is earning a livelihood." Similarly, when asked how life had changed for her when she married and moved to her husband's home, she responded, "It's always been the same. Before I got married I had to work. Now I have to work."

A New Capital low-status daughter expressed somewhat different but equally sober sentiments when in 1989 I asked her whether things had changed for women between her mother's generation and hers. Sopna, ten years old when I first knew her and now

145

thirty-two, said: "I am lucky. Unlike my parents, I did not have to stay in the village. I was brought up in Bhubaneswar with some education. In the village my parents suffered terribly. They had no food. They ate nothing but boiled tamarind leaves during the drought. I am much better off than my mother."

Sopna sees her life as an improvement over her mother's even though her husband drinks heavily and has earned little money in the past year. Nonetheless, she knows that she and her three children are not starving. In fact, they are living a reasonably comfortable village-style life on the outskirts of Bhubaneswar where they reside in a mud-walled, thatched-roofed house that is much bigger than the one in which she grew up.

Family Organization

The low-status families in my sample in 1965–67 ranged in size from four to seventeen members living together under one roof. From an outsider's perspective all the Old Town families looked like joint households: Sets of brothers, their wives, and their children resided together, sometimes with an aging grandparent. However, economically, these households were not always joint. The brothers did not necessarily pool their limited resources, and their wives might have separate *chulas* on which to cook. With no landed property to share and to pass on to the next generation of males, there was less incentive to be economically joint.[1] There was, however, much incentive to be socially joint. To reside together, sharing one courtyard, meant that women could cooperate with one another, especially in child care. Shared child care was particularly critical in families where women as well as men left the house on most days to work.

One outcaste Washerman family, in the years that I have known them, has operated as a joint family both economically and socially. Two brothers and their wives have cooperated in the laundry business, which has expanded dramatically with the building of the New Capital, and they were able to send their youngest brother

146

through college. That brother then attained a low-level government position in the New Capital. Unlike the majority of Old Town low-status families, this family has been able to invest in land as well as in education. Despite its outcaste origins, this Washerman family has in many respects moved itself into a middle-class lifestyle.

As were the middle- and upper-status households in the New Capital, low-status ones were structurally extended but not patrilineally joint. In fact, the two Sweeper families in my sample had a bias toward related sets of women residing together. In one instance, a wife's mother lived with her daughter, son-in-law, and three children. In the other instance, a wife's mother and maternal grandmother resided next door to their married daughter/granddaughter and her husband and three children. In both cases, all the adult men and women worked as government sweepers (janitors) and pooled their resources. They cooked over one fire and cooperated in child care. In this manner, they were able to survive economically.

In 1965–67, a government sweeper was earning from Rs. 60–112 per month. In these two families, joint monthly wages totaled Rs. 205 and Rs. 310, respectively. At the same time, in contrast, a middle-level government servant earned Rs. 500–700 per month, and an upper-level officer had a monthly salary of Rs. 900–1300. In addition, the higher-status families usually had landed property as well. Nonetheless, the government-employed Sweeper families had more stable incomes than the Old Town Bauris, whose work as laborers was more seasonal and irregular. They were also better off than the other two low-status families in my New Capital sample who did not have as many earners pooling their incomes.

Sopna's father, for example, worked as a government night watchman, overseeing a building in Gautam Nagar close to where I lived in 1965–67. His monthly salary was Rs. 65. His wife was not employed, and there were no other employed adults in the family. Mr. Behera supplemented his income by raising chickens and selling their eggs and by working as a part-time gardener for me. He and his two children watered the vegetables and flowers that I had planted. Although poor, Sopna's family was of middle-caste status

(Tanti), and her father was literate. He had had five years of schooling and often read at night by the light of a lantern as he reclined on the ground outside of the building he was hired to guard.

The other low-status household in my New Capital sample was a family of relatively high-caste status (Kayastha) but one that was economically impoverished. The husband worked as a government messenger for Rs. 70 a month, which his wife tried to supplement by helping in the kitchens of better-off neighborhood families – something she could do by right of her high caste. However, such work was highly irregular and not well paid. Mr. Singh was in poor health when I first knew him, and his wife constantly complained that he used up what little salary he earned on medicines and tea. He frequented the neighborhood tea stall.

A CONVERSATION WITH MRS. SINGH
January 23, 1966

Mrs. Singh began to cry today when telling me of her difficulties. She says that her husband is not a good man. He gives her no money but spends it all at tea stalls, where he eats and drinks, and on homeopathic medicines for his cough. Mrs. Singh has no money to buy food to feed herself and her children. Today, for example, there was no food in the house but a few wilted cabbage leaves and some lentils that she had been given by neighbors for whom she works. She says that she lives on the Rs. 20 a month that she earns by cooking for other families. "If I didn't have this small baby," she said, "I would just leave my husband and go back to Puri [the town where she grew up]." She also complained that her husband had sold all her jewelry. [She wears no jewelry of any kind, most unusual even for poor women.]

(Excerpt from field notes)

Mr. and Mrs. Singh have no siblings. Mrs. Singh's parents died when she was very young, and she was reared by another family. Mr. Singh's father died when he was about thirteen, at which time he dropped out of school to work and support his mother. The Singhs have two children, an eight-year-old son and a newborn daughter. (Mrs. Singh experienced three miscarriages in between the two children.) In addition, Mr. Singh's widowed mother resides with them much of the time in their small rented quarters. Although she is old and unemployed, she does assist with cooking and child care.

Portrait of an Old Town Bauri Family, 1965–67

On the edge of Harachandi Sahi is a small villagelike settlement – a row of mud-walled, thatched-roofed houses inhabited by Bauris, an outcaste group thought to be of tribal origin. Bauris provide much of the agricultural labor in the Old Town and the construction labor in the New Capital. They also work in rock quarries, helping to provide the basic building material of both the Old Town and the New Capital – red laterite stone blocks. In the Old Town, they are squatters for they do not own the land on which their houses sit.

The Patros are one family in this small neighborhood of Bauris. Thirteen family members reside together in a string of small connected rooms (see Figure 6). There are four Patro brothers, three of whom are married, and their widowed mother. First Brother and his wife have a twelve-year-old son, Chabi, a seven-year-old daughter, Santi, and a newborn son, Ashok. Second Brother and his wife have just one son, Muna, who is two, and Third Brother and his wife have one daughter, Sanju, who is one year old.

The paucity of children in the Patro home in 1965–67 was due not only to the relatively young ages of the brothers and their wives, who ranged from twenty to thirty-five years old, but also to the high rate of infant deaths that they had experienced. For example, First Brother and his wife had lost four children, and their new baby died about six months after I first knew them. They have had no more surviving children. Before Muna was born, Second Brother and his wife lost two children, both of whom died during the first year of life. Subsequent to 1967, they have had two more surviving children. Third Brother and his wife had been married only two years as of 1966 and had just the one daughter at that time.

The high rate of infant mortality among this and other Bauri

149

families is undoubtedly related to their poverty – in particular, an inadequate diet and lack of medical care – as well as to the physically strenuous work that Bauri women do. For example, during the rainy season they work long hours in the fields transplanting rice. This involves wading out in flooded fields and uprooting baby rice plants, one by one, and moving them to adjacent fields. It is backbreaking work that women engage in whether or not they are pregnant or have nursing infants.

The eight small rooms that constitute the Patro household enable each brother and his wife and children to have some space of their own. Each of the married brothers has a room in which to sleep and store food and clothing and an attached room in which to cook. Fourth Brother, who is not yet married, shares a room with his mother (Grandmother). Another room serves as an entranceway and a shed for their bullocks. All of the rooms have mud walls, dirt floors, and thatched roofs. They contain no furniture of any kind and no decorations on the walls. There is also no area set aside for *puja*. The Patros and their neighbors have no electricity, running water, or latrines. They go to a public well for their water and to the fields to eliminate. They do, however, have a reasonably spacious courtyard and backyard area where most of the household activities take place. Thus, although they are not economically a joint family, they spend most of their time at home in shared space. And Grandmother, who no longer works in the fields, helps all the parents with child care.

The Daily Schedule

Unlike other Old Town families, the Patros cannot follow a well-defined daily schedule because their activities vary by agricultural season and by the demand for rock cutting and construction. Adults tend to rise early, 5:00–6:00 a.m., have a morning snack of tea and rice water left over from the night before, and head off to work. When women are not working in the fields, they remain home and prepare a midday cooked meal, bathe young children, and tend to other household chores. From about 10:00 a.m. to noon, children may be fed a hot meal, or they may have to fend for

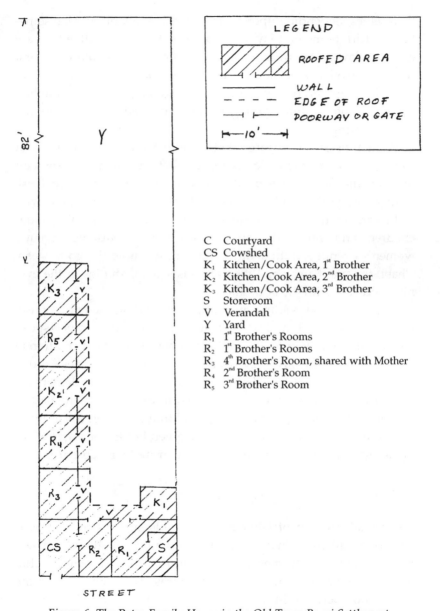

LEGEND

ROOFED AREA

WALL
EDGE OF ROOF
DOORWAY OR GATE

|←—10'—→|

C   Courtyard
CS Cowshed
K_1 Kitchen/Cook Area, 1st Brother
K_2 Kitchen/Cook Area, 2nd Brother
K_3 Kitchen/Cook Area, 3rd Brother
S   Storeroom
V   Verandah
Y   Yard
R_1 1st Brother's Rooms
R_2 1st Brother's Rooms
R_3 4th Brother's Room, shared with Mother
R_4 2nd Brother's Room
R_5 3rd Brother's Room

Figure 6. The Patro Family House in the Old Town Bauri Settlement

151

themselves, depending upon their mother's availability. Men sometimes return home midday for a hot meal, but just as often they are
gone all day, as are their wives. In the Patro household only First
Brother's twelve-year-old son goes to school. Santi, their seven-
year-old daughter, remains home and, together with Grandmother,
takes care of the three younger children when their parents are
away working.

Women begin to prepare a hot meal in the evening from about
6:00–7:00 p.m. Young children are fed first and then put down on
mats on the floor to sleep. Men tend to return home from work
during this period and to bathe and relax. They often help with
child care in the early evening as well. Cooking, feeding older
children and husbands, and then dining themselves occupy
women's evenings until about 10:00 p.m. when adults go to sleep.
Chabi, the one Patro child who attends school, studies in the evening and eats with the adult men.

In general, food is scarce and eating irregular in the Patro household. During one of my first visits to their home, the women spoke
a lot about the lack of food and the number of deaths of children in
the community. Ideally, they would like to have three meals a day
as higher-status families do, but this often is not possible. During
the seasons when women are employed in the fields, there may be
no hot cooked meal until evening. Children snack on a variety of
things during the day, and babies are given bottles of sugar water
or barley water to keep them going in their mothers' absence.

Division of Labor

The sexual division of labor in households such as the Patros is
very different from that in middle- and upper-status Old Town
households where women are home all day to cook, tend to children, and perform other household chores. There has to be more
cooperation between husbands and wives in the Patros' and other
lower-status households, especially during the seasons when the
women are employed. Not only do men assist in child care when
they are at home, but they sometimes help with the cooking as
well.

ASSISTANCE WITH CHILD CARE: THE PATRO HOUSEHOLD

May 20, 1967

This evening (6:50 p.m.) Second Brother sat on the dirt verandah in front of his room with Muna (two-year-old son) on his lap. Second Wife was away getting some rice polished at a neighbor's house. Muna closed his eyes and snuggled in his father's arms for a twenty-minute period. Then Second Brother stood up with Muna, carried him inside, and lay him down on a mat on the floor.

(Excerpt from field notes)

ASSISTANCE WITH COOKING: THE PATRO HOUSEHOLD

July 24, 1967

Second Brother, his wife, and Muna (two-year-old son) were in their cook room together at 7:00 p.m. this evening when I arrived. Second Brother was rolling out chapatis (unleavened bread) with a rolling pin and then handing them to Second Wife, who was cooking them over a fire. Muna, imitating his father, also tried to roll out chapatis.

(Excerpt from field notes)

There is, in addition, little or no sexual segregation in such households. When women must work in the public sphere and husbands and wives must cooperate in the domestic sphere to make survival possible, keeping men and women physically separate makes little sense. The greater intimacy of daily life lived in tight quarters also makes sexual segregation impractical. Not only was male-female avoidance not practiced, but wives were far less overtly deferential toward their husbands and mothers-in-law. The intimacy of the scene with Second Brother inside the small cook room assisting his wife was not unusual. Often in the evenings I would find First, Second, or Third Wife seated on the indoor verandah next to her husband while food was cooking on the *chula* inside. One evening I arrived with some photos to give the Patros and handed them to Second Wife, who was sitting outside her cook room. She was holding and looking at them when Second Brother came out of their room. He asked to see the photos, but his wife did not give them to him. She continued looking at them until Second Brother grabbed them from her, examined them, and then passed them around to other family members who were standing nearby.

This incident is illustrative of the more informal, less respectful, and less subservient relationship that existed between husbands and wives in Bauri households. Second Wife did not immediately defer to her husband's request for the photos. He had to forcibly take them from her, which he did with no word of chastisement. There generally seemed to be an easy give-and-take relationship between husband and wife in these households. The only restriction that I noted Bauri women systematically observing was the prohibition on using their husband's personal name.

Sleeping patterns also reflected the more informal and intimate relationship that existed between Bauri husbands and wives. Rather than have a separate room and/or bed, for example, each Patro husband-wife pair shared one small room (8 feet by 7 feet) with their children. They all slept together on the floor on woven mats.

Women's Dress and Adornment

The women in the Patro household, like other Old Town Bauri women, look distinctively different from middle- and upper-status women. Since they are engaged in hard physical labor much of the time, they do not dress in long, gathered saris, which would be impractical as well as not affordable. Most of the time they wear short pieces of cloth loosely wrapped around their bodies, which cover one shoulder and hang down to just below the knees. They wear no blouses or underwear, so that their legs and upper torsos are exposed. However, most of the older generation of women are covered with tattoos – from their shoulders down their arms, including their hands, and on the lower portions of their legs. Thus, most of the exposed parts of their bodies appear adorned. Instead of the gold jewelry and glass bangles that higher-status women wear, Bauri women wear heavy silver bracelets. Although their ears and noses are pierced, most of the time they wear no jewelry in them.

Some Comparisons with Old Town Washerman Women

Like Bauri women, Old Town Washerman women are also of low status, potentially poor, and required to work hard. Handling other peoples' soiled clothes and linens is considered dirty and polluting work; hence, the outcaste status of Washerman families. However, the sexual division of labor in Old Town Washerman families enabled Washerman women to remain within the domestic sphere. The men went out and collected dirty clothes and linens from other households and businesses and brought them home for laundering. The women then sorted them, boiled them in big pots of water, and wrung them out. Then the men took over the drying and ironing of the clothes and linens and their delivery back to their owners. In this manner, Old Town Washerman women were protected from the public eye and could better emulate the sexual standards of higher-status families.

Portrait of a New Capital Sweeper Family, 1965–67

The Naiks live in the Sweeper Colony, the area set aside for such outcaste families when the New Capital was built (see Chapter 2). In 1965–67, there were only about two dozen Sweeper families residing in these government quarters. By 1978, however, the area had become densely packed with squatters who had built themselves village-style mud-walled and thatched-roofed huts. The Naiks, though, reside in Type I government housing. These are one-room stuccoed brick houses with cement floors, a small cement verandah and cooking area, and small front yard (see Figure 7). They have no such amenities as electricity, piped water, or latrines. There are, however, several public water taps in front of the housing, which is a continuous line of similar one-room bungalows.

Because the Naiks are an extended family with several members employed as government sweepers, they have two Type I units next door to each other. One is assigned to Ranjit, his wife, Laxmi, and his three children. The other is assigned to his wife's mother and maternal grandmother. The Naiks use one unit principally for

155

cooking and dining and the other for sleeping. The cooking/dining side is furnished with a wooden table, two chairs, and a wooden platform bed. The walls are decorated with colorful calendars, and there is a vase of plastic flowers on the table. Ranjit, his wife, and his one-month-old son sleep in this room, while his two daughters (four and one and a half years old, respectively) sleep next door with their grandmother and great-grandmother. Other than some sleeping mats on the floor, that room has no furnishings or decorations.

The Naiks have other extended kin here as well. Laxmi's younger sister, her only sibling, lives in another unit of the Sweeper Colony with her husband and her husband's parents. Laxmi's father died when she was a baby and her mother was pregnant with her sister. Somehow they survived and are now all employed in the New Capital. In 1965–67 Ranjit and his wife's mother and grandmother worked as municipal sweepers, while Laxmi stayed home with the three young children. Previously, she had operated a "shop" – a mobile wooden shed with snacks, cigarettes, and other small items for sale. Laxmi's grandmother took over operating the shop in the evening for a few hours, often accompanied by her four-year-old great-granddaughter. The presence in their home of some Western-style furniture, as well as a radio and a tricycle for the children, is indicative that the Naiks are prospering somewhat more than are the Patros in the Old Town.

Furthermore, because the Naiks have salaried jobs with set work hours, they can have a much more regular daily schedule than the Patros and other Bauri families can. Municipal sweepers rise about 5:30 a.m., have a morning snack, and leave for work. Their work hours are from 6:00 a.m. to 2:00 p.m., at which time they return home for a hot midday meal and an afternoon rest. While her husband, mother, and grandmother are gone, Laxmi cooks, bathes the children and herself, and washes clothes. At about noon, she feeds the children. When the others return, she serves her husband his meal first and then her mother and grandmother. In the late afternoon, after their naps, the children have a snack and play until about 7:00 or 8:00 p.m., when they go to sleep. From about 4:00 to

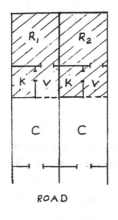

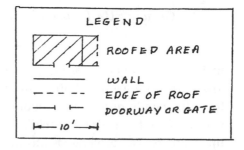

C Courtyard
K Kitchen/Cook Area
V Verandah
R₁ Dining Area and Bedroom for Mr. and Mrs. Naik and infant son
R₂ Bedroom for Naik daughters, Mother, and Grandmother

Figure 7. The Naik Family House in the New Capital Sweeper Colony

8:00 p.m. the evening meal is prepared by Laxmi and her mother, while Laxmi's grandmother works in the shop. The adults dine at about 9:00 p.m. and then go to bed.

The Naik women dress similarly to the Patros; however, only Laxmi's grandmother is heavily tattooed. She wears heavy silver bracelets around her arms just above the elbow, lighter silver bracelets around her wrists, and a small gold ornament in her nose. By contrast, Laxmi and her mother wear only a few glass bangles on their arms. Their ears and noses are pierced but unadorned; Laxmi, however, wears a black string with a gold locket around her neck.

Laxmi's two daughters sometimes wear glass bangles on their arms. Otherwise they wear no ornaments and a minimum of clothing – just underpants. Her baby son is always naked except for a string around one arm that has a charm attached to it to ward off evil spirits. During the first year of life, the time during which they are most susceptible to disease, most children in Bhubaneswar wear such charms around their necks, waists, or arms. Often the "charm" is a small locket containing a mantra (prayer) to protect the child's health.

Growing Up Poor and Female in Bhubaneswar

Early Childhood

In 1965–67 childhood was brief, as it continues to be, among poor, low-status families in Bhubaneswar. Regardless of which side of town the family resided in, economic circumstances prevailed. Unlike the Old Town Brahmin children whose physical dependence upon others was prolonged into middle and even late childhood, low-status children had their physical dependence curtailed by about three years of age, when they no longer received much care and nurturance from others. Table 9 illustrates the dramatic differences between upper- and middle-status households, on the one hand, and lower-status ones, on the other, with respect to nurturance and caretaking. A comparison of all nurturant acts recorded in my timed observations indicates that in low-status households 93 percent of such acts were directed toward infants and children under age three, whereas among upper- and middle-status households the comparable figure is 57 percent. Low-status children were expected to become both physically self-reliant as quickly as possible and responsible members of the household; higher-status children continued to receive sizable amounts of physical care into early and later childhood. The dependence of higher-status children upon others not only was tolerated, but, in many Old Town households, it was deliberately encouraged. By comparison, inculcating self-reliance and responsibility in their children was the driving force of socialization for low-status families. This process was especially critical for girls, most of whom were not sent to school but were kept home to tend to younger siblings and to help with household chores.

With most of the mothers working outside of the home, multiple-caretaking was even more pervasive in low-status households than in upper-status ones. Fathers, grandmothers, older siblings, and cousins all assisted mothers in the care of infants and young children.

Table 9. *Proportion of All Nurturant Acts[1] Directed to Different Age-Grades of Children by Socioeconomic Status*

	Status		
Age of child	*Upper (%)*	*Middle (%)*	*Lower (%)*
0–3 (N = 28)	59.5	59.0	93.0
3–6 (N = 26)	28.0	29.0	5.0
6–10 (N = 49)	12.5	12.0	2.0
Total	100.0	100.0	100.0

[1] "Nurturant acts" were defined as those actions instigated by mothers and other caretakers to respond to children's needs: e.g., offering comfort to crying or distressed children, nursing and/or hand-feeding them, bathing and dressing them, carrying them, and offering other kinds of instrumental help and care.

MULTIPLE CHILD CARE: THE PATRO HOUSEHOLD
July 23, 1967

It was late morning (10:48-11:48 a.m.), and Third Wife was the only parent home. The others were all off working in the rice fields. Santi (seven-year-old girl) sat on the floor of her parents' room, holding her baby brother, Ashok (three and a half months old). She sat immobile for six minutes with Ashok sitting on her outstretched legs. Then she called for Grandmother to come. When Grandmother did not come immediately, Santi called louder and louder. Finally, Grandmother came and took Ashok from Santi and held him for the next sixteen minutes. Muna (two-year-old boy) followed Grandmother into the room and then followed his cousin, Santi, out.

Santi, apparently, had been anxious to be relieved by Grandmother because Ashok had urinated on her shorts. They were all wet. Grandmother changed them and then went out and sat down on the front verandah.

Third Wife came out of her room holding her daughter, Sanju (one-year-old girl). Sanju was whining. Grandmother told Third Wife to put Sanju down with her. Third Wife did not do this at once, but after a moment she set Sanju down next to Grandmother, who was still holding Ashok on her outstretched legs. Sanju at first stood next to Grandmother and then sat down on Grandmother's legs along with Ashok. She tried to touch Ashok, who was beginning to fall asleep. When he was well asleep, Grandmother stood up and carried him

159

inside, leaving Sanju behind. Sanju began to cry. She cried for one full minute until Grandmother returned, picked her up, and carried her outside to the front verandah, where they sat down together next to Santi.

Muna, who had wandered off to a neighbor's house, returned. Grandmother told Santi to take him inside and feed him. Santi went off, calling to Muna to follow. He followed her slowly into the small store room that adjoins her parents' room. Santi put out some rice water in a bowl for Muna and told him to come sit down. When he did not respond immediately, Santi gave him a push, and he began to crawl in the direction of the bowl. Santi then hit him lightly on the back, and Muna fell down and began to cry. Santi told him not to cry but to eat. Muna slowly got up and sat down near Santi. For fifteen minutes Santi tried to get Muna to eat. She put out some cooked rice and began to feed herself. Muna watched her. After taking several bites, Santi gave a bite to Muna. Then she returned to feeding herself. Muna started to crawl away. Santi yelled at him to come back. When he did, she shoved some more food into his mouth. Then she hit him lightly on the face, and Muna began to cry. Santi stopped eating and told Muna to eat. She tried to pull him closer to her, but Muna would not come. Santi now put some rice in a second bowl and shoved it toward Muna, telling him to feed himself. But Muna sat crying. Santi again yelled at him to eat. Muna slowly took a bite. Santi then took some rice from his bowl, and Muna screamed. Santi, smiling, gave it back to him. Later she tried to take the whole bowl from Muna, but Muna held onto it. Santi again yelled at him to eat. Slowly, Muna, with tears streaming down his face, took another bite. Gradually, he finished his bowl of rice. As soon as he was done, Santi took the bowl and rinsed it with a little water. Then she told Muna to come. He followed her outside to where there was a basin of water. Santi washed the two bowls with water and rinsed Muna's hands and feet.

Meanwhile, Third Wife had taken Sanju from Grandmother and put her down on a mat on the floor of her room. She then lay down with Sanju to put her to sleep.

Grandmother, now joined by some neighbor women, continued to sit outside on the front verandah. Muna, having finished eating, came out and sat on the legs of one of the neighbor women. When Santi came out, Grandmother told her that she should be inside with Ashok,

160

who was sleeping. Santi responded, saying that Third Wife was inside. She did not go in and Grandmother did not insist.

(Excerpt from field notes)

I quote at some length from these field notes because they illustrative how young, low-status children are cared for in the absence of their working parents. In 1965–67, in the Patro household there were three infants with three different sets of parents. Much of the time Grandmother and Santi were the only ones home to care for them. The only other older child in this extended family was Santi's twelve-year-old brother, Chabi, who attended school and was, therefore, not available to help out during school hours. And in the afternoons and evenings Chabi was usually busy studying. Santi's principal responsibility was her tiny brother, Ashok. However, she frequently helped take care of her young cousins, especially when asked to by Grandmother. Grandmother helped care for all three young children in the extended family.

Not only does this observation illustrate how multiple-caretaking is practiced in low-status families, but it also exemplifies how very young children are taught to begin to take care of themselves – to become self-reliant at an early age. In this instance, Santi wanted Muna to feed himself and used a variety of strategies to persuade him to do so. These ranged from using herself as a role model to teasing him and using physical force. The teasing – pretending to take away his food or his entire bowl – seemed most effective.

Even when low-status mothers were home, they were usually too busy to sit down and hold or nurse a young child for any length of time. For example, they often combined holding and nursing infants and young children with other activities. In this manner, children learned at an early age that they were not the center of attention, that care came from a variety of persons other than their mothers, and that even a potentially intimate activity such as nursing was at best irregular and might be combined with household chores. They also learned that they had little control over their mothers.

Plate 21. Bauri children taking care of one another

NURSING: THE PATRO HOUSEHOLD

July 8, 1967

It was early morning and Sanju (one-year-old girl) was sitting just outside her parents' room. Her mother, Third Wife, was inside cooking. Sanju began to cry. Third Wife came out and picked her up. Sanju began to suck on her mother's breast. After several minutes, Third Wife set Sanju down and returned to her cooking. Sanju again began to cry, and Third Wife came out and held her for a moment, letting her nurse. Then she returned to cooking. This intermittent nursing of Sanju continued for half an hour as Third Wife prepared the midday meal.

(Excerpt from field notes)

Plate 22. Bauri seven-year-old girl tends to her infant brother

NURSING: ANOTHER BAURI HOUSEHOLD

July 17, 1967

It was evening (6:45–7:45 p.m.). Middle Wife sat on her inside verandah holding Rama, her two-year-old daughter. She was cleaning
Rama's ears. Then she nursed Rama for several minutes and handed
her to Grandmother, who was sitting nearby. Middle Wife went into
the cook room where she was preparing dinner. A few minutes later
Mina, Rama's ten-year-old sister, took her from Grandmother and
carried her inside the cook room to her mother. While kneeling on
the floor, Middle Wife again nursed Rama for several minutes. Rama
sat in front of her mother and reached up to her breast in order to
nurse while Middle Wife continued her food preparations. Then Mid-

163

Plate 23. Bauri six-year-old girl prepares vegetables with the help of her two-year-old cousin

dle Wife abruptly got up and left the cook room, leaving Rama behind. Rama began to cry. Mina came in and picked her up and carried her outside. Middle Brother arrived home just then. As soon as Rama saw him she held her arms out to him. Middle Brother took Rama from Mina and carried her inside with him. He sat down and held her.

(Excerpt from field notes)

July 21, 1967

It was late afternoon and Middle Wife was walking around the courtyard with her daughter Rama (two years) in her arms. Rama was sucking on her mother's breast. Then Middle Wife entered a room where rice was being threshed by two of her nieces. She took over from one niece and worked with the other one (sixteen years), using her right arm to work and the left one to continue holding Rama. Rama continued, unsuccessfully, to try to nurse. For fifteen minutes Middle Wife held Rama in this manner and then set her down on the floor. Rama urinated on the floor right next to her mother's foot. Middle Wife pointed this out to me but did not say anything to Rama.

Plate 24. Bauri grandmother feeds her one-year-old granddaughter

After several minutes, she picked Rama up and carried her to another
room.
(Excerpt from field notes)

Not only was the nursing of infants and young children handled in
a casual manner but so was toilet training, bathing, and most other
such caretaking activities. Bauri and other low-status women had
no time, for example, to engage in the lengthy massaging and
bathing of infants that Old Town Brahmin mothers performed
daily. Although Bauri children were bathed regularly, it was in a
much more perfunctory manner. In the Patro household it was
Grandmother who usually bathed her grandchildren. She would

165

fill a small basin with water and while holding the young child with one hand, use the other hand to rub her all over with a wet cloth and then dry her. Such a bath might last only a few minutes.

Young Bauri and other low-status children learned early on that their own mothers might be absent for long periods of time and that care came from a variety of family members. Furthermore, even when mothers were present, their attention was often focused on other household activities and only partially on child care. In this way, children were quickly socialized into a state of interdependence – reliance on a variety of potential caretakers – as well as into physical self-reliance and interpersonal responsibility. They were encouraged to attend to their own needs as soon as possible and to assist their older siblings, especially their older female siblings and female cousins who they could see doing much of the household work, including taking care of them. From infancy girls were provided with clear role models for how to contribute to the welfare of the family, and early in their lives they would begin to imitate their older siblings and cousins.

ROLE MODELING: A BAURI HOUSEHOLD
June 1, 1967
Mina's (ten-year-old girl) mother was not home this morning (8:20– 9:00 a.m.), and she was tending to a fire in the *chula* and preparing vegetables for a curry. She sat on the ground cutting up the vegetables. Her young cousin Kamala (five-year-old girl) came over and sat down next to her and began to peel the onions for Mina.
(Excerpt from field notes)

Children also engaged in role play that expressed the gender roles they were learning at an early age.

ROLE PLAY: A BAURI HOUSEHOLD
July 17, 1987
This evening (6:45–7:45 p.m.) Kamala (five-year-old girl) and some older cousins and neighbors (three girls and one boy) began to play together. Santi (seven-year-old girl) had a small water jug, which they

all took turns carrying. They held it under one arm as adult women do with large ones when they go off to fetch water from the well. They laughed and giggled a lot. Kamala then changed from her shorts into a "sari" (a piece of cloth), which she wrapped around her body and draped over her head. Then she sat down in front of her room and completely covered her head and face with the sari. There was much laughter as the other children tried to uncover her head. They announced to me that she was pretending to be a bride. Suddenly, Older Brother called to them and told them to go outside and play because they were making too much noise. Outside Kamala "built" a house and yard in the dirt. An older cousin (eight-year-old boy) informed me that she was "playing house." Nearby, a neighbor boy was, according to my informant, "playing store." Chabi (twelve years) had demarcated an area of the ground as a store and was selling goods [sticks, paper, and leaves] to Kamala's older cousin, China (ten-year-old girl). He [the proprietor] set the prices that China [the customer] was to pay.

Middle and Late Childhood

In 1965–67, for the children in these poor households, early and later childhood merged and were barely distinguishable from each other. Young children simply became increasingly self-reliant and responsible. Some of the boys were supposed to attend school but did so only irregularly; girls were rarely given the opportunity. Girls could be immediately helpful in the household, whereas boys had to be somewhat older and more mature before they could be assigned such "male" tasks as taking goats and bullocks out to graze, fixing lanterns, ironing and delivering clothes, and so on. Some boys who had no suitably aged sisters did participate a lot in the care of younger siblings. However, I never saw them tending to such "female" tasks as hauling water, tending fires, and cooking. By contrast, from the age of six or seven years girls might be left in charge of the household. At age seven, for example, Santi was frequently left in charge of her infant brother. In a neighboring household, two ten-year-old cousins, Mina and China, were regularly left in charge of cooking as well as child care.

167

TAKING CHARGE: A BAURI HOUSEHOLD

June 3, 1967

Both Mina's (ten-year-old girl) and China's (ten-year-old girl) mothers were away this morning (8:55–9:35 a.m.). Both girls were attending to separate fires, preparing to cook. Their younger brothers and sisters wandered around the courtyard with nothing in particular to do. China began to cook rice. She got up and down, adding wood to the fire as needed. Meanwhile, she was cutting up vegetables to make a curry. She also roasted some nuts on the fire and soaked some dried fish in water. Grandmother was out in front of the house holding Bina, China's ten-month-old baby brother. After a while China came out and took Bina inside with her. She set Bina down on the ground next to her while she continued to tend to the fire. After some minutes she took the cooked rice off the fire and put some lentils and vegetables on to cook. Meanwhile, Bina's six-year-old brother and six-year-old cousin played with him. They handed him half a mango and some matchboxes to play with. These entertained him for a while, but then he began to fuss. China was now busy sweeping the floor of the house as well as cooking. However, when she finished sweeping, she picked up Bina, held him, and fed him some rice flakes mixed with sugar and water. Later she removed the nuts she had been roasting on the fire, cracked them open to eat, and offered me some. She also offered some to her younger brother (eight years) who had just entered the house.

(Excerpt from field notes)

Mina and China often worked together inside the house in the absence of their mothers. Although their grandmother lived with them, she was very elderly and was of little help. In addition to cooking, house cleaning, and child care, the girls regularly went to the public well for water. They would haul bucket after heavy bucket of water, barely able to stagger home with them. Less regularly, they were sent to the store to purchase such provisions as kerosene, oil, and sugar. They were at the prime age to help out in the home. Not in school and not yet of marriageable age, they were available for all kinds of household tasks. China had a sixteen-year-old sister who was not yet married but who worked in the fields with her mother and aunts. Mina also had an older sister, but she had been adopted by relatives. There were no older boys in this extended family. Both girls had younger brothers, one of whom in 1965–67 was attending school. The other brother was only six and not yet in school. However, like their fathers, none of the boys in this family remained in school for more than three or four years.

Of the low-status families in my sample, Bauri girls worked the hardest. However, in poor low-status households in general girls of six to ten years of age were expected to assume numerous responsibilities and far and away outworked their brothers of similar age. They performed chores at a significantly higher rate (34.8) than their brothers (9.2), although their brothers did more child care, housework, and other household chores than comparably aged boys of middle- and upper-status families. As Figure 8 demonstrates, the children's workload increases as family status decreases. The critical factor here is the mother's workload.[2] As women have more and more work to do – especially, work outside the home – they must increasingly rely upon the assistance of their children, and it is to their daughters that they turn most readily. Thus, unlike their higher-status counterparts, low-status girls are quickly socialized into adult gender roles. They are experienced cooks, caretakers of young children, and household managers long before they marry. As Middle Wife in the Patro household (quoted at the beginning of this chapter) said, "It's always been the same. Before I got married I had to work. Now I have to work."

Figure 8 also indicates that although the workloads of low-status girls are far higher than those of other girls, the girls of each status group outperform the boys of their group. They are getting practice handling the kinds of responsibilities that they will have to assume as adult women. Thus, from middle childhood on they are being socialized into appropriate gender roles; the issue is really one of degree. Whereas middle- and upper-status girls are in school and are less available to help out at home, most low-status girls are not in school and are full-time helpers at home.

Education

In general, poverty restricts the attractiveness of formal education in India. Most poor parents cannot afford the loss of child labor that schooling would entail and cannot afford the costs – however minor they may be – for school uniforms, books, notebooks, exam fees, and so on. In addition, many poor families cannot envision the long-term benefits that sacrifices now might one day produce. However, should they consider sending children to school, patrifocal ideology makes it more desirable to send sons rather than daughters. It makes more sense to invest in sons, the future household heads and responsible agents for the care of parents and extended kin, than in daughters. If they can succeed in school and develop alternative work opportunities, it will benefit the whole family. Daughters, in contrast, will marry and probably contribute to some other family's welfare. Furthermore, until sons reach adolescence, when they can help in the fields, their contributions to a household are more expendable than those of girls.

When a low-status boy can be of use at home, his education is also sacrificed. This was particularly evident in one New Capital Sweeper family that had no older daughters. The mother, father, and maternal grandmother in the family all worked as municipal sweepers during the day, leaving their seven-year-old son at home to care for his three-year-old brother and one-year-old sister. His father, who understood the potential benefits of an education, regularly apologized to me for his son's not being in school but explained that the boy was needed at home. Ultimately, both boys and their sister received four years of schooling to give them some basic literacy skills. This was not enough education, however, to change their economic opportunities. Like their mother and father, they are now all New Capital municipal sweepers.

Most poor low-status families in Bhubaneswar have invested little in the education of their children regardless of whether they are girls or boys.[3] In my sample of low-status families, most of the boys – like their fathers – have had some limited exposure to school but not enough to change their economic opportunities. Girls, like their mothers, have generally had no exposure to school. In the

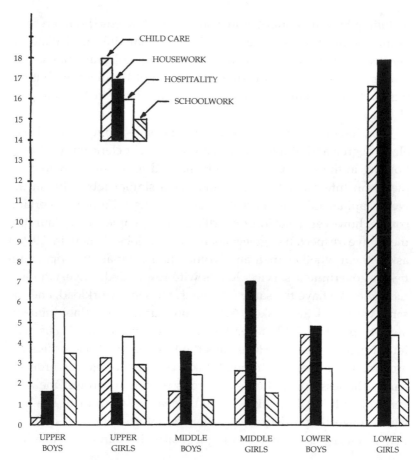

Figure 8. Bar Graph of the Average Number of Responsible Acts for Six- to Ten-Year-Old Girls and Boys by Socioeconomic Status

Bauri community, Chabi Patro is an exception, and his family is very proud of him. He passed the matriculation exams and in 1989 was employed as a typist in a New Capital government office. Although this is a low-level job, it has a regular salary and offers far more economic security than being an agricultural laborer and rock cutter like his father.

In investing in education, the principal exception in my sample is one Old Town Washerman family. The head of this joint household, the oldest of three brothers, in addition to sending his youngest brother to school, has sent all six of his children to school, including his only daughter, Reena. Although Reena did not receive as much education as some of her brothers, she did matriculate. At age twenty-two she was married to an agricultural engineer in government service. Her caste remains that of Washerman, but her husband's occupation has a very different status in the emerging class system.

Rabi, the eldest of Oldest Brother's five sons, completed a bachelor's degree and at age thirty is a government clerk with his own housing in the New Capital. He is married to a woman who completed an Intermediate degree and has a similar job to his in the New Capital. Like his parents, Rabi and his wife are a working couple; however, instead of handling other peoples' dirty laundry, they have respectable government service jobs. When in 1989 I asked them whether men and women had comparable opportunities in government service, Rabi's wife responded, "Everything is the same. We have the same schedules, the same workload, and the same wages." I then asked, "How about at home?" Rabi immediately responded, "Whatever the husband says is law." His wife interrupted and said, "He always thinks he is great! He orders me around, and I obey his orders. It takes courage to disobey orders. I am motherless and fatherless; there is no one to protect me. It is very difficult." All of this was said, however, in front of her husband, suggesting a degree of openness, informality, and intimacy that would be uncommon in higher-status husband-wife relationships.

In 1989 Rabi and his wife had their first baby, a daughter. Although no longer residing with the joint family in the Old Town, they make use of it on a daily basis. They bring their daughter there for child care, commuting together by motorcycle between the Old Town and New Capital residences, as well as to their offices. Despite the help with child care that they receive, Rabi's wife spoke to me of her heavy workload. "Now life is very difficult. Between office work, housework, and child care, I am facing much trouble." I asked if Rabi helped her at home. She said, "No. He is good for nothing!" Again, this was said, with some intended irony, in front of her husband and father-in-law. She did admit, however, that her husband helps with the baby. This young wife and daughter-in-law displayed an open and, from an upper-status family perspective, disrespectful attitude toward her husband. In a higher-status household not only would a new daughter-in-law not speak so forthrightly, but, out of respect, she would not sit in the same room as her father-in-law or have visual contact with him.

This Old Town Washerman family has realized educational goals that other low-status residents only dream of. For example, when I first knew my neighbor Sopna Behera (ten years), she as well as her older brother were attending school. One day I asked her how long she would continue in school. She said, "I don't know." But about her brother she said, "Dipu (thirteen years) will go to college. Then he will get a job as a clerk [in government service]." Significantly, with respect to education and employment, Sopna could fantasize about her brother but not about herself. As a girl, she saw no role models of improved working conditions. All she knew of was marriage and motherhood. As it turned out, Dipu completed only ten years of school and became a bicycle repairman. Like his sister, he resides in a mud-walled, thatched-roofed house in one of the villages that has been incorporated into Bhubaneswar.

Sopna completed five years of school and was married soon thereafter. She had four miscarriages before her first child was born when she was twenty-three years old. She then had two more surviving children, but each was a difficult birth. "Twice I narrowly escaped from death," she told me in 1989. "Now I have had an operation so that I will not have any more children." Sopna dreams of educating her children but says they are "donkeys." "They are not interested in studying. I would be willing to borrow money and go into debt to pay for their tuition at good schools, but their father is not supportive. He comes home once every three days and does not listen to me. He is very irresponsible."

In most poor low-status Bhubaneswar households schooling has not become much more of a reality than it had been in the 1960s. When I asked Middle Wife of the Old Town Patro household if there were any changes for women she would like to see, she responded, "Yes. I would like to see girls be able to study."

Conclusion

Caste, class, and gender are inextricably interlinked. In the caste system that evolved over many centuries in India – particularly, in North India – restrictions upon women's activities and control over their sexuality became important symbols of status.[4] Purdah – the veiling of women and restriction of them to certain quarters of the house – was simply the most extreme expression of this phenomenon. Only prosperous middle- and high-caste families could afford to so restrict their women. Poor low-status families, which constitute both the agricultural and the urban workforces today in India, must rely on the employment of women as well as of men. Such women's low status is, therefore, continually reinforced by their presence in the public realm.

Ironically, the greater equality between men and women that many upper-status women in India are currently seeking through education and employment is something that poor low-status women have always had. For example, women's relationships with their husbands and in-laws in the low-status families in Bhubaneswar that I have known are far more open and the women less subservient than in upper-status families. There is less gender hierarchy and more mutual respect within working couples when men know that they are in part dependent upon their wives' incomes. For poor low-status women, however, there is a considerable cost to this increased equality. They must work very hard in both the domestic and the public realms. They often do not have enough to eat. And they experience a high rate of miscarriage and infant mortality.

With their heavy workloads, low-status women must turn to their children for assistance, in particular to their daughters. Both boys and girls are socialized into early physical self-reliance and interpersonal cooperation, but from an early age girls are expected to assume women's domestic roles. Accordingly, they are expected to become hard-working, responsible members of their households by about six or seven years and are well prepared for marriage when they simply transfer these skills from their natal home to that of their husband and parents-in-law. Patrilocality tends to prevail

174

among low-status families as well as upper-status ones in much of Bhubaneswar, although most daughters at marriage have not moved very far away from their parents. They are still able to have regular contact with their natal families.

In 1989, for example, my husband, son, and I were invited to attend a fire-walking ceremony in a village outside of Bhubaneswar. For two hours we watched a number of young men and women go into trance and walk a path of hot coals. At the end of the fire-walking ceremony, Third Wife from one of the Old Town Bauri families I know saw me and came over excitedly, saying, "Did you see Kamala? Did you see Kamala?" It took me a moment to understand that her now married daughter, Kamala (twenty-eight years), resided in this village and was one of the fire walkers. The mother had come to watch her. Later, I observed Third Wife walking arm-in-arm with her daughter, who was still coming out of trance.

Subsequently, Third Wife explained that when she was a young wife she had made a vow to devote herself to the goddess and, as an ordeal, to fire walk annually for five years because she had lost several children. If she succeeded in her devotion and the fire-walking ordeal, she would be blessed with more children. In 1965–67, Kamala was her only surviving child. Subsequently, she had two more surviving children, a son and another daughter. Now her older daughter was in the same situation: Kamala had lost two children and had only one surviving child. Like her mother, she had made the same vow, hoping that it would ensure greater success in childbearing and the survival of her children.

This incident reflects the close mother-daughter tie that has continued in this particular low-status Bauri family. It also demonstrates the tremendous importance of having children and the pain associated with the high rate of child mortality among these families. Third Wife spoke of how frightening it was to go into trance and to walk on a bed of hot coals but how she considered it necessary to enhance her chances of having more surviving children. Women feel responsible for the deaths of their children, and although male descent is not stressed to the degree that it is in higher-status families, having offspring is still very important.

175

Daughters, as children, are valuable assistants to their mothers, just as sons, as adults, are essential caretakers of their mothers in their old age.

As in Old Town higher-status joint families, interdependence among low-status family members is highly valued. Multiple child care, which enhances emotional bonding among extended family members, is common to both status groups and is instrumental in building such interdependence. However, some of the processes by which interdependence among family members is achieved are different. Instead of prolonging the child's physical dependence upon others as is done in high-status Old Town families, low-status caretakers encourage the young child's self-reliance. However, this physical self-reliance is combined with the experience and ideology of mutual cooperation and emotional connectedness. The goal is to produce children who from an early age can contribute to the welfare of the family. It is not, as it is in much of the United States, to produce economically independent children who will go off and "do their own thing." Almost all of the low-status children in my 1965–67 sample of Bhubaneswar families continue to reside close to their parents and extended families, either in the same household or nearby where they can see one another with some regularity.

The only exception is the Washerman daughter who married a government servant and now resides in another district of Orissa. As noted earlier, this family is an exception in other respects as well. Whereas other Old Town Washerman and Bauri families continue to struggle economically, this family has prospered. The father, Gopi, attributes some of the difference to his participation as a revolutionary in the fight for India's independence from Great Britain and in his army service during World War II. He gained a broader experience by traveling around the country and working with people of different backgrounds. At the end of the war, however, he returned home to a fatherless household. His father had died, and he had to assume responsibility for his mother and younger brothers. Through industry and vision, he was able to build up a laundry clientele that extended into the New Capital and a business that prospered. For example, I first met him in 1966 when he came, unsolicited, to my house in Gautam Nagar to seek my laundry business. Subsequently, on a weekly basis he picked up dirty laundry and delivered clean, pressed laundry throughout my first stay. In 1989 one of his younger sons took care of picking up and returning my family's laundry.

Gopi and his middle brother, together with their wives and mother, worked sufficiently hard that they were able to send their younger brother through college. They operated as a highly organized joint family. Next door to Gopi his father's brother's offspring and their families reside. Although these four brothers, with their wives and children, live together, they do not cooperate economically and have not prospered in the thirty years that I have known them. Unlike Gopi's children, their children have not been sent to school and do not now have alternative forms of employment. They continue to reside in a series of mud-walled, thatched-roofed rooms like those of the Bauris, whereas Gopi has gradually converted all of his rooms to brick and cement and has enlarged the house and courtyard. He now has a sitting room with a large TV in one corner and has built a new room for himself that has a Western-style bed, a radio, and stucco walls decorated with pictures and calendars. Sadly, his wife died several years ago of diabetes and was not able to share in their prosperity.

Gopi arranged his eldest son's marriage. They have a book of photos that show the wedding ceremony as an elaborate middle-class affair. Rabi, as the groom, rode in an automobile laden with flowers. The bride and all the women in attendance wore beautiful silk saris. When I asked Gopi whether there had been any dowry involved, he vehemently replied, "No. I reject dowry. Dowry is causing much trouble." In a subsequent conversation, however, I learned that when his daughter was married in 1976 to the agricultural engineer, Gopi gave the groom Rs. 10,000 and a motorcycle. He also provided the young couple with furniture, and he spent about Rs. 50,000 on the wedding itself. About four hundred relatives and friends attended the wedding and had to be provided with food, new clothes, and so on. It had been a costly undertaking.

Often when low-status families try to move up in the caste/class system, they emulate the practices of higher castes and classes, which may involve the imposition of restrictions on women.[5] Interestingly, Gopi arranged a marriage for his son with a woman who is educated and employed in government service and whose sister is a practicing medical doctor. There had been no effort to emulate Old Town high-caste practices of purdah but rather to move in the direction that the New Capital represents. It is in the New Capital that young women are being educated and are seeking to enter new spheres of employment outside the home. However, as this Washerman family has moved up in status, they have also been forced to participate in the less desirable upper-caste/upper-class phenomenon of dowry. Although Gopi asserted that he made no dowry demands of his daughter-in-law's family, he did produce a sizable dowry when his only daughter was married. Again, he maintained that this was not "demanded" by his son-in-law's family, that he gave freely of his own will. Nonetheless, he has moved into a middle-class lifestyle in which such "gifts" are expected.

The upward mobility of this one Washerman family is the exception, not the rule, for poor low-status families in Bhubaneswar. In the thirty years that I have known them, most such families have eked out a living but have seen little significant improvement in their economic well-being. Few have invested in the education of their children, thus constraining their sons and daughters to continue their parents' way of life. For young girls, this means heavy workloads at home, followed by work outside the home in adolescence and adulthood. However, the age of marriage has risen. Low-status girls in my sample have married at between eighteen and twenty years of age rather than at puberty like their mothers and grandmothers. Subsequently, as wives and mothers, they have continued the work they practiced as children.

CHAPTER SIX

Going Out to School

Women's Changing Roles and Aspirations

In 1965–67, the only women seen in public were low-status women who worked as day laborers in rice fields and on construction jobs or as sweepers in homes and offices. Old Town middle- and upper-status women were seen out in public only on important ritual occasions, whereas New Capital middle- and upper-status women could be seen somewhat more often, discretely going to shops or accompanying their husbands out in the evening. Ten years later, the public presence of women was largely unchanged. By 1987, however, radical change had occurred: Young middle- and upper-status women were now a public presence in the New Capital and were somewhat more frequently seen in the Old Town. For instance, the large, central produce market was no longer exclusively a male domain. Whereas in the 1960s I was often the only woman at the market, by the late 1980s both men and women shopped there, together and separately. Women became a common sight, walking, biking, and occasionally riding a motor scooter along the major avenues of the New Capital. And women could be seen dining with their husbands and children in public restaurants in the New Capital, something unheard of twenty years earlier.

What could account for this striking change in one generation? Education is, I believe, the principal explanation. In 1965–67, all eligible girls and boys from middle- and upper-status families in both the Old Town and the New Capital were attending school. Twenty years later, they had come of age; most were now highly educated, including many of the young women, and many were now employed, also including many of the young women. Old norms restricting the public presence of women were having to adapt to changed circumstances.

The increased public presence of women was, moreover, an outward manifestation of other changes that had been catalyzed by allowing daughters to go to school. The nature of these changes, and how Old Town and New Capital families have responded to them, is the subject of this chapter and the next (Chapter 7). In particular, I shall draw on my 1989 interviews with grandmothers, mothers, and daughters to gain insight into the processes of change as well as the limits to change.

Educational Change

Educational change in Bhubaneswar has been dramatic over the past thirty years – especially for women. Middle- and upper-status daughters have almost uniformly surpassed their mothers in schooling (Table 10). On average, Old Town daughters have completed ten more years of school than their mothers, with many of them completing secondary school and some continuing on for Intermediate and baccalaureate degrees. Although seven of twenty-two Old Town sample girls did not matriculate (pass the secondary-level exams), most remained in school through the Eleventh Standard (end of secondary school), and five completed college. Four of those five girls have also acquired master's degrees in the arts and sciences.[1]

In the New Capital, middle- and upper-status daughters have also far surpassed their mothers' level of education (see Table 10). Whereas only one young New Capital mother in my sample had completed college, *all* daughters have done so. By 1989, twenty out of twenty-one had completed a bachelor's degree; fourteen had completed M.A.s in the arts and sciences; one had a M.S. in computer science; two held medical degrees; and one was completing a Ph.D. in the social sciences. Their mean years of schooling – sixteen years – is the equivalent of a master's degree. In other words, in the span of a single generation they have become a highly educated

Table 10. *Mean Number of Years of School Completed: A Mother-Daughter Comparison by Old Town–New Capital Residence and Status*

Status	Mothers (N = 42)	Daughters (N = 58)
Old Town		
Upper/Middle	1.5	11.4
Lower	0.5	1.4
New Capital		
Upper/Middle	9.7	16.0
Lower	0.0	3.5

elite in a society where only a small fraction – less than one percent – of women acquire a higher education.

Among low-status women, in contrast, there has been little educational improvement (Table 10). Out of fourteen Old Town low-status daughters, only four attended school at all, one through matriculation and the other three only as far as the Third or Fourth Standard. In the New Capital, two of four daughters attended school, through the Fifth and Ninth Standards, respectively. The educational record of low-status sons has not been much better.[2] As described in Chapter 5, most low-status families had not yet envisioned the benefits of education. Even if they had, they could not afford to have children away at school when they were needed at home to care for younger siblings and to help out with other household chores while their mothers and other adult kin were away at work. By adolescence most low-status sons and daughters had become workers like their parents.

Old Town Conservatism

The figures in Table 10 indicate that Old Town middle- and upper-status families have responded somewhat more conservatively to educational opportunities for their daughters than have New Capital families. In addition to curtailing schooling earlier, they have also insisted that their daughters attend all-girls' schools, where they can be safe from contact with boys. Whereas all-girls' schools are available in Bhubaneswar at all levels of education except the postgraduate, they do not include the elite English-language schools. Old Town girls did not, therefore, have access to the same kind of education that some New Capital girls did. Furthermore, most Old Town families were quite explicit that a son's schooling took priority over that of a daughter. As one father expressed it during a conversation in 1987: "Girls don't get the same educational attention as boys. I try to keep an open mind, but a 'matriculation' or 'Intermediate' is enough. Then they are ready to marry."

In this conversation, Mr. Gauda, a Cowherder by caste and a retired clerk in the state government, was speaking spontaneously in his home of many years in the Old Town, close to where his family has resided for generations. He and his wife of forty-three years still keep cows and sell milk as part of their livelihood. Married at eighteen, Mr. Gauda's wife has only a rudimentary education – four years of schooling – whereas her husband completed secondary school and qualified for a government job. The couple produced eight children, all of whom have surpassed their parents educationally. Two of their four grown sons have M.A.s and two have Intermediates; two daughters have also completed Intermediates and one has only matriculated. The eighth child, a son, is still in school.

Two years later, when I was interviewing Mrs. Gauda about being a wife and mother, she continually stressed the importance of caring for her children, educating them, and marrying them:

We had to concentrate on our sons' education both because of expenses and because of dangers. It's a jungle out there, and we live in an isolated house. I had to go with a lantern to meet my son every evening when he came home from college. I have always had to think about my children's safety.
(Excerpt from March 7, 1989, interview)

Like her husband, Mrs. Gauda emphasized the importance of a son's education over that of a daughter when there were limited resources, but she also identified another area of concern, that of danger. Sending a girl off to school, especially to a college not in the immediate area (all the colleges are in the New Capital), is considered a major risk by many Old Town families. The Gaudas' third daughter, who was not yet married, was participating in the interview. I turned to Ritu (twenty-five years) and asked her whether she would have liked to complete college.

No. I was not interested in continuing beyond the Intermediate. My father was supportive, but there was too much housework, it was difficult to study at home, and there were problems with safe transportation back and forth to school.
(Excerpt from March 7, 1989, interview)

While Ritu also identified safety as an issue, she introduced two other factors relevant to having discontinued her education. First, she was needed at home to help with the housework. At the time, the Gaudas had just one daughter-in-law to assist Mrs. Gauda with work within the home as well as with feeding and milking a herd of cows. Second, Ritu was not that interested in her studies and found it difficult to concentrate on them at home where there was other work to be done. She felt ready for marriage; and, in fact, her marriage was being arranged in 1989 while I was in Bhubaneswar and was celebrated the following year.

As Mr. Gauda's earlier statement implies, education and marriage are closely connected in the minds of most Old Town families. Parents determine where and for how long their children will attend school and when and whom they will marry. These are important parental responsibilities especially because there is only a narrow range of years during which girls are considered marriageable. Previously, that narrow age range was linked to puberty, but today to be attractive to a suitable bridegroom a middle- or upper-status girl should have the level of education that Mr. Gauda had indicated. Too little or too much education can be a problem in arranging marriages, and to remain unmarried is still *not* a viable alternative for women in Bhubaneswar.

Although the Gaudas represent a fairly characteristic attitude toward girls' education in the Old Town, interviews with some mothers and grandmothers revealed a deeply felt desire for change – for girls to have access to education. A number of older women spoke of wishing that they had been able to continue their schooling and of how they wanted things to be different for their daughters.

Mothers' Aspirations

I was the only daughter of my father. He was not interested in educating me. Now things have changed. I want to educate my children, and girls in this generation have equal schooling to boys although they should not learn more than boys.
(Excerpt from March 19, 1989, interview with Mrs. Badhei, an Old Town Carpenter mother)

My ultimate aim in life was to make my children educated. My father prevented me from studying when I wanted to continue. I don't hold this as a grudge against my children. I wanted them to get an education. I got them educated and then married. I brought them up differently than I was. . . . With an education women can manage themselves. Also, the cost of living is high. If both men and women are employed, they can manage better.
(Excerpt from February 26, 1989, interview with Mrs. Mahapatra, an Old Town Brahmin mother)

Mrs. Badhei's daughter completed an Intermediate degree and was married at age twenty to a twenty-three-year-old man with a bachelor's degree; her mother had had a Fourth Standard education and married at age fifteen to a man five years her senior. Although the differential in age and education between husband and wife has been greatly reduced in this next generation, it has nonetheless been maintained. The Badheis' daughter is experiencing another kind of change, however: She now resides in a nuclear household with her husband and children on the other side of India, whereas her mother resides with her husband's extended family in the Old Town.

Two of Mrs. Mahapatra's three daughters have acquired graduate degrees. Mita (forty at the time of the interview) holds a master's in science and, although married with children, is employed outside of the home. Sita (thirty-eight years) has a master's in education, is married with children, and teaches school. The third daughter is somewhat less highly educated, having completed an Intermediate, and is a full-time wife and mother who resides in her parents-in-law's home together with her husband and children.

Both Old Town mothers attribute their lack of education to their fathers – the authority figures in their childhood. However, both women suggest that *they* have been able to have a voice in their daughters' schooling. Conditions have changed. Some schooling is now a requirement for arranging a good marriage for daughters, and women as mothers feel they must help oversee the process. Mrs. Badhei expressed the concern that girls, while deserving an education, should not become more educated than boys. Here she was stating a fundamental principle of patrifocal family structure and ideology – that husbands should be more educated (and older) than their wives. Mrs. Mahapatra, however, expressed a very different perspective. She linked a woman's education to her potential independence – an unusual view in contemporary Bhubaneswar but one into which, as someone who was widowed with young children, she may have had special insight. Furthermore, she pointed to the economic advantages of an educated women who can work and help contribute to the family welfare as two of her daughters and a daughter-in-law did – a new phenomenon in Bhubaneswar.

The idea of female employment outside of the home is still unacceptable in most Old Town families. Regardless of their education, most Old Town women continue to observe purdah. Those few who work are carefully escorted back and forth from home by male kin; they are not allowed out on their own. One young Brahmin man, a participant in my original study, complained to me that his parents would not even allow his wife out to accompany their

children back and forth from school. Harish (thirty-two years) believed that his children's schooling should have the highest priority,
but his parents – still the authority figures in this extended family –
disagreed.

I regret not being a matriculate. I want my wife to be concerned with
our children, to get them ready for school, and to collect them after-
wards. I want to emphasize their studies, unlike in my childhood. My
parents took no interest.
(Excerpt from April 9, 1989, interview with Harish Mahapatra and his wife)

This particular Old Town Brahmin family was unusually conservative. Harish's sister had been married at age twelve, having had
only a rudimentary education, whereas most of her age-mates did
not marry until they were eighteen to twenty-five years old. Harish
and his wife, however, represent a new and different point of view.
Harish was openly critical of his parents and of what he perceived
to be an unsupportive family and neighborhood in which to rear
children for fitting into a new world where an education was essential. Nonetheless, he continued to reside with his Old Town extended family, which included two other grown brothers.

More Radical Change in the New Capital

In 1967, in the course of conversation one day, Mrs. Tripathy mentioned her educational goals for her then young children. Her two
sons, she said, would definitely go to college. After that, they would
do some kind of government service. They would, in other words,
do very much what their father had done. "Perhaps," she added,
"the girls will also go to college if they pass their matriculation
exams. They might go for a while, anyway."

By 1989, it was clear that six of the seven Tripathy daughters
had outperformed their brothers educationally. The eldest had
completed a B.A. and had then been married. The next four had
completed master's degrees and were teaching, three of them at the
college level. The sixth was completing medical school, and the

seventh was still studying at the Intermediate level. Their brothers, by contrast, were not outstanding students as were the sisters and had not gone as far educationally.

Mrs. Tripathy's ruminations in 1967 were characteristic of patrifocal family thinking: It was assumed that sons should have educational and occupational priority and that daughters should have enough education to be marriageable. At that time most New Capital families were not thinking about careers for their daughters; rather, arranging a good marriage for a daughter was their prime concern. How, then, had this transformation taken place, not just for the Tripathy daughters but for many other New Capital daughters?

An educational philosophy about girls' schooling evolved during the 1960s and 1970s as Bhubaneswar became an established center of education. Unlike in some parts of India where schools for women were established some hundred years ago, in Orissa – one of India's most rural and least economically developed states – schools were slow to be established, and little formal education was available to women before Independence in 1947.[3] Thus, unlike in nearby Bengal, no educated female elite had emerged by the time of Independence. For example, my 1965–67 landlord was the first Orissan to receive a higher education during the British Raj and to join the Indian Administrative Service. For his generation he was the exception, not the rule, and he was male. Some members of his generation did begin to invest in the higher education of sons but rarely of daughters. It was this next generation that constituted New Capital parents in my 1965–67 study. They were rearing their children during a new historical era of political independence from Great Britain, of nationalism, and of democratic commitment to improving conditions for all, which implied a greatly expanded educational system and increased gender equity.

Orissa, as a newly established state of a new nation, was a microcosm of changing values, one of which was a commitment to education. Providing educational opportunities for those who had been deprived of them in the past was a part of that commitment.[4] Accordingly, the school attendance of girls and low-status, "scheduled caste"[5] children was encouraged by exempting them from tuition and other fees charged to middle- and upper-status boys and by opening many new girls' high schools and women's colleges. Bhubaneswar, as Orissa's newly established capital, thus became the state's educational center and a model of educational opportunity. Between 1950 and 1965, for example, two universities, three colleges, and a special college of education that served the entire eastern region of India were opened there. (Subsequently, more colleges, research institutes, and institutions of specialized training have been established, including a culinary school and a women's college specializing in computer science.) Primary and secondary schools were built throughout the newly constructed New Capital, while in the Old Town and surrounding villages schools were expanded and upgraded. By 1965, residents in all parts of Bhubaneswar had access to education from the primary to the postgraduate level. Women were no exception.

In 1965–67, the ethos among most middle- and upper-status Bhubaneswar families was that daughters as well as sons should attend school. The only question was for how long. Beyond their concerns about marriage, most parents had not thought through the implications of higher education for daughters. For sons the advantage was obvious: They needed as much education as possible to compete for government jobs, as well as for jobs in the private sector, because they would be the economic supporters of their extended families. That in 1967 Mrs. Tripathy thought more concretely about her sons' education and careers than those of her daughters is quite understandable.

Eleven years later, when I returned to Bhubaneswar in 1978, it was evident that most of the Tripathy daughters were academically talented. Mr. Tripathy, who in 1965–67 had remained a somewhat distant and austere figure in my presence, greeted me eagerly and immediately proceeded to cite all of his daughters' accomplishments in school. He was clearly very proud of them. They were winning many "Golds" and "Firsts" in state and national examinations and were being encouraged to continue their schooling into the college and postgraduate levels. With the exception of the first daughter, who was married at age twenty, the others were allowed to continue with their education. As one daughter explained to me in 1987: "Our father was an ambitious man. He wanted his children to look good in society; he wanted to feel proud of them. He did this by encouraging our educational achievement. The marriage of his daughters was not that important to him."

Mr. Tripathy was willing to set aside his concerns about marriage to allow his daughters to become highly accomplished educationally and professionally. Perhaps, in addition to taking pride in their accomplishments, he realized that with so many daughters he could not provide much dowry for them. Their accomplishments and employability were going to have to substitute for dowry. However, he did not anticipate the crisis over marriage that would ensue.

Because of the number of daughters involved, the Tripathys are a striking – but not a unique – example of educational change for New Capital women. Daughters in other families were also receiving high levels of education. But it was not until I interviewed mothers and grandmothers in 1989 that I began to learn the degree to which previous generations of women had desired an education, had become literate, and had encouraged their daughters' education. I shall begin with the Panda family, introduced in Chapter 4.

A THREE-GENERATIONAL PERSPECTIVE: THE PANDA FAMILY

GRANDMOTHER: I only attended school a few days. I saw the teacher cane a child and never went back. I was self-taught at home. I was always interested in higher studies and was able to teach my own children in Oriya up to matriculation. I am literate in Oriya. I opposed my husband marrying our daughters and urged him to allow them to get highly educated first – to complete their studies. I was always interested in my daughters studying music and dance. [Their father was opposed.] I myself was interested in philosophy and aesthetics. Now [in my old age – late seventies] I enjoy reading the *Gita* and the *Romayana* [sacred Hindu texts].
(Excerpt from February 20, 1989, interview)

MOTHER: I was allowed to continue my education after marriage. [She had a B.A. at the time of marriage and then, after having three

189

children, returned to graduate school to get an M.A.] I have tried to rear my own children to be independent, especially my daughter. I have done what I can for them, what I thought best at the time [i.e., encouraged higher education for both her sons and her daughter].
(Excerpt from April 9, 1989, interview)

DAUGHTER (Laxmi, twenty five years old; M.Sc.; unmarried): I am very lucky to have been born into my family, with no younger sisters. I am very free, I have free time and free choice. . . . Lots of girls get an education because they want to have a good marriage. . . . You can stay with tradition, but you should not accept it blindly.
(Excerpt from March 19, 1989, interview)

These brief excerpts from more lengthy interviews with three generations of women from the same family reveal a number of interesting themes with respect to women's education. The maternal grandmother reflects back to her village childhood where she was actually sent to school but found it frightening and never returned. Her parents did not insist, presumably because at that time schooling for girls was not considered important. Nonetheless, Grandmother was interested in learning and became sufficiently literate to assist her own children, three daughters and a son, with their studies. More importantly, she pushed for her daughters' education, countering her husband's inclination to arrange their marriages before they had completed a college education. The first two completed B.A.s before marrying and the third an M.A. Subsequently, Grandmother assisted one daughter with child care when she returned to graduate school.

Mrs. Panda, the mother, refers to being "allowed" to continue her education after marriage. This required the cooperation of her husband and parents-in-law, as well as her own parents who provided housing and child care. When I first knew her she was attending graduate school while caring for three children. Her husband, a government official who was posted outside of Bhubaneswar, visited on weekends. It was an unusual arrangement for

190

the times. What is particularly interesting in her narrative is her concern with rearing her children to be "independent" (her term). From their early childhood (see Chapter 4), Mrs. Panda had stimulated her children to learn and to think for themselves rather than emphasize familial interdependence. They had all been sent to prestigious English-language schools. She was particularly concerned that her daughter feel sufficiently independent and self-assured to pursue a graduate degree and a career before marriage, and she fretted whenever her daughter displayed any uncertainty, any "weakness." Happily, her daughter achieved academic success and excellent employment outside of Bhubaneswar. In fact, she was the only New Capital daughter I knew who was allowed to take a job far away from home, and now she is even further from home. She is married to an Orissan, and she and her husband reside in the United States, where he is employed.

Laxmi, the daughter/granddaughter here, has clearly benefited from this educational philosophy and experience. She speaks of being "free," meaning free from the pressures to marry, which, if she had had younger sisters, would be present. Because sons and daughters normally marry according to birth order, if she did not marry in a timely fashion, she would be holding up the marriages of younger sisters. And because she has been encouraged to pursue higher education and a career for its own sake, Laxmi is critical of those young women who, she believes, get an education only to enhance their marriageability. Furthermore, she is critical of following tradition in a nonreflective fashion. She has been provided with the personal space, education, and experience to critically reflect about issues of gender in India – a topic we shall return to, along with Laxmi's perspectives, in later chapters.

The theme of women's aspirations for more education also emerged in a group interview with Mrs. Tripathy, her mother (Grandmother), and four daughters. In that conversation I learned that Grandmother had had her marriage arranged when she was seven and consummated at twelve. "I wanted to be more educated, to learn more music. [She still sings well.] I did not want to marry. My parents cooperated with me, but my grandparents objected." And thus her marriage was consummated as soon as she reached

191

puberty, and she proceeded to bear many children. "I wanted only two children, a son and a daughter, but I had thirteen. She [pointing to Mrs. Tripathy] was the first. I had wanted to be like my brother and sister-in-law, who are musicians and have traveled to the United States." There was still regret in Grandmother's voice as she reported her girlhood dreams. Now she is a widow and dependent upon her various children.

Similarly, Mrs. Tripathy had wanted more education. "In my time what I wanted could not be. Some of my friends went on; some became doctors. Our family was very conservative." Thus, despite her own and her mother's aspirations, Mrs. Tripathy had only six years of schooling and at the age of fifteen was married to a widower with one child. She proceeded to bear nine children. As her children were growing up, however, attitudes toward girls' education began to change, and her daughters were able to accomplish what their mother and maternal grandmother could only dream of. Although the Tripathy girls attribute to their father the desire to see them educated, it is clear that they come from a family heritage of unfulfilled female aspirations. Undoubtedly, their mother was also instrumental in allowing them to continue their schooling and to postpone marriage.

In another New Capital family with three daughters and a son, all three girls were also highly accomplished. By 1989, the eldest had a Ph.D. and had recently been appointed a professor at a local college. Her two younger sisters both had M.A.s and were seeking employment; one was joining the Indian civil service. None was yet married. (By 1995, however, all three had married.) In this instance, their mother, Mrs. Misra, had not had personal aspirations for a higher education, although she had been exposed to it and had encouraged her daughters to pursue their studies.

My mother was very much eager to read me more, but I was not interested at all. . . . I had lost my father when four years old. My older sister studied and became a doctor. My brother became an engineer. . . . But things have changed. Girls should have an education. It gives them a choice. They can be economically independent.
(Excerpt from February 23, 1989, interview)

In this family there had already been a heritage of female education on the mother's side although not on the father's. Mr. Misra came from a small village where schooling was limited and not expected for girls. He had had to leave the village to pursue his studies. Mrs. Misra, in contrast, grew up in a town where girls were beginning to attend school and where higher education was available. Both parents, however, were committed to their daughters' education and had sent them to the best English-language school in Bhubaneswar. In fact, the girls grew up speaking principally English and complained that their Oriya was not very good. With respect to education and careers, they said that their mother had always encouraged them to go on – to complete their education and establish careers before marriage – and *not* to be like her.

Mrs. Misra, like Mrs. Mahapatra in the Old Town, mentions economic independence as one of the incentives for a higher education for girls. This idea is new and contrary to patrifocal family ideals and the expectations that men will be the earners, that everyone is economically interdependent, and that women are totally dependent upon their husbands and other male relatives. It is not that Mrs. Misra opposed marriage. She was, in fact, quite concerned about getting her eldest daughter married. But both she and Mr. Misra had a new view of marriage as more a partnership between husband and wife and as compatible with women having careers. They also recognized the importance of being able to earn an income should it be necessary. The Misras reared their daughters to think that they had some choice in how they would live as adults: that they could, if they wished, combine marriage with careers.

Not all New Capital sample families exhibit the same commitment to women's education and careers. The Das family, for example, arranged the marriage of their daughter, Lili, when she was only eighteen and a half and still had a year to go before completing her B.A., which she finished after marriage. They explained that their daughter was not a serious student so that when a good marriage offer came along, they felt they should take it. Mr. Das said that his extended family had urged him to accept it because of his poor health; if he were to die, then arranging Sita's marriage might be a problem.

A DIFFERENT THREE-GENERATIONAL PERSPECTIVE: THE DAS FAMILY

GRANDMOTHER (maternal): My marriage was fixed twenty-one days after my birth. I moved to my father-in-law's place when I was twelve. I was literate; I had five to six years of school. [Later in the interview, when I asked Grandmother what had been her greatest satisfaction in life, she responded:] Getting my children settled. Now I enjoy reading the *Ramayana* and the *Mahabharata* [*sacred Hindu texts*]

MOTHER: There has been a lot of difference [since my mother's time]. I studied up to the Intermediate. At that time graduation [bachelor's degree] was not here [available in Bhubaneswar]. You had to go to read at Cuttack [a town twenty-five miles away]. Our father looked after our studies. But at that time in our families they were very much interested in getting the daughter married. By the time I got married I was nineteen. But even after the generation gap our daughter also got married at the age of eighteen and a half. [This was said with laughter.]

DAUGHTER (Lili, twenty-four years old; married): A woman must be accommodating and self-sacrificing. Her role is to keep the family running smoothly. It is different for working women. They are economically independent and can have more of a say in decision making. Women like myself and my mother are very dependent.

(Excerpt from April 20 and April 24, 1989, interviews)

In this family the grandmother does not speak of unfulfilled educational aspirations, although she is literate and enjoys reading in her old age. Her daughter (Mrs. Das), however, had wanted to continue her studies beyond the Intermediate, to become a doctor. Her family was not supportive and arranged her marriage when she was nineteen, nearly the same age that her daughter married. The Dases might have postponed Lili's marriage had she been a more ambitious student and had Mr. Das not experienced poor health. In the course of conversation both Lili and her mother professed traditional attitudes about women's roles and the danger of becoming self-centered – something that many families fear occurs with too much education. Nonetheless, Lili can imagine things differently for employed women. Despite the attitudes of gender

194

hierarchy expressed here, both Lili and her mother are instrumental in running the household and participating in family decision making.

Education, Marriage, and Employment

In one generation middle- and upper-status women in Bhubaneswar have moved into higher education, and for some women, with such education has come a desire for employment and careers outside the home. These aspirations challenge the traditional marriage system and with it certain aspects of patrifocal family structure and ideology. Most obviously, the age of marriage for women has been greatly delayed – from early childhood and puberty to late adolescence and early adulthood. Old Town families have responded more conservatively to these new educational opportunities for women than have New Capital families. They have stopped their daughters' schooling sooner and arranged their marriages before they have become "too old" and "too educated." Some education is beneficial in negotiating marriages today but not so much that it jeopardizes a girl's modesty, decorum, and willingness to adapt to her husband's family.

Most Old Town families have been quite sensitive to the need to provide their daughters with enough education to make them more desirable marriage partners to increasingly better educated young men. However, they have not wanted to jeopardize their daughters' marital, and hence, their economic, security by allowing the girls to become too educated and potentially too old and independent to be selected as brides by suitable grooms and their families. To do so would also jeopardize their own family honor and status.

Many New Capital families, in contrast, have allowed their daughters to continue onto college and graduate school, and some now face a marriage crisis: They have highly educated daughters who are in their mid to late twenties for whom they must find older bridegrooms who are even more highly educated. If a daughter has become career oriented and the family wants to encourage her ambition or just be sensitive to her desires, they must also try to

195

find a bridegroom and parents-in-law who will be supportive of her working outside the home. Furthermore, the more educated a prospective bridegroom is, the more dowry his family can demand. Arranging a suitable marriage can, therefore, become increasingly difficult and expensive.

Arranged marriages are still the accepted practice in Bhubaneswar – as they remain in most of India – and because all sample children were eligible for marriage by the time of my 1987 and 1989 visits, conversation in many households focused intensely upon the topic of marriage. By 1987, 76 percent of the daughters in the Old Town were already married, but in the New Town only 52 percent of them were. This meant that there were still a lot of marriages to be arranged, and some families had become very concerned. In the Old Town, the mean age of unmarried girls was only twenty years – very much within the acceptable age-range (eighteen to twenty-four years) for marriage, however. In the New Capital, the mean age of unmarried girls was twenty-seven but ranged into the early thirties. Some families were in a state of turmoil, even crisis, over marriage.

In the Misra household, for example, by 1989 there was much tension over finding a suitable groom for their eldest daughter, aged twenty-six, who had a Ph.D. and a position as a college professor. Mr. Misra was personally not an advocate of arranged marriages and wished that his daughter had found a suitable young man herself, but that had not happened. In fact, it is very difficult for it to happen because there is no system of dating. Quite the contrary, even in coeducational schools girls and boys have little contact with one another. They sit on opposite sides of the classroom even in graduate school, and for a young woman to maintain her reputation she cannot be seen talking with young men, let alone socializing with them outside of the classroom. Thus, although Mr. Misra was an advocate of "love" marriages, it was not a realistic expectation for his daughters, nor was it something that his wife and extended kin would support.

In 1989, the Misras were searching hard for a compatible bridegroom for their academically inclined daughter. Citing my husband and myself as models, they hoped to find a young man who was also a professor and would like an academic wife. However, there were not large numbers of eligible men in Orissa of the right age, education, profession, and caste, and the Misras had, on principle, decided not to participate in dowry. "Now we have decided that we should not at all give *any* dowry," Mrs. Misra said. This decision will further restrict their search.

The Pandas, too, were concerned about their twenty-six-year-old daughter, Laxmi. Although they had encouraged her career and even her distant employment, they felt responsible for ensuring a good marriage for her before she became much older. And despite the independence with which she had been reared, Laxmi agreed that arranging her marriage should be her parents' responsibility and expressed confidence that they would make a good choice for her:

My parents have left me free. . . . But I have left the responsibility to them [of finding her a suitable husband]. I don't want to take any such project on for myself because I know my parents are very capable in this matter, and their choice I know.
(Excerpt from March 19, 1989, interview)

Like the Misras, the Pandas oppose dowry and had refused to accept any when their first son married. They spoke of the hypocrisy of many friends and relatives who criticize the dowry system, on the one hand, but then accept substantial gifts from the groom's family or endow their daughters, on the other. Mrs. Panda cited the example of relatives who maintained that they had given no dowry yet had provided each daughter with land and a sizable bank account at the time of her marriage. However, Mrs. Panda said that she now found herself in the uncomfortable position of possibly having to provide dowry if she and her husband want their daughter to get married: "We cannot count on finding suitable candidates who stand by the same principles." I asked if Laxmi might not find her own husband in her place of employment. Mrs. Panda said, "No. Laxmi does not like any of the young men she has met there. She finds none of them compatible."

The Pandas also have concerns about caste. A suitable man these days means someone of the right age, education, and profession, who is also of the right caste. They were apprehensive that if they waited too long, Laxmi might select by herself someone whom they considered unsuitable. "We cannot prevent a love marriage. It is not the same as in our day when we did not question our parents' authority. While we do not oppose love marriages in theory, we would be unhappy if our children married out of the Brahmin caste. A love marriage is all right so long as it is with the right person." The Pandas appreciated the irony of this statement and went on to speak at some length about the inconsistency of their views on the topic. Such issues and contradictions present dilemmas for many contemporary families who are in principle opposed to the inequities of caste but who find it difficult to ignore this still pervasive sociocultural system when it comes to marriage. These are not unlike the contradictions that many Americans express regarding interracial marriage.

In the Tripathy household, the issue of marriage had reached crisis proportions by 1987. Only one of seven eligible daughters was married. By 1989, only one more had married, and this was accomplished more by chance than through planning. Mr. Tripathy had grown old and somewhat senile and was of little help, leaving his wife and two younger sons with the responsibility of trying to find suitable grooms for their highly educated and potentially too old daughters/sisters. As one daughter put it, "Now there are no suitors available. We're too educated and there's a scarcity of educated boys in Orissa. We would like to meet more educated men, but there's no way to do it. Furthermore, they must be of Brahmin caste."

Not only were comparably educated suitors of the right caste and background scarce in Bhubaneswar and surrounding areas, but young men and their families reportedly complained that the Tripathy daughters were too old and independent (i.e., they had graduate degrees and were pursuing careers). These young women had another disadvantage as well: With so many daughters, their parents could not afford large dowries, but their daughters' earning potential was not considered a suitable substitute. As one of the daughters expressed it, "Candidates come to our house but do not choose us. It is our fate, our fortune." At other times, however, she was less fatalistic and bitterly complained that "men just want less educated wives whom they can dominate; we are not supposed to out-achieve our husbands."

During my 1987 visit to Bhubaneswar, I was asked by the family to come consult with them about an unexpected visit from a potential suitor and his father. The young man worked and resided in the United States but had returned home to Bhubaneswar to find a bride. The Tripathys reported that he wanted to make a decision and get married within a week. They were eager to have a suitor for their next-to-oldest daughter but concerned about the rush he seemed to be in. They wanted me to come evaluate this young man and his employment in the United States. As it turned out, however, the young man decided against the Tripathy daughter.

My mother, who was with me on this trip to Bhubaneswar, tried to console Mrs. Tripathy and the girls, pointing out that they were all beautiful and talented. Mrs. Tripathy poignantly responded by saying that she now wished she had had only a few children as my mother did. Her pride in her daughters' accomplishments no longer seemed to compensate for the marriage crisis she confronted. She took very seriously her parental duty of getting her children – especially her daughters – well settled. And she was hurt by gossip that she and her husband were delaying their daughters' marriages in order to let them work and support their parents. It is sons, *not* daughters, who are supposed to help support their parents and extended families, and the Tripathys made sure that their daughters' earnings were set aside for their futures. As one daughter explained, "We are working and getting money, but we do not use it to live on. We live on our father's pension and our brothers' contributions. Nonetheless, people gossip and say our parents want their daughters' incomes."

The one marriage that occurred between 1987 and 1989 was unusual in that a young man who was a college lecturer wanted to marry a college lecturer – someone of similar age, education, and profession. He had heard through a friend about one of the Tripathy daughters who fit these criteria and arranged to meet her and then her family. He ended up displeasing both his father-in-law and his own parents by taking marriage arrangements into his own hands. However, it was a serendipitous union for the Tripathy daughter. Subsequent to 1989, one more daughter has married, leaving four yet unmarried, one of whom is older than two of her now married sisters. This means that this young woman has been bypassed in the marriage market and has a bleak life ahead of her in Bhubaneswar, a town where marriage and family prevail and where there are no activities for unmarried women. For example, women are expected to be accompanied by men to the theater, cinema, or other such cultural events. Although women now go to the market alone and commute to work, they are not expected to attend public events without husbands, fathers, or brothers. And to be unmarried and childless is considered a tragedy for a woman.

Conclusion

In contemporary India, education, marriage, and women's new-found career aspirations are intricately interconnected. A transition that began in a few parts of India a century ago is currently in process in Bhubaneswar. With the introduction of education for women – particularly higher education – comes, on the one hand, an increased desire for such education and, on the other, certain challenges to patrifocal family structure and ideology. New-found convictions that girls, as well as boys, should receive an education must accommodate older beliefs that women ought to be secluded within the home, their chastity protected, and their marriages arranged at an early age. The potential for conflict between old practices and ideologies and new ones has been set in motion, and different families have responded in somewhat different ways.

In both the Old Town and the New Capital, most middle- and upper-status families have responded positively to these new educational opportunities for women. In one generation, for example, the normative age of marriage for daughters has risen from fourteen to fifteen years to from eighteen to twenty-six years. An older, educated, and potentially employed daughter, however, implies a more independent, less docile, and less subservient wife and daughter-in-law. Although most young middle- and upper-status men and their families now want an educated wife and daughter-in-law, they generally would like her interests to be secondary to theirs. She is still expected to be the person who makes the major adaptation ("sacrifice") at the time of marriage, working to fit into her husband's family. Thus, a woman's education is more often valued for its status enhancement potential than for its own sake.[6] A bride should still be younger and less educated than her prospective husband, and she should pursue a career only if it fits in with his career plans and his family's lifestyle. In one Old Town Brahmin family, for example, where a marriage was being arranged in 1989 between a son in the military and a young woman with a medical degree, it was not clear that the new daughter-in-law would be allowed by her parents-in-law to practice medicine. They expressed pride in her degree but considerable ambivalence about letting her go out to work. From her prospective in-laws' point of view, this young woman's high level of education, especially her science education, enhanced her marriageability status, *not* her employability status. And her personal aspirations were not considered relevant.

In the New Capital, where many young women have been encouraged to pursue careers before marriage, the challenge to patrifocal values is more dramatic. A young woman with her own income has the potential to act independently – even to leave an unhappy situation. Particularly sensitive is the mother-in-law–daughter-in-law relationship. As one New Capital mother expressed it: "A serious problem all over India is that mothers-in-law want to dominate their daughters-in-law and tell them everything to do. But daughters-in-law are now educated and have their own ideas about what they want to do; they have their own creativity. Mothers-in-law must adjust to this and back off, but most have not adapted to these new conditions. Husbands must also adapt." Chapter 7 will explore these new challenges to the patrifocal family system. Where husbands and in-laws have been supportive, new familial relationships seem to be thriving; however, where they have not been supportive of more independent and employed wives/daughters-in-law, marital and family strife has resulted. By

1989, in my sample families, three separations and one divorce had occurred – all involving highly educated, employed women.

The extensive education and employment of young Bhubaneswar women has also had other effects, often unintended, upon patrifocal family structure and ideology. For example, daughters who remain with natal kin into their late twenties and even early thirties build, to a degree not formerly possible, long-term, close ties with their parents and siblings. After marriage, they want to retain those close ties, and there is much evidence that they are doing so. Many Old Town and New Capital girls have married within Bhubaneswar or close by, making frequent visits to their natal families possible. Some adult daughters even reside with natal kin. For example, one divorced sister resides with an older married sister in Bhubaneswar and her three children. In another instance, a set of elderly parents live much of the time with a daughter, who is separated from her husband, and one grandchild. Their other grandchild resides with his father and paternal grandparents.

There is much evidence that significant change in women's aspirations and roles has occurred in Bhubaneswar – change that has serious implications for patrifocal family structure and ideology. For some women, this has resulted in a changed self-awareness and a new reflectiveness about gender roles and gender and age hierarchies. Although a changing gender ideology has not been directly promoted by schooling, where gender issues are not part of the curriculum, their being in school along with boys has allowed girls and young women to envision themselves in jobs and careers for the first time. Furthermore, girls who have done well academically have been encouraged by teachers to continue their educations. Schooling has also made a generation of young women literate and given them access to newspapers, magazines, and other printed materials. While such materials are still rare in Old Town households, they are commonly found in New Capital households. For example, many New Capital women read magazines in Hindi and in English from such cosmopolitan centers as New Delhi, Bombay, and Calcutta, and many of these magazines consciously address women's issues.[7]

There are, however, limits to how far families and related institutions have as yet been transformed. For example, parents remain in control of their children's marriage arrangements, thus preserving caste as a principal criterion of marriage and effectively preventing "love" marriages. Dowry continues to be an issue – one that no one admits liking but that persists nonetheless. Because a daughter's earning potential has not yet been accepted as a satisfactory substitute for dowry, a good marriage is still viewed as the way to ensure her economic future. Thus, a girl's marriageability remains a major concern of her parents, who continue to socialize their daughters to think of being a good wife, a good daughter-in-law, and a good mother as their principal responsibilities in life. In addition, girls are still expected to make the major adjustment in marriage – to sacrifice their interests in favor of others and to become the preeminent caretakers of children and aging parents-in-law. And although large discrepancies in the age and educations of husbands and wives have been reduced, differences persist, thereby preserving the principle of male authority. How the different generations of Old Town and New Capital women, and women of different socioeconomic status, perceive these kinds of issues is the topic of Chapter 7.

Change and the portent of further change in Bhubaneswar is well symbolized by the enactment of Saraswati Puja, the annual festival honoring the Hindu goddess associated with speech and learning and considered the patroness of the arts and sciences. In 1965–67 Saraswati Puja was primarily a private celebration within the home, especially in the homes of those families who believed that education was important. While it continued to be celebrated within the home and at school, by 1989 Saraswati Puja had become a citywide event. Massive images of the goddess were erected in several key areas of the New Capital. At night, these images were illuminated by blinking lights and surrounded by musicians whose playing was electronically amplified. There were dramatic visual and sound images, and young people – both men and women – came by the hundreds to parade and dance through the city in honor of Saraswati. Times had changed, formal education had become paramount, and women were becoming full participants in this public celebration.

CHAPTER SEVEN

Change and Continuity in Women's Lives

A Three-Generational Perspective

Previous chapters have introduced a cultural model of the Hindu patrifocal family as a context for understanding women's roles and statuses and the child care practices predominant in Bhubaneswar in the 1960s. They have also examined some of the sources of dramatic change that have been occurring in family and gender systems in Bhubaneswar during the last thirty years. This chapter will explore aspects of change and continuity in patrifocal family structure and ideology from the perspectives of three generations of women enmeshed in them. In 1989, when I returned to Bhubaneswar to systematically interview women, I began with the question, "How have the expectations for women's education changed?" I tried to encourage women to reflect about the potential effects of formal education upon marriage, the dowry system, patrilocal residence, husband-wife relationships, the role of daughter versus the roles of daughter-in-law, wife, and mother, the preference for sons versus daughters, and other aspects of the family and women's lives. Although I had an interview schedule in mind, I used it loosely, allowing women to take the dialogue where they wanted to go. In the course of several hours of conversation, however, most of my topics were addressed, along with many others.

The information presented here comes directly from these interviews, many of which included women from several generations of the same family. They involve forty-four mothers, daughters, and grandmothers, as well as a few fathers, sons, and grandfathers who participated at times, from thirteen of my original sample families – six from the Old Town and seven from the New Capital. The women I interviewed represent new and old Bhubaneswar as well as the different caste/class systems in each side of town. Interview sessions which I received permission to tape record, lasted anywhere from one to four hours, with some interviews continuing over several days. I conducted the interviews in both Oriya and English, with young people helping me to translate their elders' Oriya when I did not fully understand it. One highly educated New Capital daughter helped me extensively with translation.

Reflections on Educational Change

I begin with a discussion of educational change for women with members from three generations of the upper-status Misra household – a conversation that was alluded to in Chapter 6. Mrs. Misra (Mother), two of her daughters, Menaka (twenty-six years old) and Nakima (twenty-three years old), and their very elderly paternal grandmother (Grandmother) were present. While talking, we sat together on the spacious front verandah of their Type VIII home in the New Capital.

MOTHER [speaking for her elderly mother-in-law]: She (Grandmother) received no formal or informal education. Isn't that right? [This was directed to Grandmother and confirmed by her.] She married at thirteen, maybe fourteen years. [Again, Mrs. Misra stops to confirm with Grandmother, who indicates that she was twelve years old.]
MENAKA: She (Mother) married at nineteen when a graduate.
MOTHER: No. I completed my B.A. exams after one year of marriage. My father-in-law did not want me to read any more.

I indicate that in contrast her three daughters had continued their educations as far as they could go, earning either master's or Ph.D. degrees. Nakima responds first.

NAKIMA: Well, because we lived in a town from the very beginning and since the culture thinks we should go to the best of schools, we were admitted to public [private] schools – the Convent – and we had the best education possible in Bhubaneswar. Since we were reading there, we could work higher. We could complete our graduate and postgraduate degrees.

MENAKA: But Mummy was also staying in town. During her times things were different.

MOTHER: I had lost my father when I was four years old. My older sister studied and became a doctor. My brother became an engineer. He was very intelligent, and he has completed a four-year Ph.D. in engineering. My mother was very much eager to read me more [have me study more], but I was not interested at all. [Mrs. Misra became the child who remained at home with her widowed mother even for several years after she was married.]

NAKIMA: In a way, I think education gives you a choice – to be economically independent. Certainly, a future. We at least, within certain limits, have a chance to make our own living, to make our life. I think things have changed.

Grandmother did not participate actively in this part of the conversation but became fully engaged later, when the topic shifted to early marriage and moving to one's in-laws' house. Nonetheless, a contrast in generational perspectives is evident in the preceding remarks.

Kalpana Mohanty, a New Capital upper-status daughter and now herself a mother of three daughters, confirmed these generational changes in expectations for women's education.

Yes, girls are now equal to men. They should have postgraduate degrees and work. My mother married at fourteen, after only four or five years of schooling, and that was viewed as important only for carrying our rituals. For me, marriage came right after I completed my B.A. I wanted to go on for an M.A., but it was expected that I be married by twenty. I don't expect any of my daughters to marry until they have had all the education that they want and have held jobs for a while.

As described in Chapter 4, Kalpana's marriage was arranged during my 1965–67 field trip. Negotiations with her prospective par-

ents-in-law and husband included the stipulation that she be allowed to complete her M.A. after marriage. Kalpana did this and
has been an employed wife and mother ever since.

In another New Capital middle-status household, two daughters-in-law spoke with me about women's education. They had
married into the Mahapatra household. The interview took place
on the front verandah of a newly built house that accommodates
what is now a joint family – parents, three married sons, and a
granddaughter. Mrs. Mahapatra, who was not feeling well, remained indoors watching a Hindi film on television.

FIRST DAUGHTER-IN-LAW [replying to my question about women's
    education]: Definitely, it has had an impact. We have our own
    thoughts now. We don't have to depend on anyone. I was married
    at twenty-four, whereas my mother was married at nineteen after
    only the Ninth standard.
SECOND DAUGHTER-IN-LAW: I, too, was married at twenty-four,
    whereas my mother married at twenty-one.
FIRST DAUGHTER-IN-LAW: I have an M.A. in history. I was interested
    in a career, but there was no opportunity. My parents wanted me
    to get married. [She then expresses the hope of doing something
    with a career later on. Now, however, she is a new mother.]

These excerpts from New Capital interviews underscore the educational changes for women that have occurred over the past two
generations – from the little or no schooling and very early marriage that grandmothers might expect, to more extensive schooling
for mothers, to the postgraduate degrees and the potential – even,
for some, the expectation – of careers for daughters. Marriage, however, continues to be an important consideration. In the Old Town,
the response to schooling for girls has been generally more conservative than in the New Capital, with considerations of the safety,
purity, and marriageability of daughters outweighing other factors.

My interview with the Old Town, middle-status Gauda family
took place in the inner courtyard of their home with Mrs. Gauda
(mother) and her youngest daughter, Ritu (twenty-three years old).
Ritu and I sat on the floor of the courtyard, with Mrs. Gauda

coming and going as she prepared, with the assistance of a daughter-in-law, the morning meal.

In response to my question about higher education for girls, Mrs. Gauda said that there were too many dangers in sending her daughters to college.

I always had to think about their safety. Women should not go out to work. In other houses that may happen but not in our house. If a husband has a job, why does the woman need to go out? I am not in favor of women working [outside the house]. Women should always stay at home.

[Then Mrs. Gauda proudly exclaimed:] My older daughter-in-law has not once stepped across that gate in the twelve years since she came to us! All she does is go to her father's house. If my son goes out, sometimes he takes her, but she has never gone on her own or with friends to the market or cinema. I do not approve of women gallivanting. They should be concerned with self-respect. They should eat well and sleep well.

Mrs. Gauda then demonstrated with her sari how a woman should veil her face when going outside, launching into a speech about her disapproval of many women and their obscene displays in films. Her second daughter-in-law was nearby preparing the midday meal and remained silent throughout this interview. The Gaudas' only other daughter-in-law, the wife of their oldest son, does not reside with them. She and her husband moved to a house of their own so that they could live more independently, and Mr. and Mrs. Gauda have never forgiven them for this act of defiance.

As reported in Chapter 6, poor low-status women have had little opportunity to pursue an education, although they express the desire to. For them, a career is not a relevant topic. That they work inside and outside the home is expected of them from early childhood. In answer to "Are there any changes for women that you would like to see?" one Old Town Bauri informant responded: "Yes, of course, but does it ever happen? I have already grown old. What kind of advancement can there be for me?"

I repeat the question. Mrs. Patro then speaks of a social welfare program for mothers and children that she once learned about:

You could send your children, and they would get one meal and learn something. Women were told how to keep latrines clean. The social worker suggested some kind of work to me. If the government would give some kind of work and provide us with some prosperity, then that would be good, don't you think? But I am alone in this house and I have grown old. Our work is in the fields. That is how we survive.

Education and Changing Marriage Practices

At the time of my interview, Ritu Gauda's marriage was being arranged. One day when I arrived at the house, Ritu seemed both excited and nervous and indicated that she wanted to tell me about something. She took my hands in hers and began talking rapidly about the surprise visit of a prospective father-in-law.

RITU: I was in my nightie when he came. I didn't know who he was. He had been roaming the neighborhood visiting houses of appropriate caste families. I was brought out to meet him. He tried to reassure me, telling me I was like a daughter. On this first visit he was just inquiring about what household skills I had.

I asked Ritu if she had met the prospective groom.

RITU: No. I saw him but did not talk with him. We were introduced, but I felt very shy. I kept my head lowered and did not get a good look at him. We did not talk, but when they left, I saw him from the window. I thought he looked handsome.

I ask what it felt like to be marrying a stranger.

RITU: I am scared. I am wondering how I will spend my time. Will he turn out to be good or bad?

209

The prospective father-in-law had liked the Gauda family well enough to return the next day with his son and another male relative. This time Ritu was dressed in her best sari. She explained that they wanted to see photographs of her and her certificate of matriculation from school but that they had not exchanged photographs. I asked her about the groom's education and learned that he was not a college graduate, that he had been recruited into the air force after two years of college and would receive a special diploma. Ritu's state was one of great excitement – that this might actually be the person whom she would marry – mixed with a certain amount of fear and trepidation. At this point her mother joined us and spoke:

MOTHER: I was married as a little child, at nine years, and went to live with my in-laws at fourteen or fifteen.

I ask what that had been like.

MOTHER: How should I feel? I just felt the same.

I ask, "Were you a little scared?"

MOTHER: Yes. It was not a question of happiness. I cried a lot.

"How did your in-laws treat you as a new bride?" I ask.

MOTHER: They received me very well; they had spent so much over the wedding. I went as a bride so they had to accept me!

"But that does not always happen, does it?" I ask.

MOTHER: Yes, that is true. But I was given affection and attention. [Mrs. Gauda's in-laws, as it happens, were known to her. They lived in the same locality in which she grew up. Although she and her husband had never spoken to one another before their marriage, they knew about one another.]

210

I then ask Mrs. Gauda what her husband's age had been at the time their marriage was consummated.

MOTHER: I don't know. I wouldn't remember anyway. I don't even remember the ages of my children. He was away in the air force at the time. Later he resigned and returned to Bhubaneswar.

I ask if her family had given a dowry at the time of her marriage.

MOTHER: Yes, a bicycle, a watch, some jewelry, and money.

"Will there be a dowry for Ritu?" I ask.

MOTHER: Yes. The family comes from Berhampur [a southern region of Orissa] and people there are very greedy. However, the dowry is not yet set. I am going to tell the bridegroom to take whatever is offered happily, otherwise go away. I cannot offer any more! [She adds,] Ritu's father will be the main spokesman for the family. He may ask me some things [confer with me].

I then ask if anything has changed with respect to arranged marriages.

RITU: Yes. Now women have a say. At that time [referring to her mother's marriage], they had to marry blind. The groom could be blind or crippled. Nowadays people have more say.

I then direct the question to Mrs. Gauda, but she turns it back to me, asking what marriage is like in the United States. I briefly explain that young people meet and choose one another.

MOTHER: What a peculiar system, where parents have so little say!

Regardless of residence in the Old Town or the New Capital, or of class/caste status, marriages of this generation almost universally continue to be arranged, with some participation by the sons and daughters themselves in the selection of their spouse. Love marriages – the selection of a spouse by individual choice rather than either *by* one's family or *together* with one's family – are distrusted. Only one sample family spoke in support of them. However, most people recognized that love marriages, once extremely rare, were becoming more common and anticipated that they would eventually receive greater acceptance. As one of the New Capital Mahapatra daughters-in-law put it, "People are meeting each other and getting married, but society does not yet accept it."

The initial marriage arrangements as described for Ritu Gauda are representative of a fairly traditional process, but one that differs from the experiences of women of Ritu's mother's and her grandmother's generations in that the prospective bride and groom are allowed to meet. Two days after the preceding discussion, Ritu met the prospective groom. He came to see her, and they had an hour alone to talk. "I really liked him," she said. "He is a very nice man." Having met and talked with the groom, Ritu now seemed reassured, happy, and no longer anxious. She threw her arms around me several times and asked my son, who accompanied me on this occasion, to take photos of us together. We also took photos of her in several of her best saris so that she could send them to the bridegroom.

Several Old Town and New Capital sons described a somewhat different process. They had actually met a suitable young woman and liked her and had then gone to their parents, requesting that they arrange a marriage with the parents of the preselected young woman. One son referred to this as "an arranged marriage in form only." It was not, however, a love marriage in the Western sense. There was no dating or means of getting to know one another other than very superficially. In all instances, the girl was of the right caste, and the parents agreed to the arrangement.

One New Capital mother said that she had initiated such a marriage for her son. She was eager for him to get married before he left to study abroad and had encouraged him to marry a girl who was his younger brother's classmate and whom he knew slightly. "Instead of seeking extensively for a bride," she said, "consulting lots of people and taking much time, I suggested to him a girl he had known for some years. I would not have proceeded had my son not agreed. I would never force him into such a decision." Another member of the family referred to this as a "love-cum-arranged marriage."

In trying to better understand why most young, highly educated women whom I have known in Bhubaneswar continued to prefer arranged marriages over love marriages, I spoke at length with several of them. One was Laxmi Panda, then twenty-six and a scientist employed in a major city. I asked whether in her workplace, where male and female scientists did research together, love marriages occurred.

That happens. It depends on the family. If they are very particular for that, in that case it will be there. People arranging for themselves, that is there. My parents have left me free. They have told me that if I want to have anybody of my choice, then I should tell them. I don't want to take any such project on for myself because I know my parents are very capable in this matter. It will be according to my choice. [What Laxmi means here is that her parents would not force her into a marriage that she did not want.] In some houses where the parents are a very different type, it's the parents [only] or your choice, then you arrange for yourself. But I know that my mother will arrange for me what I want, so I don't have to search for myself. I have myself seen that my parents are very proper in that matter.

Laxmi, although leading an unusually independent life for an unmarried Bhubaneswar woman, did not want to assume the responsibility of selecting her own husband. She was confident that her parents would make a good choice of marriage partner for her. Without exception, the young women whom I have watched come of age in Bhubaneswar have accepted marriage as both inevitable and desirable. Lacking any dating experience or way of meeting suitable young men, they have looked to their parents to make this very significant decision for them. However, unlike most of their mothers and grandmothers, they entered marriage with sufficient maturity and sense of choice that fearfulness has been greatly reduced.

In contrast, in recalling their own arranged marriages at an early age, many grandmothers emphasized their feelings of fear. During the New Capital Misra interview, for example, Grandmother recounted some of her unhappy memories of her marriage at age fourteen.

I was very unhappy [in my parents-in-law's home]. I felt distinctly uncomfortable because I was so young. My new husband had diarrhea. It was blamed on me, the new bride. Also, my husband's older brother, aged twenty-two, died at the time of the wedding. No, I did not feel good about it. When I first came, I was only fourteen years old. I did not care for him [her new husband]; he did not care for me. I used to sit alone all the time and weep uncontrollably [literally "tears would beat me"]. Then my father-in-law, he took me aside. He told me many things. He tried to make me understand. . . . There was a reception on the fourth day after our wedding. People came and remarked on everything – my jewelry, my looks, etc. They made me feel very uncomfortable. . . . My husband recovered, and things got better until I gave birth to two daughters. Then the unhappiness started again and continued until I finally had a son [Mr. Misra]. I never did get along with my mother-in-law.

Mother-in-law–daughter-in-law problems continue to be chronic regardless of how marriages are arranged. Just before my 1989 arrival in Bhubaneswar, the third Tripathy daughter had been married under unusual circumstances. Kalika (thirty-three) had been selected by a young man over her older sister, Padmini (thirty-five). Sitting together, cross-legged, on her wedding bed in her new apartment, I listened as Kalika poured out her problems.

There are some problems. I will tell you now. You can know the problems I face after my marriage. Why I am here alone with no help from anywhere. I don't want help from my parents. I want to be independent. But I should get help from my in-laws; yet I don't.

214

Kalika went on to explain the almost miraculous circumstances of her marriage, given her status as an older woman from a family with many unmarried daughters. Her husband had learned about her from a friend and had come to her home by himself to discuss marriage. Her father, now old and senile, became very angry with him because he was acting on his own, but the young man returned a second time. He was a college lecturer and wanted to marry a college lecturer. He liked what he had heard of Kalika and persevered. On the second visit, Kalika's father became even more angry. He learned that the young man was a Brahmin but of a lower *jati* than the Tripathys. The young man came a third time, this time with a mediator and after having already spoken with Kalika's mother. This was the first time that he actually saw Kalika. He asked in what year she had passed her B.A. exams in order to determine her age and learned that she was slightly older than himself. She assumed this was the end of things. Two days later, however, he came to see her at work and explained that he wanted to marry an educated woman like her from a cultured family. He asked for her horoscope and proposed marriage.

I said no, that he must speak to my mother. I told him that in our society arranged marriages are not like this, that he's so liberal, and I'm afraid. I must have my mother's and my family's opinion.

That night Kalika's mother went to visit the young man's father, and the father came the next day to meet Kalika. He did not object, so a wedding date was set. "I got married with no dowry, no arrangements, just a few friends and family," Kalika said. Following the wedding, she went to her parents-in-law's house to reside.

The bride never returns to her own house after the wedding. But I am unlucky that my mother-in-law did not come to welcome me. [Normally, the new bride and bridegroom are welcomed by the women of the household.] My husband is everything to me. At first he did not take this [slight] seriously. On the fourth day [after the wedding] there was a reception in a big club. The groom's party. Our honeymoon was also in his [her husband's] house. On the eighth day the bride goes to her own house for the first time. It is an auspicious day. When she returns to her in-laws, she can be asked to work. My mother-in-law is not so good to me. So adamant. My husband's sister is also adamant. They forced me to work [that day], to prepare work in the kitchen. They wanted to torture me. My husband came to my defense. He explained that his wife is educated – a servicing [working] woman, who cannot prepare food for the whole family and work. How is that possible? It is indecent to send a daughter-in-law to the kitchen on the eighth day. My mother-in-law wanted, like other mothers-in-law, a girl who will cook for them, prepare meals for them, and who will serve them.

In a short time it became clear that Kalika's mother-in-law resented her – a daughter-in-law whom she had had no role in selecting – and wanted her to behave as a more obsequious and traditional daughter-in-law. Ironically, this mother-in-law is herself an employed woman who had a love marriage. Despite Kalika's teaching responsibilities, she was expected to do all the cooking for the extended family. On the tenth day after the wedding and while her husband was away at a conference, his sister came into Kalika's room when she was worshipping and demanded back all the jewelry that her parents-in-law had given her.

I was afraid. I cried and sobbed. They were taking back the engagement ring that my father-in-law had given me on his first visit and that I wanted to wear until death. My father-in-law heard my sobs and came. He tried to protect me and offered to give me comparable ornaments in five to ten days. I said that I would return what I had but would not take any more. When my husband returned and learned what had happened, he was very angry. He threatened to return the ornaments and not to take any more food from his parents.

Relations with Kalika's in-laws continued to deteriorate. After the jewelry incident, her mother-in-law and sister-in-law suddenly took a trip to Calcutta without telling her.

216

They left me alone without telling me where different foods were stored, and I was expected to cook for my husband and father-in-law without any help. After three months my husband called his mother back, explaining that I had to grade exam papers. I still didn't have any time. I had to prepare food in the early morning, go to work, and then prepare food at night until midnight. In addition, my mother-in-law resented any time that my husband and I spent alone in our room. She accused us of being a king and queen. My husband got very angry and said that he would never take food in their house again. Why was she torturing us?

Kalika's parents-in-law called her mother, complaining that she was not being a good daughter-in-law. Her mother told them that their son and daughter-in-law were educated and independent and suggested that they be allowed to live separately. Kalika and her husband then moved out and set up their own small household. Kalika's parents-in-law, meanwhile, accused her of "breaking our house."

My problem now is that my husband wants to live with his family [there has been a reconciliation], but I do not want to. This is a problem for us now. He is their son, and he wants it. But as I am not their real daughter, so that when they have no love and affection for me, how should I be obedient to them?

Kalika's dilemma is that she understands her husband's feelings of obligation to his parents, especially as the eldest son. Nonetheless, she does not want to return to a very difficult situation in which she is expected to be a dutiful daughter-in-law and her education and professional responsibilities are not respected. As will become evident shortly, her dilemma is not unique. The increased education and independence of young people has made joint family living potentially more hazardous. Kalika's husband is torn between his feelings of love and responsibility toward his parents and his love and concern for the wife whom he selected.

Patrilocal Residence

The expectation that sons will continue to reside, whenever possible, with their parents and that daughters-in-law should adapt to their husband's family remains strong in Bhubaneswar. In the Old Town all sample families that were joint in 1965–67 have continued to be joint at my later visits, with several of the households that were nuclear becoming joint as sons have matured and married. Despite new occupational opportunities, joint household structure has remained extraordinarily stable. Many Old Town young men have found employment in the New Capital, which allows them to remain at home and to commute.

In the New Capital, where middle- and upper-status children have been educated for professional lives, there has been more mobility and less emphasis upon patrilocal residence. Nonetheless, the ideal remains that at least one son live with or near elderly parents. It is too early in the lives of many New Capital children to determine just how this will work out. However, two upper-status New Capital households in my sample have become joint, with at least one married son residing with his parents, and two other families have designated an unmarried son to remain home, overseeing family property and caring for aging parents while the other sons pursue careers outside of Bhubaneswar. A fifth household has married sons and daughters living nearby; a sixth, sonless, family has elderly parents residing with a daughter and granddaughter. As of 1989, only one set of New Capital middle- or upper-status parents lived alone.

All lower-status families in my sample have continued to be extended in a diversity of ways as they were in 1965–67. One set of elderly parents, the Beheras, were residing in 1989 with their married daughter, Sopna, instead of their son. From their perspective, this arrangement was a tragedy – a serious breach of patrifocal family rules that delegate the care of parents to sons and daughters-in-law, not to daughters. During my interviews with Mrs. Behera and Sopna, it became clear that there was great bitterness about this situation. Both mother and daughter repeatedly returned to the topic.

SOPNA: My brother does not have a respectable job because he
   won't speak nicely to his elders or use the right connections. He is
   sullen and rude. Right now he has no job but lives off his father's
   retirement pension, which he uses to pay rent, etc.
MOTHER [breaks in, crying]: I can't forget my son despite all this. I
   have had to scold him a lot. I have been trying to knock some
   sense into him. I still feel unsettled having to live with my daughter
   and her family.

In the course of our conversation, it became evident that Sopna's
parents, after Mr. Behera's retirement from his job as a government
night watchman, went to live with their married son in another
part of the New Capital. However, their son and daughter-in-law
"stole" from them instead of taking care of them, using Mr. Behera's retirement funds for their own interests. Ultimately, the Beheras left and moved in with Sopna, who was living with her
husband and children in a small village outside of Bhubaneswar.
This would not have been possible earlier in Sopna's marriage
when she resided with her parents-in-law.

SOPNA: I lived for five years with my parents-in-law. Everything was
   very happy until I had an operation [after several very difficult
   births] which required that I have milk and other foods. And I
   couldn't do as much work as I did formerly. This led to tension
   with my sister-in-law. You know the kind of tension that exists in
   Oriya households. So we moved out.

Sopna then explained that her parents-in-law were very nice,
that they lived nearby, and that she would like me to visit them.
   Things between Sopna's parents and brother, however, had de-
teriorated so badly that the Beheras wanted to leave their small
savings to Sopna rather than to their son. They had a certificate of
deposit with the Bank of India that would mature in five years.
They feared they might not be alive then and that, following rules
of patrilineal inheritance, it would go to their son. They asked me
how they could ensure that the money would go to Sopna. I was
able to arrange a meeting between them and a bank official, during

which Sopna was made the legal recipient of their small investment.

When I asked mothers, daughters, and grandmothers about the tradition of patrilocal residence, most confirmed that it remained very important and that most contemporary daughters would reside with their parents-in-law for at least some period of time. One New Capital daughter asserted, "Things have not changed!" However, patterns of residence after marriage have grown increasingly dynamic as young educated sons and daughters mature and marry. In the Old Town an eldest son in one family moved to a separate house with his wife and children after having disagreements with his father. The father remains bitter and will have nothing to do with his son and his daughter-in-law, whom he accuses of being "poorly raised" – that is, raised to be selfish rather than put the interests of family first. Kalika Tripathy's difficulties with her in-laws have already been described. In yet another New Capital family a troubled marriage, exacerbated by mother-in-law–daughter-in-law tensions, has led to a formal separation of husband and wife that will be described later.

Although most Old Town and New Capital daughters have been reared to believe that it is their responsibility to adjust to their husband's family and to be accommodating, some are also being reared to expect a limited amount of autonomy as they pursue higher education and careers. The value placed upon female accommodation and self-sacrifice as underlying tenets of the patrifocal joint family has come into conflict with the new value placed upon individual motivation and accomplishment as well as upon a more companionate marriage. Kalika Tripathy's husband, for example, wanted a wife of comparable education and profession to himself who could be a companion. He found someone who met these criteria but then encountered difficulties with his parents, especially his mother, who, it seems, wanted to be in control of her son and daughter-in-law. She complained that they spent too much time together and that Kalika was not a "good" daughter-in-law – not sufficiently dutiful and domestic. Kalika, who worked hard as a college lecturer, resented being asked to cook for and wait upon her husband's extended family in a servile fashion. Although she had grown up in a large family where everyone helped with household chores, she had been reared to put her studies first and had come to expect respect as a professional woman – as someone who would share in household duties but not have to perform them alone *for* everyone else. In this instance, as in others that will be described, two different expectations for marriage and family had come into conflict.

Dowry

The topic of dowry (gifts given by the bride's family to the bridegroom's family) came up repeatedly in my interviews whenever mothers, daughters, and grandmothers discussed marriage arrangements. Some of the women asserted that dowries were a recent phenomenon whereas others maintained that dowry expectations in earlier generations had not been onerous – that what parents-in-law really wanted was a "good" daughter-in-law, *not* material goods. "Now," as Mrs. Das of the New Capital put it, "dowry is a big problem. It takes Rs. 60,000 – to a lakh [Rs. 100,000] to marry an ICS officer, Rs. 80,000 for a doctor, and even for small jobs they take a lot."[1]

Most middle- and upper-status families maintained that they did not want to participate in the dowry system, and those with sons asserted that they did not make any demands for dowry. However, as one Old Town Brahmin son explained:

Yes, the demand for dowry has increased. I was not in favor of it and my family did not demand any, but my wife is an only daughter and her parents insisted upon giving her some.

Another Old Town Brahmin son criticized dowry:

In our family we don't like dowry. We have seen the burning of brides on TV. We like to get something, but we don't demand anything. We don't like to force dowry – just whatever the bride's family can give. We want educated and good girls.

He explained that his wife had brought with her Rs. 8,000 in cash, some gold jewelry, and some household utensils. In comparison, for the dowry of one of his sisters, the family had paid Rs. 15,000 and had not recovered any of it when the marriage did not work out. And his mother described her own dowry as gold that was much less expensive then, fifteen gold rings, a bicycle, and a watch.

Dowry is emerging as an issue among low-status families as well. When I asked Sopna Behera and her mother about dowry, they replied:

SOPNA: No. There was nothing for my mother.
MOTHER: [interrupts]: I was married for Rs. 3.
SOPNA: Nowadays one would need Rs. 50,000.

I ask about dowry when she was married.

SOPNA: There was some jewelry. Not a lot. And no cash.

An Old Town Bauri informant said that there was no dowry when she was married but that now a dowry is required for daughters.

Yes. Demands are there. Cycles, watches, and so forth. If these are not there, Rs. 5,000 at a minimum are needed. If that's not there, then too bad. You can't get your daughter married.

In the upwardly mobile Old Town Washerman family, dowry has also entered marriage transactions. Although Mr. Dhobi maintained that there was no "dowry" per se when his only daughter was married, he did give her in-laws a motorcycle, household furniture, and Rs. 10,000. In addition, he added:

The wedding cost Rs. 50,000 [in 1976]. Now it would cost Rs. 80,000–90,000. Three to four hundred relatives come and must be fed, given new clothes, etc.

222

I ask if he had received any dowry when his son was recently married.

I made no demands. I forbid demands. My daughter-in-law's family gave freely. [I learned, however, that they had given Mr. Dhobi's family Rs. 10,000 and some household materials, but no motorcycle.]

Among most sample families it has become politically incorrect to speak openly or positively about dowry, but there is agreement that dowry demands are real and can be onerous – especially for New Capital middle- and upper-status families with highly educated daughters whom they wish to marry to even more highly educated professionals. This becomes a particularly serious burden for a family such as the Tripathys, with seven educated daughters and not a lot of wealth. It becomes a moral problem for other families such as the Pandas and the Misras, who would like to stand by principle and not participate in a system they find repugnant. Mrs. Panda spoke of the hypocrisy of those who criticize dowry but nonetheless endow their daughters:

One of my relatives said that they had given no dowry, but it turned out that they had provided each daughter with land and a bank account. We refused to accept any dowry or gifts from our daughter-in-law's family [when their first son was married], and we were criticized by many – even our own relatives. Now I find myself in the difficult position of possibly having to provide a dowry if I am to get my daughter married. I cannot count on finding suitable candidates who stand by the same principles.

Like her mother, Laxmi Panda was critical of dowry:

Dowry is just a tradition. How it evolved is a different story. Personally, I don't like the concept at all. It is not proper. The logic is not there. It's done only because of custom. Girls' parents give into it, especially those with several daughters who are not well educated. Those families must get the older ones married in order to marry the younger ones. They cannot take risks by revolting against dowry. If their daughters do not get married, they cannot support themselves. If a daughter has no sisters and is doing a good job, then the family can go on waiting until they can get a proper choice. They are lucky. They can stand by principle and not give in to dowry demands.

Here Laxmi describes a scenario similar to her own – an only daughter with a high level of education and a professional job. Her mother, who is actively engaged in trying to find a suitable husband for her, seems less optimistic.

In the Mohanty family, a somewhat different mother-daughter dialogue ensued when the topic of dowry arose.

MOTHER (Kalpana): There is no dowry anymore. What women bring is their employability.
DAUGHTER: What about all the dowry burnings!
MOTHER: It is only a weak husband who lets it happen. In my family there have never been any dowries given. My father gave some small gifts, but nothing like a motorcycle or a house. He opposed dowry on principle.

One of the new issues raised by Laxmi Panda and Kalpana Mohanty is the employability of brides. As living costs for middle-class, urban families have dramatically risen in India in recent years, acquiring a daughter-in-law/wife who can earn money has become increasingly attractive. However, as already noted, it is not clear that a woman's earning potential has replaced expectations for dowries among such families.[2]

The issue of dowry is complex. Some anthropologists have argued that in a predominantly patrilineal society like India, where sons inherit family property, a dowry constitutes a daughter's inheritance – her share of the family wealth.[3] The problem with this argument is that women rarely get to control the dowry their family provides at the time of their marriage. Because most of the dowry goes to the groom and his parents, it is not comparable to a son's inheritance. Furthermore, as long as sons are viewed as the rightful heirs to family property, dowry becomes a family burden that can negatively affect the status of daughters. However, dowry is also a way in which families can express their wealth and status. If a daughter is a sacred gift, then her dowry constitutes the material transaction that helps to bind different families together. One wonders whether in the case of Kalika Tripathy the absence of a dowry exacerbated the situation with her parents-in-law. Not only did their son marry a girl of his own choosing, but he refused a dowry and therefore brought into the family a wife with no endowment to help secure her position there.

Husband-Wife Relationships

A topic that I was particularly interested in exploring with mothers, daughters, and grandmothers was expectations for husband-wife relationships. Had these changed with the increased education of daughters, their later age of marriage, and the emergence of love marriages as a part of popular culture in India if not as a reality for these young women? Predictably, I received a diverse, yet patterned, set of responses.

In the Old Town household of the upper-status Mahapatra family, the interview took place on the second floor of Mrs. Mahapatra's (Mother) house, which she now shares with her married son, his wife, and two young daughters, as well as with her daughter Sita and Sita's two children. We all sat together in Mrs. Mahapatra's small, crowded room, some of us on her bed and some on the floor.

MOTHER: At that time the husband's ability was like a god. Wives would pray to God but take care of their husband first. That's no longer so.
SON: A wife would never reply, never speak back to her husband. Nowadays they do. They have their education.

I ask Mrs. Mahapatra what it had been like to move to her husband's household.

MOTHER: I came from a large family to one where there was only my husband and in-laws. I was so young. I had to fear my in-laws. I came from a large family but came to a household with only in-laws there. I was very lonely. . . . At that time a husband was god. Nowadays things have changed, but I had to worship my husband.

In another Old Town Brahmin household I chatted with the oldest son, Harish (thirty-two years), and his wife (twenty-three years), who reside with his parents, younger brothers, and their two young children. They remain in the same house where I knew them as young children. Harish spoke of generational changes in husband-wife relationships:

Yes. The difference in husband-wife relationships is like heaven and hell. My father never listened to my mother. He treated her like a fool. They had many arguments. By contrast, I listen to my wife when she points out my mistakes. Why did my father never do this? Women were treated badly in society until now, although things are only marginally better. They were not treated even as well as outcastes. I used to feel sorry for my mother but I couldn't do anything. There was no understanding between my parents. There should be give and take, especially after a new marriage. I do not want any friction in front of our children. It is bad for them.

I ask Harish if he can imagine his daughter, now five years old, working outside the home and not observing purdah as his mother and wife do.

Yes. Women should not be married young. That was difficult for my wife [who was seventeen at marriage]. She came from a small family into a large one and was expected to do everything. Daughters from uneducated families [who marry] into ones in 'high society' do not know what to do. It is very difficult for them. Daughters-in-law should be talked to and treated with sensitivity. One should try to understand others' needs. . . . I was very young when I got married. Initially, I didn't understand what adjustments my wife was having to make.

Harish's remarks are particularly interesting because he comes from an Old Town family that did not invest in their children's education. His older sister, unlike most girls of her generation, was married at twelve. Harish completed eleven years of school but did not matriculate (pass the exams), and he holds a low-level job in the New Capital. His wife completed only eight years of school and is nine years younger than her husband. The discrepancy in their ages, and by implication in authority, reflects one traditional tenet of the patrifocal family. Despite Harish's lack of higher education and his upbringing in a conservative, Old Town, Brahmin family (his father is a temple priest), he seems to have developed a great empathy for women and a sensitivity to women's rights. He and his wife sat side-by-side during the interview, exhibiting a kind of husband-wife intimacy rarely observed in the Old Town. Although Harish has developed some new attitudes about women and about husband-wife relationships, his parents still wield authority and do not allow him to take his wife out of the house.

For several Old Town mothers it was difficult even to respond to a question about husband-wife relationships when, in their generation, there had been no expectation of anything approaching a conjugal relationship. They had been married young to a stranger many years their senior and into joint households where the emphasis was upon mother-in-law–daughter-in-law relationships, the production of sons, and contributions to household work. For example, when I asked Mrs. Gauda what kind of understanding there had been with her husband, she could not respond. Finally, she said:

My husband is much older than I am, by ten to twelve years. [Then she redirected the question to me, saying,] Why are you asking me about this? You used to be here watching me and the children. You know these things!

Similarly, when I asked Mrs. Badhei (Old Town Carpenter family) what makes for a good husband-wife relationship, she at first could not respond either. She looked uncomfortable with the topic and finally said:

Both members should be the same mentally [i.e., compatible].

227

I ask whether the husband should be the one in authority, the one who makes decisions. Mrs. Badhei responds firmly,

I make the household decisions.

Neither of these middle-caste women responded about having to worship their husbands as did the elderly Mrs. Mahapatra. However, none of these women could or would speak emotively about a relationship that was based upon patrifocal principles, *not* ones of intimacy and companionship. New Capital grandmothers made the same kinds of comments. When at a very young age one marries a much older man and moves into his household, there is little or no "conjugal relationship" in the Western sense of the term.

I interviewed Mrs. Das and her daughter Lili (New Capital, upper-status family) one day. On a subsequent day Mr. and Mrs. Das accompanied me to Mrs. Das's parents' home, which they share with their widowed son and his children, to interview her mother (Grandmother). The interview took place in a sitting room with Mr. Das (Father) and Mrs. Das's father (Grandfather) also participating. I began by asking Grandmother about her marriage.

GRANDMOTHER: I was married at age seven.

I ask what she remembers of it.

GRANDMOTHER: Just a little.
MOTHER: Marriages then took seven days.

I ask Grandmother if she was frightened.

GRANDMOTHER: No.
GRANDFATHER: My marriage took place a long time, continuously for ten days. I was seventeen. My wife came to the house at fourteen to fifteen years, when I was twenty-three. [This was when the marriage was consummated.]

228

MOTHER: My mother's marriage was fixed when she was twenty-one days old to another family in the same village. The families were known to each other.[4]

FATHER: There was no dowry at that time. But they used to give lots of gold to daughters. That could not be taken away from her, unlike money today.

I ask Grandfather what it was like to have such a young wife.

MOTHER: That was the custom, that's all.

GRANDFATHER: Marriage was being fixed by the parents. The boy or the girl had no voice.

MOTHER: They looked into the family background, etc.

I ask Grandmother if there had been adjustment problems for her in moving to her in-laws at such a young age.

GRANDMOTHER: No difficulty. My in-laws were very nice.

FATHER: It must be the girl's submissiveness. That's one of the important reasons.

GRANDFATHER: I visited my wife's house, and she visited mine for years before we actually lived together. Although we did not talk to each other, we got used to one another's families and homes.

FATHER: The husband is the leader, the deciding factor.

GRANDMOTHER: My husband took all the decisions. [She and Grandfather nod in agreement.]

MOTHER: Today things are changing. Women are looking after their children's education. They are taking a lot of responsibility.

FATHER: I feel a different way. The circumstances have changed. The demands of the profession, of the office of the man have increased. In bigger places they are busy from 9:00 a.m. to 9:00 p.m. The result is that the girls are forced to take more responsibility.

Using his daughter Lili, as an example, Mr. Das continues with occasional interjections from Mrs. Das. Much of their conversation is overlapping:

229

FATHER: Lili must take her son back and forth to school, talk to the principal, and all of these kinds of things, certain banking operations.

MOTHER: Making all the household work.

FATHER: In other matters, suppose, in my daughter's case, I can say, my son-in-law wanted to purchase a black and white TV, but she said, "No. We should get a colored TV." They got a colored one. She's having a voice. Her husband wanted to get a refrigerator, but she said, "Let us not go in for the frig now." . . . Slowly the domains are passing into the hands of the girl.

I ask what happens when both husband and wife are employed outside the home – is there greater shared decision making?

FATHER: That's beginning to happen in the case of families where the girls are working.

MOTHER: Yes. Economic independence.

FATHER: In some important cities – with one hundred thousand population or more – some girls have now started working.

MOTHER: They work.

FATHER: So there the sharing of the domestic responsibilities is slowly being felt. . . . But the steps are imperceptible. They are slow. . . . And wife beating is declining. Slowly, it is coming down.

MOTHER: In lower-class families.

FATHER: It is there. In bigger towns it is not there. . . . It was common in the old times, even in the 1930s. . . . In spite of being a backward country, women have made great strides. They are in high positions – female ambassadors, head of the UN, prime minister. India is a land of incongruity.

I quote from this interview at some length because of the numerous themes that emerged in response to my question about marriage and my effort to get people to reflect upon husband-wife relationships. The latter question has been addressed in a variety of ways, none of them indicative of an emotionally laden, intimate relationship in the Western sense. However, these two couples were comfortable with one another and comfortable speaking with me. Not surprisingly, given her age, lack of education, and the presence of her husband, Grandmother was the least articulate member of the group. However, she felt comfortable coming and going from the room, participating in the conversation as she liked. She was also overseeing cooking that was going on in another room at the same time. Mr. and Mrs. Das represent a different generation in that they are both more educated, were older at the time of marriage, and have established a relationship of sharing. In the early years of their marriage, when I first knew them, they shared a bedroom and dined together at the same table. While they maintained a traditional division of labor, there were few overt expressions of male dominance and authority.

Nonetheless, when I asked Mrs. Das and Lili what makes for a good husband-wife relationship, their response emphasized traditional gender roles:

MOTHER: Lili's husband and mine make the big decisions. Lili runs the household. She does the shopping, the food preparation, looks after the children's schooling, and so on. In former times the men did all the shopping. Our husbands are too busy with work for either shopping or overseeing the children's education.

LILI: It would be different if I were employed. Then they [employed women] are economically more independent. They have more of a say in decision making. Women like myself and my mother are very dependent. We cannot assume an equal role on that account. We must tend to the home and the children. The husband has the final word.

MOTHER: Women must be accommodating and self-sacrificing. What's most important is to keep peace in the household. One should look to the family's welfare first. If women are self-oriented, then it will lead to quarrels in the family. Their role is to keep the family running smoothly.

At this point, Mrs. Das eloquently expresses a basic tenet of the patrifocal family – the need for women to put their interests behind those of their husband's family. This can be more difficult for young women in an era when many of them are being reared to excel in their studies and to assume jobs in the world outside the home. It can also be more difficult because they are older and more mature when they marry. All of these factors are relevant to the highly accomplished New Capital upper-status Misra daughters.

Mrs. Misra, when responding to my question about husband-wife relationships, said:

I just obeyed my husband's ideas. I was not a working woman. I didn't know anything. I had no say. I want my daughters to be able to make their husbands understand that both opinions count. I am afraid of arranged marriages. We must look for men, see them and get to know them well, and try to determine if they will make our daughters happy.

Kalpana Mohanty and her daughter expressed themselves somewhat differently:

MOTHER (Kalpana): Give-and-take is what makes a good relationship.
DAUGHTER: Mutual understanding. Both husband and wife must want to work together.

I ask what happens if there is a difference of opinion between husband and wife.

MOTHER: The wife should give way.
DAUGHTER: No. There is no reason why the wife should give in any more than the husband.
MOTHER: The husband's voice should come first.
DAUGHTER: I disagree.

Kalpana represents the transitional generation of the children whom I began studying in 1965–67. Whereas Kalpana uses the mechanistic term "give-and-take," her daughter uses the more expressive term "mutual understanding" to characterize an ideal husband-wife relationship. However, when confronted with the issue of potential disagreement between husband and wife, they take separate paths. Kalpana follows the traditional path of female self-sacrifice and male dominance. But her daughter is not willing to accept that position for women. She represents yet another generation of women in Bhubaneswar, some of whom are more egalitarian than their mothers were in their attitudes toward and expectations about gender roles.

First Daughter-in-law in the New Capital middle-status Mahapatra household also represents a transitional point of view. To my question about what makes for a good husband-wife relationship, she responded:

I think it's adjustment – adjustment with one another – with your husband. Both should adjust – the wife 80 percent and the husband 20 percent. There is more making of decisions together. Still the major decisions lie with husbands.

I ask what happens if husband and wife should disagree.

If he has a mind to buy something, he'll buy it. I should not say anything.

I ask if men have more authority because they are the earners.

I don't think so. It's a totally man-dominated society. But it's changing. When the age difference was great between husband and wife, men totally dominated women. Today, with the age difference less, there is less of that. My father is twelve years older than my mother. There's only four year's difference in my own case.

Laxmi Panda (New Capital, middle-status family) raised another set of issues with respect to husband-wife relationships. It was in response to my question about the possibility for young women like herself to combine marriage, children, and a career. Concerning child care she said:

It is nice to have a husband who can understand and can share work with [you] properly. The commitment to children for the woman is because the woman gives birth to them. Men cannot give birth. Women can't help it. It is a natural thing. They cannot neglect their children and go for their studies [the way men can]. If you've got a good person who is understanding and who can devote his time for these things, who can share very properly, then you're very lucky. You can do very good research and things like that. If you're not lucky, then you can't help it. Then you have to stay home and take care of children. . . . Men are supposed to assume responsibility for their own children also. But many men don't bother that much, but women always take over. . . . In every country that happens, backwards or not.

Then Laxmi raised a very different issue, that of potential husband-wife competition when the wife also has a career.

Men know the fact that women can do as well as they can [at jobs outside the home]. If women do a good job, the man feels threatened. Many times they [husbands] get so much of a complex for that reason – because the woman has become too equal at that job. There is no reason to think like that. No reason for such separations [between men and women]. They [some men] don't get enlightened. I have two friends who do everything at home, still their husbands have complexes and feel threatened. . . . The main reason is a question of psychology. There are a few men who are very broad-minded, but many can't think properly. They don't need to compare themselves with their wives. There's no need for such competition.

Laxmi could articulate an ideal husband-wife relationship for someone like herself, with an education and a career, but she was not very optimistic about achieving it.

One of the most articulate exponents of gender equity and a companionate husband-wife relationship was Laxmi's aunt, Gitali

Panda. At age twenty-six, Gitali had entered a traditional arranged marriage in which she and her husband had not met before the wedding. Like her niece, Gitali had a master's degree and was employed before marriage. For the early years of her marriage, she resided in another town with her husband and parents-in-law. By the time of this interview she had left her husband and in-laws and was residing in Bhubaneswar with one daughter while her second daughter remained with her husband and parents-in-law. Gitali's parents had retired to their natal village but stayed in Bhubaneswar with her much of the time. In response to my question about husband-wife relationships, she said:

It should be one of commonality, of cooperation. Women and men should have the same rights. The only difference between them is physical, although women are more sensitive. They consider everything for their children.

There were two major problems with my marriage. My husband and I never had any time together. I had to rise early and leave by 8:00 a.m. for my job in Bhubaneswar. My husband never rose before I left the house and was usually out in the evening when I returned home. So we never saw one another. My husband is to blame for this. He wanted me to work, but he also wanted me home catering to him. When I came home, however, I was obliged to spend time with my parents-in-law. Besides, my husband was always out.

The second problem was that he [her husband] wanted to be very dominant – to order me around, not discuss things together, not have a cooperative relationship. I could not accept this kind of relationship. My father-in-law had liked my personality and had selected me because I had a strong personality, and he hoped that I would set right his unruly son. But my husband was dominated by his mother for his first twenty-nine years and feared being dominated by a wife, so he tried to be very dominating [with me] from the beginning. He expected me to carry out his orders. His friends teased him, saying "that wife's nose is very sharp. She may dominate you, so be careful." He would become very angry with me. . . . My father-in-law is very considerate, but he has no voice in the family. My mother-in-law is very dominant. My husband is very attached to her. He's like a child.

When I began living separately, he had to have his mother's permission to visit me. . . .

Women feel that they should sacrifice, that they would lose respect in society if they leave their husband. I don't feel so. I don't care [what society thinks]. Sincerity is what's most important. I am sorry that I was not born to participate in the fight for Independence. I would have been a follower of Gandhi. One of my close friends – I admire her intellect, but she is afraid of her husband. "Whatever he orders, I should carry it out," she says. She is afraid of his anger. . . .

In my day I was too fast. I was out of step with society.

Gitali is unusual in that she chose to leave her husband rather than endure an unhappy marriage. Clearly, she valued a companionate, conjugal relationship more than she did the coherence of her husband's joint family. She did not want to be dominated by either her husband or her mother-in-law. After eight years she left and set up a separate household in Bhubaneswar. She is not legally divorced because she is worried about the impact that might have on her older daughter who stays with her father and grandparents. She receives no financial support from her husband and in-laws. Her marriage did not involve a dowry, but what household belongings she took with her at the time of marriage she left behind. "I don't want to live a luxurious life," she says. "Struggle – I think that is the theme of my life." Nonetheless, she worries about the daughter who is with her because she is a "fatherless child." Gitali says that this daughter has become very dependent upon her, which is "not good for her future."

Gitali views herself as a kind of rebel, as someone who will stand up for what is right regardless of societal pressures. She reminisces about her childhood when she was very interested in dance. Her father opposed dance for a girl but her mother, who loves music, was supportive and allowed Gitali to study dance secretly. After some years, her father saw her perform in a dance recital and changed his mind. "He could take pride in me," she says. Clearly, Gitali's mother was also capable of acting independently of her husband and must have served as a role model for her daughter.

When I interviewed Gitali's mother (Grandmother), she reflected on her early life:

I attended school only a few days. I was self-taught at home. I was married at twelve, and moved in with my husband and mother-in-law at sixteen. It was an arranged marriage with another family in the same village. That was the system then. My father-in-law was dead, and my husband was an only child. Life with my mother-in-law was not difficult. She was very kind and considerate. She had no daughter, and she treated me as her own daughter. She did not expect a lot of respectful behavior. She was very affectionate. But she advised me to observe customs before other village women. Otherwise, she told me to wear flowers in my hair and to keep my head uncovered so that she could see and enjoy how I looked. I would sing her songs, and she listened. . . . She died after the birth of my second child.

I ask how much older than herself her husband is.

Ten years.

"How does that affect the husband-wife relationship?" I ask.

I had to adjust to the customs of the time. My husband was quite considerate. The wife's role was to do housework and care for the children – look after their health and studies. There was a division of labor between men and women. At that time [women's] brains were not so developed, so they could not realize that they were suppressed. We were simple. We had to adjust to conditions, showing much devotion and respect to our husbands.

A predominant theme in the Panda household, distinguishing it from many others in Bhubaneswar, is that of independence. Gitali's older sister always emphasized the importance of her children's learning to act independently and worried when her daughter, Laxmi, seemed to be insufficiently self-assured.

I have done what I can for them. Maybe, it was not always what was right but what I thought best at the time. Each of them is different; each has their own fate, their own destiny. They must take their own path in life. As their mother, I can only express my opinions and let them make their own decisions. I should not impose my will on them. That would only lead to rebellion. I have raised my children to be independent. Thus far, none of them has been disobedient. . . .

All of my sons have gone out [studied and/or worked away from home]. My daughter has been the most difficult one. In Bhubaneswar she did not even like to walk to the square without a friend. She was very dependent upon her parents. She always walked between us. Thus, I urged her to accept the job in another city. I went with her and helped her get settled [two years ago]. She cried a lot when I left; she didn't want to be left behind on her own. I told her that she must learn her own mind and to make decisions. How was she otherwise going to cope with marriage and in-laws? So often the husband is weak and sides with his mother. My daughter must learn to be strong, but she tends to have a quiet nature and not to express her own feelings. I am very worried about her, especially with respect to marriage.

As a wife, Mrs. Panda often acted independently of her husband – for example, taking the initiative in such important matters as arranging her children's marriages. She complained that her husband was often indecisive and left things up to her. And Gitali acted unusually independently in leaving her husband. Although her parents were upset by this, they did not abandon her. While they and other members of her extended family remain very concerned about her welfare, they have supported rather than rejected her.

Whether Gitali's behavior represents the future or is simply an aberration in the context of the patrifocal family remains to be seen. However, these interview materials do document a change in expectations for husband-wife relationships in middle- and upper-status families over the last three generations. Increasingly, young people desire more say in the choice of a spouse and a more openly expressive and companionate marriage. How effectively the patrifocal family adapts to these changed aspirations may be critical to its future.

Lower-status husbands and wives have already experienced less formal and more egalitarian relationships. For example, Mrs. Patro (Old Town Bauri family), when asked about husband-wife relationships, said:

There is always give-and-take of suggestions and advice. My husband is a mistri [trained builder]; I am an agricultural worker. He does not work in the house, but he does help with child care.

I ask if she feels that she is an equal contributor to the household economy.

Yes. I make enough to tide us over, but my work is seasonal. Otherwise we would starve. Even my husband's work is periodic. Sometimes it is difficult when there is no income from either side.

I have already described how in the Old Town Washerman family, when I asked about husband-wife relationships, their new daughter-in-law complained that her husband liked to order her about and expected her to obey and was not very helpful in the house. However, the fact that she said these things openly in front of her husband and father-in-law implies that she had a far more informal and expressive relationship with her husband than is possible in most middle- and upper-status Old Town households. Similarly, Sopna Behera complained openly about her husband's irresponsibility and drinking habit but said that her married life was not unhappy.

My husband takes no responsibility. He turns over his earnings to me. It is up to me to decide how to spend it.

When I asked Sopna if a woman should have the right to leave her husband if she is unhappy, she replied:

No! They'll be quarreling one hour and make up the next. That's how things are.

Attitudes Toward Separation and Divorce

Husband-wife separations are not new in India. It is rare for a married woman to leave her husband and in-laws, but married men have historically had more prerogatives, although these have varied by caste status, region, and era. Hindu sacred law, as observed by high castes, makes marriage indissoluble. Rama and his faithful wife Sita, from the epic *Ramayana*, continue to symbolize the Hindu ideal of marriage. Nonetheless, there is evidence from ancient times both that divorce was possible and that a man could have more than one wife, especially in the case of a first wife's death or barrenness.[5] In contemporary times, however, legal divorce is new to families in Bhubaneswar. I tried to explore these issues with mothers, daughters, and grandmothers to assess changing attitudes – particularly, given that by 1989 three married daughters in my original sample of families had experienced separation and/or divorce.

Regardless of their generation or education, Old Town middle- and upper-status women had very negative views of separation and divorce. They maintained that a woman should never leave her husband even if she is very unhappy. As one young woman put it, "A woman has no right to leave an unhappy marriage. She can go to the police station [to get help], but she cannot leave."

In the upper-status Mahapatra household, one daughter, Sita, has been forced to return to her natal home because her husband threw her out and took in another woman – "a kept woman." Her family is distraught and very much ashamed of this. Her mother, in the context of discussing husband-wife relationships, said, "My daughter is living in an unnatural way." Sita would like to fight – to go to court to demand a share of her husband's salary and property – but her family is adamantly opposed to any such action because "neighbors would talk." It is, they think, improper for a Brahmin family to engage in such litigation.

BROTHER: Our family is opposed to going to court. My sister's husband's salary would be divided and his property shared if we went
to court. My sister has nothing from her husband – none of the Rs.
15,000 in dowry, the 150 grams of gold, the Rs. 20–30,000 of
furniture, clothing, etc.
SITA: I want to have [my husband's] salary divided. But my brother
does not support this. He is concerned about the talk of others in
this village [Old Town neighborhood].

This young woman must try to support her children with no help
from her husband and with no access to her dowry. Fortunately,
she is employed and she and her children have been taken back
into her natal family.

In contrast, in the New Capital there was some acceptance of
separation and divorce among the younger generation. When I
asked Kalpana Mohanty and her daughter if a woman should be
able to leave her husband if she were very unhappy, they replied:

DAUGHTER: According to the Constitution, she can.
MOTHER (Kalpana): She should not, in my opinion.
DAUGHTER: Even if the husband tortures her?
MOTHER: First, they should try to understand each other. Are there
circumstances when a woman must leave? Women should com-
promise.
DAUGHTER: I disagree.

This was a particularly sensitive conversation because one of
Kalpana's sisters is divorced and has lived with her for the past
twelve years. The sister had an arranged marriage in which she
was very unhappy. According to Kalpana, the problems were with
her sister's husband, not her parents-in-law. Clearly, the sister has
not been thrown out by her own family. Nonetheless, family members were reluctant to talk about the circumstances that led to the
separation and divorce.

Mrs. Das and her daughter, Lili, who in general took relatively
conservative positions on gender roles, highly disapproved of separation or divorce for a woman. "Where would a woman go?" they

asked. She would have to be economically independent to contemplate such an action. Again, they stressed the importance of a woman's trying to adjust to the circumstances of marriage, even if it takes years. Mrs. Das described one of her sisters who had had a difficult time in marriage. "She was unhappy for seven or eight years, but now she is adjusting."

The Misra family also had a negative view of separation and divorce even though Mrs. Misra's sister, who was unhappy in marriage, had committed suicide.

MOTHER: Divorce is not acceptable for the parents. They feel very sorry. [She continued, speaking of her sister:] She never told us why she was unhappy. After that [the suicide] my mother never had any peace of mind. She grew weak and died. [She paused a moment and then continued more philosophically:] I think something like that [divorce] is coming to pass here, too. When people approach matters in a spirit of "I-ness," [some] people say it's just modernity, but they don't really understand modernity. They do not have a clear understanding of modernity. They're portraying themselves in an angry, impatient manner. A girl must learn tolerance.

DAUGHTER: We are made to believe from the beginning that whatever we do, our actions will have an impact on the family. That is how women are reared – to work things out quietly and to think of the family first.

Despite the widespread distaste for separation and divorce in a society where most marriages are still arranged and where the well-being of the family is emphasized over that of the individual, such events are beginning to occur, and attitudes are gradually changing. The three New Capital Mahapatra daughters-in-law, like Kalpana Mohanty's daughter, all agreed that women should have the right to leave an unhappy marriage.

FIRST DAUGHTER-IN-LAW: Nowadays, a woman is going to leave if she does not have an adaptive husband. Society has not accepted

242

this up to now, but it will have to. Some women are even going to court and getting their share of their husband's income.

Mrs. Patro, speaking as a lower-status woman, indicated a far more casual and egalitarian attitude toward divorce than most middle- and upper-status women. In response to my question about whether a woman should be able to leave an abusive husband, she said:

Of course, but does it ever happen? If a husband is wicked, then a woman can leave and go away, taking some clothes with her. For six months the husband must provide her with food and clothes. After that she is on her own. But who will take care of the children? So she will have to willingly stay and take the abuse and beatings.

In other words, yes, a woman *may* leave, but it is not practical to do so.

Women's Roles

In addition to exploring changing attitudes toward husband-wife relationships and, by implication, the role of wife, I asked mothers, daughters, and grandmothers to reflect upon their other roles as women – those of daughter, daughter-in-law, mother, and mother-in-law. Many of their responses have already been described in previous chapters. Here just a few additional insights will be reported.

When I asked about the two major transitions that Indian women experience – from the status of daughter to daughter-in-law and from wife to mother – all Old Town and New Capital middle- and upper-status women responded uniformly. "Responsibility" was the word used over and over again. As Mrs. Das (New Capital, upper-status) and her daughter, Lili, expressed it:

MOTHER: Responsibility! There is no responsibility as a girl in one's father's home. After marriage there is much responsibility.
DAUGHTER: Yes. Responsibility.

I ask about becoming a mother.

MOTHER: Further responsibility and work!
DAUGHTER: Yes!

Similarly, in the New Capital upper-status Mohanty household, Kalpana answered:

Responsibility. As a daughter there is very little. The focus is on one's studies. Then suddenly you are thrust into a position of responsibility at marriage and expected to cook, take care of children, etc. My mother-in-law was very patient with me. However, the shift today is at an older age and less dramatic than it was with my mother. And if you have been employed, you already have assumed some responsibility.

I ask about motherhood.

If one's children are quite qualified in all respects, motherhood is very satisfying. If they do well in school, read well, get a good name in sports, etc. Then I am satisfied, not happy. I am waiting until I see them grown up, with their own careers, etc. Then I can be fully satisfied. And I will be happy if they are satisfied with their husbands.

Kalpana's responses reflect her highly educated, upper-status, New Capital background. For herself and her daughters, their studies, rather than domestic duties, have come first. As an employed wife and mother, however, she is also cognizant of the responsibilities acquired in the work place.

In the Old Town upper-status Mahapatra household, the conversation went somewhat differently. Mrs. Mahapatra, after speaking about the loneliness she experienced going from being a daughter

244

in her natal family to a daughter in her in-laws' household, focused on motherhood.

MOTHER: Once I had children, life was full.
SON: My youngest sister told me that when she got married [and moved to her in-laws' house], she would have to wake up, crying, early in the morning and take a cup of water to her father-in-law. He would put his toe in the water. Then she had to take it to her mother-in-law who put her toe into the water. Then she had to drink the water and start the household work.

In upper-status families a way of formally honoring one's parents-in-law is by drinking water that they have defiled with their feet. In addition to being a sign of respect, ingesting such substances from older women is a way for young women to become empowered.

I ask if such things happen in the Mahapatra household.

MOTHER: No.
SON: No. She [Sita] is a B.A. She's [wife] an M.A. We're not so strict a family.

It is significant that the son, in this instance, refers to the college and postgraduate degrees that his sister and wife hold as if to say, With their education, who would expect such deprecating behavior of a daughter-in-law? Nonetheless, I have observed highly educated New Capital daughters-in-law bow down before their parents-in-law and kiss their feet – also a traditional sign of respect.

In the Old Town middle-status Gauda household, Mrs. Gauda also responded to my question about women's role transitions by emphasizing responsibility.

As a mother, I had to care for my [eight] sons and daughters, marrying them, building a [new] house. I was very busy. I was very content with family life. Responsibility is still there even more than ever. Despite my sons being married, they still rely on their parents. Bringing up eight children was very tough. It is better now than earlier. My oldest son had to drop out of a special military school because of financial problems. He could have become a big officer. I am very sorry about that. Even then, though, we were quite well off. If we hadn't been well off, how could we have married off our daughters? But responsibility doesn't end there. There's the responsibility for grandchildren.

Mrs. Gauda's sense of responsibility continues through the generations of family that she has helped to produce.

Mrs. Behera, a New Capital lower-status grandmother, responded similarly to my question about the transition from daughter to daughter-in-law and mother. "Can't you see the differences from the freedom of being a girl?" she said. Then she began reciting all the work she must do. In contrast, Mrs. Patro (low-status Bauri) of the Old Town, responded:

It's always the same. Before you get married you had to work. Now I have to cook for my in-laws. When you become a mother, there have to be a lot of changes. I had to know all about housekeeping from my own family. We are not expected to learn at our in-laws like upper-caste girls!

The difference in perspective between these two lower-status women may be attributable to the Beheras' residence in the New Capital, where Mr. Behera received a fixed government salary. Although it was small, this salary meant that Mrs. Behera did not have to work outside the home and that their daughter, Sopna, could attend school. Although Sopna did perform some work outside of school – child care for neighbors and gardening for me – she did not have the heavy load of household responsibilities that Bauri girls have and that prevent them from attending school. Mrs. Patro's somewhat snide remark about when lower-status girls, as distinct from upper-status ones, learn household responsibilities is important to note.

Preferences for Sons versus Daughters and Differential Child-Rearing Practices

In earlier chapters I have described differences in the rearing of sons and daughters. Patrifocal family structure and ideology create significant differences in families' expectations for sons and daughters. It is assumed that daughters will marry out and will become responsible for their husbands and parents-in-law, whereas sons will remain home or will at least assume financial responsibility for their parents and extended patrilineal kin. I wondered how mothers, daughters, and grandmothers would express themselves about these differences, and so I asked them whether they had any preference for sons over daughters and whether or not they believed daughters should be reared differently than sons.

Most women denied that they had any gender preference for children. Mrs. Das, from the New Capital, responded:

No. If anything, there is a preference for daughters in my family. [The Dases come from southern Orissa where women have higher status.][6] They care less about sons. My sister had three daughters and then a son. She doesn't care about the son. There was no familial pressure to have sons. I go on caring about Lili (daughter) and wanting to give her gifts. I give much more to her than to my son.

When I asked this question of Mrs. Das's parents, however, I received a contrary view:

GRANDFATHER: My first child was a boy, so I was not concerned.
MR. DAS: At that time there was a preponderance of wishes for sons.
GRANDFATHER: Without a son there is no salvation.

When I asked Grandmother whether daughters should be reared differently from sons, she responded:

No. My children were nice. There was no problem in bringing them up. They heard everything, and I treated them the same. The same affection was bestowed on all of them. There was no discrimination.

247

Mrs. Das, however, asserted that there were important differences between sons and daughters.

Daughters are more obedient and compliant. They stay at home and do what their parents say. They are much easier to raise. Boys are out of the house more. They're off with friends, engaged in outside activities. They are harder to control. At times I worried about my son, but he turned out well. He is obedient.

Kalpana Mohanty of the New Capital responded to my question about preference for sons over daughters, saying:

Absolutely not! Why should there be? My in-laws did wish for a grandson, but my husband and I did not submit to this pressure. [They stopped having children after the births of three daughters.]

I ask if there were any handicaps to having only daughters.

MOTHER (Kalpana): "No. Perhaps, in rural areas there are."
DAUGHTER: "There are still high female infant mortality rates."

This refers to the evidence that mortality rates are significantly higher for girls than for boys – particularly in North India – indicating that infant daughters are given less good care than sons because they are less valued.[7]

When later I asked about who cares for parents in their old age, Kalpana responded:

It is the daughter-in-law's responsibility. My daughters will look after me. I think so.

First Daughter-in-law of the New Capital Mahapatra household was somewhat more equivocal in her response.

No. I had no preference for my first child [a daughter]. The first child is always welcome. My husband felt the same. But society still goes for sons. Once sons got better treatment, but no longer.

I ask whether she will rear her daughter differently than a son.

No, I don't think so. My husband thinks she should take up a career, that she should learn mathematics. Others of us are more inclined to art.

In the New Capital Misra household, some preference for sons has continued over the last two generations. Grandmother, in an earlier quote, referred to the difficult time she experienced at her in-laws when she first produced daughters rather than sons. Subsequently, her daughter-in-law, Mrs. Misra, produced three daughters before bearing a son.

MOTHER: There is still a strong preference for sons. Even my in-laws have it. I experienced the same thing [as had Grandmother] when I had three daughters before a son. My parents-in-law were very unhappy with both the first daughter's birth and the second and third. The last one was named "Bitter" by my father-in-law!

NAKIMA: He liked me a lot once I began to grow up. Then he began to tell me I should be like Indira Gandhi. He began to take pride in me.

MOTHER: My mother-in-law had a strong conviction that the fourth child would be a boy, and it was.

I ask whether daughters should be reared differently than sons.

MRS. MISRA: We Oriya women, actually, we have given a lot of education for that [training for becoming a wife and daughter-in-law] to all our daughters. It is also from childhood onwards they're preparing – "Do this, do that." They're preparing – for example, how to prepare food cleanly, how to preserve it cleanly, don't

249

waste food, all these things. You have to give them some advice about *pujas*. . . . Now it is changed. Sons also must be responsible in the house and must learn things about housekeeping.

MENAKA: Our grandmother was brought up to believe that sons are providers only. Father is very handicapped. He can't even make a cup of tea. Now things have changed.

In the Old Town upper-status Mahapatra household, my question about preference for boys was met with acquiescence.

SITA: Yes. There are differences in some families but only in backward families.

SON: Yes, there is still a preference for sons.

SABITA: Sons are very much freer; daughters must be prepared for married life.

In contrast, Mrs. Badhei (Old Town, middle-status) responded by saying that she preferred sons and daughters equally.

It's the same pain to give birth to boys and to girls and the same trouble rearing them.

I ask whether girls and boys are reared differently. Mrs. Badhei finds it difficult to answer at first. Finally, she says:

Girls work in the house, boys do only outside work, depending upon their education.

I ask if girls can do employed work outside the home, and Mrs. Badhie answers:

No. They're not interested.

Sopna Behera (lower-status, New Capital), like most other Bhubaneswar women, denied that there was any preference for sons over daughters and reported that sons and daughters were treated the same. "They all work." Earlier in the conversation, Sopna had talked about how helpful her older son (ten years old) was: "He helps with shopping, bringing water from a tube well a mile away – he helps with all the work." When I asked her whether her daughter's life would be any different from her own, she responded:

Ultimately, it will depend on fate, not on what I think. I would like her to be educated, to get a job, and then to marry – to a good son-in-law.

As I had found in my initial 1965–67 child-rearing research in Bhubaneswar, it is difficult for most women to articulate what they do differently in rearing sons and daughters. There were sporadic references to indoor versus outdoor work, which they believed differentiated girls and boys. Only Mrs. Das raised the issue of obedience, and yet in 1989 an explanation for why girls were outperforming boys in school achievement related specifically to that issue. Many people argued that because girls are more obedient than boys and are restricted to the home, it is easier to get them to study than to get the boys, who wander out-of-doors and are less amenable to direction, to do so. I suspect that the patrifocal family structure, which results in girls leaving their natal families and boys remaining at home, is so fundamental that most people did not think about it in response to my question. Also, the emphasis most middle- and upper-status families place on education has reduced gender role differences somewhat. Parents are committed to their children's academic performance rather than to training their children for specific gender roles; in such households, children are allowed to focus on their studies rather than on gender-differentiated domestic chores.

Similarly, the patrifocal family ideology that prefers sons over daughters is something that, as mothers, most women denied, although some admitted that the bias existed at a societal level. Some women had even experienced it with their parents-in-law. Since

Independence, India has officially endorsed gender equity, and most educated Bhubaneswar families in my sample had adopted this ideology. "Gender equity," however, does not mean "sameness." As in the United States, it often means equal access to education with a delay in the assumption of more traditional gender roles until marriage. The expression of those more traditional gender roles by highly educated, older, and sometimes employed brides/daughters-in-law/wives is currently in transition.

Observance of Menstrual Restrictions and Birth Pollution

Determining whether or not women observe special restrictions and practices at the time of menstruation and childbirth is one way of measuring their adherence to traditional gender roles. Other research in India indicates that the observance of menstrual restrictions has declined as a woman's primary role has been redefined as marital partner rather than as bearer of children.[8] A focus on special restrictions surrounding menstruation and childbirth tends to emphasize the biological function of women as the bearers of descendants for the patrifocal family and patrilineage. As discussed in Chapter 3, however, "biological function" must be understood within an agrarian world view in which women's menses are associated with the fallow earth before the rains come and the earth is replenished and once again becomes productive. This world view conceptualizes women as distinct from but complementary to men and as essential to the earth's well-being. The regeneration of the world is seen to be a human, natural, and divine activity.[9]

With increased education of and participation by women in an increasingly urbanized and industrialized society, such biological markers, with their ritual significance from a more agrarian era, are declining in importance. The once clear associations between a woman's bodily rhythms and the seasonal rhythms of an agricultural way of life are being lost. As has happened in the industrialized West, in India women are beginning to abandon special

252

practices associated with menstruation and childbirth that formerly symbolized and dramatized their biological functions. Discussing with mothers, daughters, and grandmothers their observance of and beliefs about restrictions at the time of menstruation and childbirth was, therefore, one means of gaining insight into changing gender roles and ideology in Bhubaneswar.

I had my first discussion of practices associated with menstruation in 1987 while visiting the Tripathy family with my mother. My mother and I sat together on a bed with Mrs. Tripathy, her mother, and four of the Tripathy daughters, talking about a lot of the issues that gave rise to my 1989 field trip and systematic interviews. When I raised the topic of practices related to menstruation, it set off a cacophony of talk – Grandmother, Mother, and the girls all talking at once and then arguing with one another. Although they had difficulty agreeing and then in explaining their disagreement to me, it was clear that I had touched on an issue of some significance. The group conversation went as follows:

GRANDMOTHER: Among our Brahmin *jati* when menstruation comes the first time, the girl is not allowed to step over the threshold [go outside]. This used to be so with all castes. In those days girls never studied very much. They never got beyond the seventh class. For three or four days [following the onset of menstruation] they do not bathe. They are kept apart.

MOTHER: Seven days the first time – at night in a room alone. Other women come and sit with the girl in their midst and decorate her with rice. Then she bathes and wears a new sari and sits decorated like a goddess.

"So it is really a day of honor?" I ask.

Someone then uses the word "shameful," and I inquire, "Why does the girl feel shameful?" I am corrected. The word in Oriya is *laja* and is difficult to translate into English. It really means a time of self-awareness – of a girl's learning about her fertility and her need for modesty and about how to comport herself in a mature way so everyone will know that she is grown up.

MOTHER: They're scared initially. They must be pacified by their mothers and aunties. They should be pampered – given new clothes and jewelry. They will cry and weep, and their mothers must make them feel better. The tears do not end for even seven days in some cases.

KALIKA: After the first time, every month for seven days that means she will not do housework, not cooking. She'll sit in a corner of the house. Her meals will be there. After seven days she will take her bath.

MOTHER: On the first time on the seventh day there will be a big feast.

PADMINI: She becomes very sad. . . . She becomes very shy. . . . In her [Grandmother's] time, after seven days, for the first time, she got ready to marry. She would already be married to a man, but she would not move to his house until after the first menstruation.

GRANDMOTHER: "Nowadays things have changed."

Then there is more group discussion.

KALIKA: In the time of our mother, marriage came one year later [one year after the first menstruation].

PADMINI AND MOTHER: [overlapping]: Nowadays, [it's] been changed. . . . It's different because girls go to school, they study. No one knows about it [menstruation]. It has no value any more. It has gradually lost its value.

KALIKA: Society says, "Why expose a girl to this shameful thing?"

MOTHER: Everything has changed. Now [menstruation] has become private. It is not announced publicly to the family. Only the mother knows. The husband doesn't know. The extended family doesn't know.

According to the Tripathys, by 1987 much change had occurred in this realm of women's lives. In 1989 I asked other women about practices at the time of menstruation and childbirth. Kalpana Mohanty (New Capital, upper-status) and her daughter made very strong statements opposing such practices.

254

KALPANA: I never accepted the idea of menstrual impurity, although my mother did. Underlying it was the idea that a menstruating woman should be separated from the gods for the first three days of her period. She should not pray, not go to temple. I do not believe in this. I go to the temple, and I have not passed on these ideas to my daughters.

I tried to talk with Kalpana and her daughter about women's feelings of shame and/or shyness at the time of menstruation, employing terms that the Tripathys had used, but they were unresponsive. These were practices that they had totally discarded.

The response from Mrs. Misra and her daughters, Menaka and Nakima, was somewhat different. As members of a highly educated, upper-status New Capital family, they had discarded some but not all traditional beliefs and practices associated with menstruation. Mrs. Misra's initial answer focused on a secular interpretation of menstrual taboos, but her daughter immediately raised the sacred dimension of the restrictions – that of not offending the deities by entering *puja* rooms or temples at the time of menstruation.

MOTHER: It [menstrual restrictions] provides a period of rest in the joint family. Others take on the jobs of the family system.
MENAKA: Even now I feel that I shouldn't enter the *puja* room. Even if given an option, I would like to stay out of the *puja* room. But Nakima, probably, would like to go in.
MOTHER: No. It's not a question of liking to go in.
MENAKA: You [directed to her younger sister, Nakima] won't feel you're doing anything wrong if you feel like going in.
NAKIMA: Even now I normally don't go in because I guess it's been ingrained from childhood not to do it. It's become a habit. It's not a question of liking.

As it happens, in this household of educated women the only restriction observed at the time of menstruation is the one of not entering the *puja* room – of separating oneself from worship and from the deities. Nakima, however, indicated that she observed this

255

restriction not out of belief so much as habit. The Misras maintained
that prohibitions on handling food and on having contact with
other members of the household are not generally observed anymore. Furthermore, the girls explained that such practices have not
been part of their family tradition for several generations because
their mother comes from an educated, urban family. In addition,
residing in a nuclear family makes the prohibition on handling food
very difficult to observe. As Mrs. Misra pointed out, if she did not
enter the kitchen, there would be no one to prepare food. (She does
not rely on her studious daughters or her elderly mother-in-law for
cooking.)

In discussing childbirth, Mrs. Misra said that after giving birth
she spent seven days in the hospital. When she returned home, she
and the baby had to be "washed properly," and then they stayed
in a particular room for some days.

MENAKA: Is it still practiced now?
MOTHER: Yes. This is our custom. It is more or less hygienic, also.

I ask if Grandmother also observed the same customs.

MOTHER: Yes, although she cannot keep the way we do. She had no
  education. It was not done properly.

Mrs. Misra uses modern and secular interpretations – efficiency,
rest, and hygiene – to explain menstrual and childbirth practices.
What is considered "proper" now has changed from her parents'
generation.

The New Capital middle-status Panda family expressed a variety
of attitudes. Young, educated, and employed, Laxmi said that menstrual restrictions were not practiced at all in her family and that
she was even "freer" in the city where she worked. However, her
Aunt Gitali asserted that Grandmother had observed restrictions
for a week but had taught her own daughters to observe them for
only two days. They were not to perform *puja* (prayers at home in

the *puja* room or at temple) during this period or to eat meat, fish, eggs, or salty and oily things. Gitali has not yet decided what to do about her own daughter, who was only nine at the time of our interview. Following childbirth, Grandmother said that she had observed restrictions for a week for both ritual and hygienic reasons. Gitali reported that she had done the same, but she asserted that many women have shortened the restrictions to three to five days and observe them "more for scientific and hygienic purposes" than for ritual ones.

Among middle- and upper-status New Capital women, the observation of traditional restrictions on behavior at the time of menstruation and childbirth, along with the accompanying ideology of untouchability and ritual defilement (Chapter 3), has greatly declined. What restrictions remain have been transformed into a more modern ideology of hygiene, except that most women professed that they would not enter the *puja* room to pray while menstruating. In contrast, in Old Town middle- and upper-status families these restrictions are still largely observed, along with purdah. Like purdah, however, such restrictions are not practical for low-status, working women. These practices, principally the prerogative of higher-status women, are changing as women become better educated and lead more active lives outside the home, as households become increasingly nuclear, and as husband-wife relationships become more companionate.

Conclusions

As I concluded each interview, I tried to elicit from the mothers, grandmothers, and daughters with whom I was speaking their views of gender roles in general and the relative status of women and men. This kind of broad question was difficult for some of these women to respond to, especially the older and less educated women of the Old Town. However, those responses that I did receive are illuminating about both continuity and change in gender ideologies.

In the Das family, for example, there was an unusual degree of continuity among generations, considering their educated New Capital status. In response to my question, Grandmother said:

Women should get a good husband and reside in the in-laws' place. They should be confined to the home. Women should do everything in the house.

Her answer focused on the traditional division of labor and set of restrictions that confine women to the home. Although her daughter and granddaughter – Mrs. Das and Lili – are not restricted to the home, they also support the traditional division of labor. Their response to my broad question about relative status was that men have a higher status and are dominant. "Only working women could begin to be equal with men," they said.

In the New Capital household of the upper-status Misra family the relative status of women and men set off the following mother-daughter dialogue:

MOTHER: It depends on what a woman wants.
MENAKA: You [referring to her mother] might be ruling the affairs. I think that at home Mummy's status is definitely higher than Daddy's. She has a say in everything.
MOTHER: I always had to consult with my husband about your studies, your futures, your marriage.
MENAKA: What about the relative status of women and men?
MOTHER: These little things. How can we connect to that?
MENAKA: [answers for her]: Always things are talked out between Mummy and Daddy. We also have a say.
NAKIMA: We always discussed. Any decision Daddy made he consulted with all of us, including my [younger] brother.
MOTHER: He always do it. Sometimes I refused. Why always do it? It is not necessary, but he always insisted on that.

Then the daughters began to compare how their household is run with that of their uncle (father's brother).

MOTHER: He is autocratic, a little bit of a tyrant.

Two things are of particular interest here: First, Menaka recognizes that a woman like her mother, who is principally a wife and mother, can be dominant in one sphere of life – the home. A gender-based division of labor need not lead to pervasive male dominance. And, second, it is clear that Mr. Misra, while potentially dominant in other spheres, tries to run a democratic household and engages his wife and children in much decision making. In previous conversations, both Mr. and Mrs. Misra showed that they are sensitive to what their daughters will experience in marriage. They are very concerned about finding for their highly educated and employed daughters husbands who will respect their careers and share household work and decision making. This kind of concern distinguishes the Misras from the Dases, for example, whose daughter Lili married at a younger age and had less education and no career ambitions.

In a New Capital family like Kalpana Mohanty's, where there has been a tradition of female employment, the response to my question about the relative status of women and men was somewhat different:

MOTHER (Kalpana): Yes. They [men and women] do have equal status now. Not always, but in most things.
DAUGHTER: Higher education is the main cause.
MOTHER: In general, women look older than men. Therefore, they needed to be much younger to start with [in marriage]. Now the age [of husband and wife] is very close, only one year, two years, or three years. That's why they [men] were once dominant. They never cared about the wife's opinion. Nowadays we have our opinion. Husband and wife talk over problems together. Now they have a discussion, have respect for each other's opinions. If there's a problem, both come together and decide, find a solution.

Similarly, in the Tripathy family, where the daughters are all educated and some are employed, the response was

PADMINI: Yes, the status of women is changing. Nowadays, there are many houses where women are working. They have to go out. They will not do all the household work. They get respect. They don't have to go under the dominance of the husband.

I ask about how things were in their mother's and grandmother's time.

PADMINI: It was different among different people. Some [men] were more dominant than others. Our grandfather was a very simple man. He did not want to dominate his wife, so my grandmother was somewhat free. But my father likes to dominate my mother.
KALIKA: Yes, that's true.
MOTHER: A lot. I want to go out but there's not time. I want to be a person in my own right, arrange marriages, etc.
KALIKA: In our society, too [a reference to my description of what is happening in some American households], the men are cooking and helping the wife.
MOTHER: Some husbands are willing to help, but society does not look kindly on that.
KALIKA: Society does not like it. It likes to see men in a higher position.
PADMINI: If the husband does housework, he will be called "henpecked."

In the New Capital Mohanty family, by contrast, where the three daughters-in-law are highly educated but are not employed outside the home, gender ideology is more conservative. All three agreed that women are inferior to men. As First Daughter-in-law put it:

They're still considered of inferior status to men.

I ask if they are troubled by that.

FIRST DAUGHTER-IN-LAW: No, No. We don't have that. We don't feel it personally. We are educated and so you can feel an equal with your husband. That has become a great change because you have studied, you have a great perspective towards life.

Laxmi Panda, employed but not as yet married, answered in a more philosophical fashion:

Yes, they [men and women] are equal. But not everybody is doing in that way. Generally, we don't feel that much about it [gender inequities]. Everyone has their own personal nature.

I ask if higher education makes a difference, and Laxmi responds thoughtfully and critically:

Yes, but not always. For some, it is of no use. They are still limited, not reasoning and analyzing. They just accept what they learned earlier. How can they become scientists? Lots of girls are becoming educated because they want to have a good marriage. They're not really interested in their studies. . . . You can stay with tradition. That is not a bad thing. But you should accept tradition with your own reason and heart. You should think what it is before you can accept. You should not accept it blindly.

In the Old Town, where joint family life remains strong and where sample parents responded to the idea of girls' education more conservatively than parents in the New Capital, there are nevertheless indications that gender ideologies are changing. For example, in the Mahapatra family, Mita and Sita are both employed, as is their brother's wife. Nor are these women restricted to the house. Nonetheless, as members of a high-status Brahmin family residing in a conservative town, they worry about other peoples' opinions. When I asked if a woman should have the right to leave her husband in an unhappy marriage, they responded:

GRANDSON: She has the right, but not every woman prefers that. They don't like that.

SITA: The atmosphere is not supportive. Women prefer to suffer.
BROTHER AND SITA TOGETHER: Women must accept [their situation].
They are afraid of other people, what they will say.

I ask if they see any changes in society's attitudes.

DAUGHTER-IN-LAW: A man does not want her [his wife] to go against
him.

These responses are particularly poignant given Sita's unfortu-
nate marital situation. Although they seem to uphold the status
quo, these remarks were made with different generations of women
and men sitting together and discussing matters in a way that
would not have happened in previous eras and still does not happen in many Old Town households. There was an unusual degree
of openness and intimacy demonstrated among generations and
between genders in this Old Town Brahmin family.

Mrs. Maharana (Old Town, Carpenter's family) found it difficult
to respond to my broad inquiry about the relative status of women
and men. Her son (twenty-six, unmarried) spoke for her:

Nowadays there is no difference between a man and a woman. Nowadays a woman is likely to be the same to a man. They do the same
type of work as men. There are girls doing screw tightening and
electronics work. One of my friends has a woman assistant. There is
no difference in an educated family. In our family there is a big
difference. We are a traditional family.

This son matriculated and works as a technician in the New
Capital. I ask him if he would like to have an employed wife.

Yes. If she's interested, there's no problem for me. I would be supportive of [her work]. My parents might not approve. My mother may
complain. She might not allow.

I ask who would decide whether a wife/daughter-in-law could work outside the home.

My parents have that power because our marriage would be proposed by them, by my father and mother. We don't have any love marriage. We are powerless.

This young man's comments capture well the intergenerational tension that has developed in some Old Town households in which parents remain very conservative about women's roles, but their sons have a changed ideology. However, this son is unlikely to challenge his parents on the issue of female employment. He will probably marry an older girl who has a comparable education to his and with whom he can have a more companionate relationship. His work in the New Capital has exposed him to radically different gender roles than those he experienced growing up in the Old Town. Furthermore, he may get a government house in the New Capital when he marries, which would free him and his wife from the daily supervision of his parents. His older sister is married and resides in a nuclear household in a major city elsewhere in India. Although she is not employed, her life must be dramatically different from her mother's life in her husband's Old Town joint family.

Harish Mahapatra of the Old Town also responded to my broad question for his wife:

I am in favor of women being educated, becoming economically independent, and standing on their own feet. A woman who worships her husband and blindly believes in him is foolish. If educated and independent, she can take care of herself and her children, even if her husband is a drunkard and beats her. If she is clever and capable, then she can escape from the clutches of her husband.

Harish, however, continues to live with his very conservative parents who will not allow his wife to leave the house. He referred to his mother as of the "old culture" and as not accepting of change

263

of any kind. His wife, he says, is more amenable to change, and his daughter will be very different. Meanwhile, he has purchased a separate piece of land in the Old Town on which he plans to build a house and to which he will one day move his wife and children. He says that other members of his joint family will be welcome to stay with them. Thus, he is not rejecting his joint family but is contemplating a change of residence that will give him greater autonomy.

Transformations in women's roles and in gender ideology are clearly underway in Bhubaneswar, and they have implications for patrifocal family structure and ideology. These excerpts from interviews with mothers, daughters, and grandmothers – as well as with some fathers, sons, and grandfathers – attest to such change. The theme of women being able to take greater charge of their lives, of having their own voices and opinions, pervades these interviews. And education is often cited as the explanation for this change. These interviews also exemplify the complexity of changing practices and beliefs in India. Change is never uniform, and in Bhubaneswar it is very much affected by Old Town versus New Capital residence, by caste and class status, and by different levels of education and exposure to new ideas.

CHAPTER EIGHT

Systems of Family and Gender in Transition

At the conclusion of my interviews with mothers, daughters, and grandmothers, I always inquired if there were something I should have asked about that I had not. This question usually resulted in women asking me questions about women's and men's roles in the United States and in our then making comparisons between Indian and American systems of family and gender. One of the most poignant responses to this question, however, came from the New Capital Misra family.

MOTHER: You have not asked about family obligations, what we should do, that which is there in family life, like my husband's older sister who was widowed just before we were married. She had to come, together with her sons, to stay with us. They had to come here to get a good education and all, to get their family settled. This was for seven or eight years. Other family members had to be given money, too.

When she paused, I ask, "So you had to help out?"

MRS. MISRA: [correcting me]: [It's] not that we had to. Not true, because my brother-in-law is also there, and he also has a lot of money, but he doesn't spend it. . . . Indian families – you must look at their difference. I never thought of [not taking on my husband's family responsibilities]. I never asked anything to my husband [in the early years of marriage]. I always asked to my parents, my mother.
MENAKA: Out auntie (Mother's sister), since she was earning, she always gave us the best of dresses . . .

265

MOTHER: I never asked Mr. Misra for anything. How could I do it?

MENAKA: That's where self-sacrifice comes in.

MOTHER: Because I know that he's in difficulty.

NAKIMA: But I'm sure the same would not be true for a girl, even if she's not working, a girl of today. She would certainly put her foot down. I mean that things have changed to a certain extent.

MOTHER: That was one of the reasons why we wanted you to work, to stand on your own feet.

NAKIMA: Even if a girl's not earning, even if she's just a housewife, she would certainly rebel.

"You mean there would be less acceptance of the husband's earnings going to other relatives?" I ask.

MOTHER: That's why my in-laws . . .

NAKIMA: [cuts her off]: Especially nowadays, the mentality is you give money as a type of investment. You give somebody some money, and you expect a return back.

"Rather than an expectation that it's just a responsibility to help out with relatives?" I ask.

NAKIMA: Yes.

Embedded in this dialogue are several assumptions relevant to understanding systems of family and gender as they ideally should be and as they are changing in parts of Bhubaneswar and elsewhere in India. It is significant that Mrs. Misra's immediate response to the question What had I failed to ask? was to begin talking about "family obligations." She put our discussion of changing women's roles and marriage practices back into the patrifocal family context in which the well-being of the extended family unit is supposed to take precedence over the needs of the nuclear unit of husband, wife, and children. She spoke of the heavy financial commitment that her husband assumed when they were first married. It was sufficiently heavy that she was reluctant to make any special requests of him. He was, of course, supporting his wife and children, but she looked to her mother and to her older, employed sister for anything not essential. Also, for several of those first years of marriage she resided with her mother while her husband was being transferred from one government post to another, which must have saved further expense. As Menaka appropriately expressed it, her mother had exhibited "self-sacrifice," an essential ingredient of being a good wife. Traditional patrifocal family values stipulate that as a wife a woman should put the needs of her husband's extended family above her own and those of her own children.

When I used the words "had to help out" to describe this situation, Mrs. Misra differed, pointing out that her husband's brother had not assisted despite his ability to do so. She was making a distinction between the moral responsibility of supporting extended kin and the actual behavior of some individuals. Not all family members, she suggested, observe this code of morality, and I should be aware of such differences among Indian families.

Finally, this mother-daughter dialogue addresses a potentially significant change in attitude toward family and gender roles. Nakima, Mrs. Misra's youngest daughter, asserts that "a girl" (a woman of her generation) would no longer silently accept the financial sacrifice as her mother had done. She would "put her foot down," meaning she would not be willing to sacrifice her own well-being or that of her children in favor of the well-being of the extended family. Furthermore, Nakima asserts, even an unemployed housewife – a wife who is not contributing directly to the economic welfare of the family – would rebel. Her words are in dramatic contrast to those of Lili Das, who said that only an employed wife would have the power to oppose her husband in such a situation. Both young women, however, identify a locus of change: that is, educated wives who are capable of asserting themselves and opposing the collective interests of the traditional patrifocal family. It is fear of such threats to the unity and coherence of the joint family that makes some men reluctant to educated their daughters and other men hesitant to have highly educated daughters-in-law.

Arenas of Change and Conflict

Orientation toward Interdependence or Independence and Personal Autonomy

Placing value upon interdependence, rather than upon independence and personal autonomy, is widespread in India and integral to the successful functioning of the traditional patrifocal family. Studies of the family organization and child-rearing practices in several regions of India all agree on this fundamental principle.[1] Children are socialized, as described in Chapter 3, to identify with the family as a whole and to put the interests of that collective unit ahead of their individual interests. Margaret Trawick (1992), in her in-depth analysis of the emotional bonds among the members of one South Indian family, uses the term *"de* individuation" to capture the complex web of interactions that discourage the development of an autonomous self in favor of what Alan Roland (1988) has called a "we-self" – a person whose sense of identity is based upon a deep-seated emotional connectedness with others.

> Hence it would seem that, as life proceeds, what happens to the self is neither individuation (i.e., increasing differentiation of self from others) nor internal integration (i.e., crystallization of a stable sense of self), but rather a continuous *de* crystallization and *de* individuation of the self, a continuous effort to *break down* separation, isolation, purity, as though these states, left unopposed, would form of their own accord and freeze up life into death.
> *(Trawick 1992, pp. 242–243)*

A current debate in psychological anthropology and cross-cultural psychology concerns concepts of self and how they vary from one society to another. Western psychology, in theorizing about human development, has tended to assume that individuals strive for autonomy from others, for independence of action and thought, and for personal self-development and fulfillment. Hence, the focus in Western psychoanalytic models upon "individuation" – the assumption that successful early socialization moves a child away from its intense emotional, symbiotic bond with a single caretaker (the mother) toward an individuated selfhood, that is, someone capable of mature autonomy. Individuals in the West are conceptualized as independent, self-contained, autonomous entities who, ideally, are capable of developing one-to-one emotional bonds with others. In contrast, some anthropologists and psychologists have recently identified a number of non-Western societies that are more group-oriented. In these societies the ideal self is not an autonomous individual but a person who is emotionally bound to the group – someone who will subordinate his or her personal desires to the collective interests of a larger body.[2] These two general types of societies, which seem to cultivate contrasting concepts of selfhood, have been variously labeled "sociocentric – egocentric," "other-focused – self-focused," and "collectivist – individualist."[3]

Although it is important to recognize that societies may construct quite different conceptions of the individual and of selfhood from one another and may, therefore, select from the range of human potential different qualities for emphasis, it is also important not to overdraw the distinctions.[4] Western "egocentric" individuals must also be capable of becoming social beings; they can never be totally autonomous and independent of others. Reciprocally, non-Western "sociocentric" individuals cannot be totally interdependent and other-oriented. They must be capable of at least some autonomous thought and action.[5] Interdependence–independence might best be conceptualized as a continuum along which cultures fall according to the particular mixture of collectivist and individualist elements that they exhibit at any one time.[6] One must, however, always remember that the effort to charaterize such societal orientations requires building cultural models with which to examine the actual behavior that different members of a society exhibit.

In these two models it is, in fact, the tension between the two different constructions of self that often becomes culturally salient. In the West, for example, in Euro-American culture individuals are expected to be capable of independent action but also to be able to form stable and intimate emotional bonds with others – a prerequisite for establishing nuclear families. There is a culturally formulated tension between "selfish individualism" and "mature

individualism."[7] In Hindu culture, in contrast, the tension is between the "selfish desires" of the individual and the interests of the
joint family.[8] *Renunciation* of personal desire is therefore culturally
lauded and elaborated. As Mrs. Misra so poignantly pointed out,
there are differences among Indian families and the degree to
which individuals act morally where what is "moral" is culturally
defined as giving precedence to family obligations over personal
interests.

Theorists such as Kurtz (1993), Roland (1988), and Trawick (1992)
are right to recognize the individualist assumptions of Western
psychology and psychoanalysis and to identify the powerful collective experience that underlies patrifocal family structure and ideology. In fact, my systematic observations of family organization and
child-rearing practices in Bhubaneswar lend much support to such
theories.[9] However, my observations also address the diversity of
family structures existent in that one town and the subtly different
experiences that children have growing up. On the whole, New
Capital middle- and upper-status children received more focused
maternal attention than did Old Town children and were given
more opportunities to be self-reliant in early and later childhood. A
significant shift was occurring in child care practices and ideology –
from those that were adapted to an agricultural way of life and
focused upon a child's health and survival to ones that prepared a
child for a world of competitive schooling and competition for jobs.
LeVine et al. (1994) refer to the former as a "pediatric model" and
the latter as a "pedagogical model" of child care.

Changing child care practices were producing more self-reliant
and potentially less interdependent and group-oriented individuals. When such changes in child care are combined with an intense
focus upon Western-style educational achievement and professional goals, one might predict some movement away from the
culturally ideal interdependent self toward a more independent
and autonomous self. Such would be compatible with Nakima's
description of the wife who would "put her foot down" as opposed
to the wife who practices "self-sacrifice."

Western theories of modernization, beginning with Durkheim
and Weber, have tended to associate modernity with increased

individualism – individual autonomy, individual freedoms, and individual rights.[10] An increase in emphasis upon individualism rather than upon group identity seems to be the result of such factors as the development of a market economy, increased sociocultural heterogeneity, movement from ascribed to achieved roles, and increased geographic and social mobility.[11] A critical sociological question, however, is whether increased individualism is necessarily linked with modernization – that is, industrialization, urbanization, and Western-style schooling. Japan, for example, seems an exception in having industrialized but retained many of its collectivist values. However, Japan is a small and homogeneous society that is only recently beginning to exhibit a shift toward individualism – a shift spearheaded to some extent by young women.[12] In India, which is a much larger, more complex society than Japan and less industrialized and urbanized, it is too early to determine whether a significant shift from a more interdependent/collectivist society to a more individualist one is occurring. My research in Bhubaneswar does indicate, however, some movement in the direction of increased independence and autonomy for women.[13]

Some of those women in Bhubaneswar whom I have observed coming of age in the last thirty years have experienced conflicting signals about women's roles and identity. Whereas on the one hand, they have been taught the cultural ideals of modesty, deference, and self-sacrifice – especially with respect to husbands and parents-in-law – on the other, they have been encouraged to achieve in school and to develop career aspirations. Rather than being rapidly moved at puberty into the roles of daughter-in-law, wife, and mother, they have been provided with a prolonged adolescence during which to formulate a more distinct sense of self. In addition, some of them have had mothers and grandmothers who regretted not being sent to school and who have supported them in their individual endeavors, and others have had sympathetic fathers as well. The result has been young women like Laxmi Panda, who had the courage to leave an unhappy marriage despite heavy social disapprobation, and like Kalika Tripathy who, with the help of her husband, was able to stand up to a punitive mother-in-law.

The process of change, however, is neither uniform nor monolithic. Most young women in Bhubaneswar try to balance old ideas and practices with new ones, and few have overtly rebelled against tradition. Their widespread acceptance of arranged marriages is perhaps indicative of this. In contemporary Euro-American society there is evidence that significant gender differences exist in independence and autonomy – that women are more emotionally interconnected and relational in their interactions with others than are men. In these respects they more closely approach the ideal Indian self.[14] If this is the case in a postmodern society such as the United States, perhaps we do not need to postulate significant intrapsychic change for Indian women as they adapt to conditions of modernization. And, as I argued in Chapter 3, what Westerners often misconstrue as passivity in Indian women is deferential behavior appropriate to some circumstances that can be transformed into assertive and dominant behavior in other circumstances. The complex training in the joint family for both interdependence and dominance may serve women well as they move into the modern hierarchical, bureaucratic workplace.

Hierarchies of Authority versus Egalitarianism

The traditional patrifocal family is based upon age and gender hierarchies of authority: Older members have authority over younger ones, and males have authority over females. Since these two hierarchies cross-cut each other, both men and women have authority in some contexts but are subordinate in other contexts. Ideally, these relationships of dominance-subordination should take precedence over relationships based upon emotional bonds such as love. As previously described, emotionally intense dyadic bonds, as between mother and child or husband and wife, are carefully guarded against. Such pair-bonds, especially exclusive ones, are considered potentially threatening to the collective well-being of the extended family. Thus, mothers should not openly exhibit love for their children, nor should husbands and wives openly exhibit love and affection for one another. Love should always be contained.[15]

With husbands and wives, the principle of authority is given precedence over love through the parental arrangement of a marriage between strangers in which the groom is significantly older and better educated than the bride and can therefore be dominant. Furthermore, the young, immature bride is inducted into a strange household where she is expected to be docile and subservient in her demeanor and to obey her mother-in-law, who also continues to wield authority over her son. She becomes the most subordinate member of the household's female hierarchy. Sexual segregation of the household and gender-differentiated roles and responsibilities further operate to keep husbands and wives apart much of the day, and the cultural belief that love between spouses should develop only gradually through habitation and the production of children also serves to contain this potentially disruptive pair-bond. Spontaneous feelings of romantic love for another individual, so highly valued and culturally elaborated in the West, are considered a dangerous emotion in much of India.[16]

These two principles – age- and gender-based hierarchies of authority and the containment of pair-bonds – which underlie the traditional patrifocal family, are being contested in contemporary Bhubaneswar, especially in middle- and upper-status New Capital households. As described in Chapter 4, a more conjugal husband-wife relationship had already emerged in the 1960s among some young parents who, in the absence of parents-in-law, had begun to dine together, to occasionally socialize together with others, and sometimes even to share a bedroom separate from their children. Thus, some New Capital children experienced growing up in non-sexually segregated households in which a husband-wife pair-bond was evident.

With the young, highly educated women of the next generation marrying at significantly later ages, the dominance of husbands over wives is being further eroded. Although some disparity in age and education between bride and groom has been retained in arranged marriages, it has been greatly reduced, thus creating the potential for a more egalitarian and affectionate relationship between a husband and wife. By 1989, this was noticeable in both the Old Town and the New Capital. Young husbands and wives felt comfortable sitting together and talking with me, sometimes openly teasing one another and laughing together. Furthermore, the cultural ideology with respect to husband-wife relationships has been changing. Interviews with young women, as well as with some young men, made it clear that they wanted companionate marriages.[17] They wanted to marry someone with whom they could share decision making, *not* someone who would try to dominate them. And many young women also wanted to marry men who would respect their career aspirations. For the New Capital Misras, this was an important consideration in selecting suitable husbands for their highly educated, employed daughters. In the example of Kalika Tripathy, a college lecturer, it was her husband who had wanted a wife with whom to share careers and thus he personally selected her.

Although there are significant differences in the degree to which such new desires and aspirations are being realized in Old Town and New Capital middle- and upper-status families, the fact is they are occurring. And most parents have built into the process of arranging marriages participation by their sons and daughters. Neither women nor men of this generation are being forced to marry someone whom they find physically or emotionally distasteful; some mutual attraction is expected.

There is, nonetheless, evidence from both Old Town and New Capital families that making the transition from age and gender hierarchies to increased egalitarianism, especially between husband and wife, can be problematic. This is dramatically illustrated by the cases of Gitali Panda, who left her husband and set up a separate household, and Kalika Tripathy, who with her husband left the household of her parents-in-law. The tension between the principles of gender hierarchy and gender equality is also evident in those interviews involving mothers and daughters in which they disagreed about the rights of women – for example, about the extent to which a wife may differ with her husband or the right of a woman to leave an unhappy marriage. Such tension is also evident in Harish Mahapatra's struggle with his conservative Old Town parents over the issue of his wife's seclusion.

Women in Culture: Reflections on the Psychocultural Development of Indian Women

The government's 1974 landmark report on the status of women in India, *Towards Equality*, makes the following remarkable assertion:

> The contrasting norms of behaviour for the daughter and the daughter-in-law tend to make the life of a woman alternate between freedom and restrictions, between harsh and soft treatment and . . . does not allow her to become a person. She has roles but no personality.
> *P. 65*

What is remarkable here is not the report's contrasting of the roles of daughter and daughter-in-law but its conclusion that Indian women lack personal identity. The statement conflates "roles" with "personhood" and "personality," implying that a strong cultural focus upon the one somehow denies the other. The approach taken here, in contrast, is that concepts of "selfhood" and "personhood" are culturally constructed. In collectivist-oriented societies this involves a strong orientation toward roles – especially toward kinship roles and obligations – whereas in individualistic societies the pursuit of personal goals outweighs the importance of kinship roles and obligations. Nonetheless, all societies – whether individualistic or collective – try to socialize and enculturate children so that their outward behavior, as well as their internalized attitudes, values, and predispositions, conforms to what is expected of them as adults. One's personal identity is, therefore, very much a product of sociocultural factors. Implied in the quote from *Towards Equality* is a preference for Western-style individualism over the collectivism of India's traditional patrifocal family system. No doubt, the ways in which that system has tended to constrain women's behavior and limit their opportunities underlies the authors' sentiments. Nevertheless, women are not merely passive agents who are acted upon by sociocultural circumstances.[18] As this book has tried to demonstrate, they are also actors who help to shape (reproduce) and reshape (transform) their sociocultural system. But they must do so *within* their culture – within the constraints of the prevailing social order and belief system in which they find themselves.

There are seeming paradoxes in Hindu society and culture. For example, the status of male-female relationships is complex, ambiguous, and unresolved within Hindu cosmology. Male deities cannot act without the female force, *shakti*. Female deities, with their divine power, can be both creators and destroyers. Human females, who are by nature endowed with *shakti*, are also believed to be inherently powerful. Their powers, of course, include the giving of life. They are also believed to be endowed with strong sexual appetites – stronger than men's – and women, unlike men, whose semen supply is limited, are believed to have unlimited supplies of blood and milk.[19] These and a myriad other images of males and females get constructed differently in different regions of India and at different historical moments. The significant point for our purposes, however, is that, in general, females, whether they are human or divine, are considered inherently powerful. In Hindu theology, in contrast to Judeo-Christian beliefs, male forces are not inevitably dominant.[20]

In everyday Indian life, however, in which the predominant kinship system depends upon male descent and inheritance, female power has had to be channeled to meet the needs of the patriline – the patrifocal family, the patrilineage, and the *jati* or subcaste that is based upon ties of kinship. For the sake of society, therefore, women's sexual appetites have had to be brought under control and their reproductive capacities directed toward the right patrilines. In this conceptual system, women have to be controlled because of their inherent powerfulness, not because of their inherent weakness.[21] Practices such as child marriage, or arranged marriage at puberty, and purdah help to ensure that women's reproductive powers will maintain the social order and thereby bring honor to their families. If women were allowed free rein in fulfilling their sexual desires, if they were allowed to have sexual relations with the wrong men (men from inappropriate kinship and caste groups), they would indeed disrupt the established social order. Accordingly, especially among higher-status families where there is much at stake in honor and property, women's power is construed as potentially dangerous and in need of control.

Gender-based control mechanisms such as those just mentioned tend to raise the flag of "sexual inequality," and in modern India they have certainly served to restrict women's access to Western schooling, to occupations outside the home, and so on. They do not, however, inevitably produce feelings of inferiority and inadequacy in women.[22] On the contrary, the several generations of women whom I have known in Bhubaneswar all take pride in their lives and accomplishments, however restricted these may seem to more Westernized Indians and to outsiders. Sudhir Kakar (1982, p. 60), the eminent Indian psychoanalyst, in theorizing about the psychocultural development of Indian women, asks why it is that in such a patriarchal society "the cultural devaluation of women" does *not* get translated into "a pervasive sense of worthlessness in individual women."

Kakar overstates the "cultural devaluation" in a society rife with examples of powerful females, both human and divine. Furthermore, much of his thesis about the psychocultural development of men rests upon the powerful influence that mothers exert over sons. Kakar does, however, identify two significant sources of self-esteem for Indian women: First, he suggests that despite their not being of the preferred sex, daughters receive enough attention from their mothers and extended kin to feel loved and secure. And, second, he points out that their growing up in well-defined communities of women provides daughters with a context in which they can experience some degree of autonomy and power. My studies of family organization and child-rearing practices in Bhubaneswar confirm both of these hypotheses.

The significance for women's self-esteem of growing up within communities of women needs to be emphasized even though, ironically, two indicators of sexual inequality – purdah and sexual segregation – help to create these communities. Carol Gilligan, the noted feminist psychologist, and her colleagues have recently explored problems of female adolescence in the United States, and they have concluded that if girls are to develop and maintain self-esteem during adolescence it is important for them to remain connected to their families and female role models, maintain close relationships with older women, and retain distinct voices from those of men.[23] These are all conditions that characterize the patrifocal family in India. Similar circumstances prevail in Morocco, according to Susan Schaefer Davis (1994), where girls experience their adolescence as unstressful and emerge with a clear sense of self-confidence. Davis argues that in Morocco's male-oriented society, where families are organized by hierarchies of age and gender, the culture of women is highly valued. Girls grow up in intergenerational groups of women in which interdependence, not autonomy, is valued and the separation of the sexes may help to enhance their self-esteem. One is reminded of Rita's and Sita's efforts in 1967 (Chapter 2) to explain to me that relationships among women are more important than a woman's relationship with her husband.

According to Kakar (1982, p. 72), the stage of life following daughterhood is characterized by "an Indian girl's struggle for identity and adult status" in the "alien, often threatening, and sometimes humiliating" household of her husband and parents-in-law. There is no question that marriage to a stranger and a shift of residence to a potentially strange household in a strange village or town constitutes an emotional challenge for many young women. This transition could result in widespread emotional disorders if most women were not psychologically prepared for it, having achieved what Catherine Ewing (1991) describes as "intrapsychic autonomy" (as distinguished from "interpersonal autonomy"). An emphasis in childhood on interdependence rather than on autonomy does not inhibit the development of an inner sense of self, Ewing argues.[24] And that sense of self, I would assert, is further secured by a girl's firsthand knowledge of the roles that she will assume throughout her life. Thus the transition in roles is not a "struggle for identity" as much as it is an integral part of a woman's identity.

It is relevant here that middle- and upper-status mothers, daughters, and grandmothers in Bhubaneswar all referred to this transition as a time of "assuming responsibility." They spoke little of personal feelings – although I was able to elicit a few comments.

Instead, they described what it was like to assume the household work and responsibilities of a daughter-in-law and wife and later of a mother. They viewed life as more a progression of changing roles and responsibilities than a process of personal development – something that underlies Western psychology and has become part of American popular culture. For Old Town women, in particular, life was a process in which the level of their responsibility for others continued to increase until their middle years, when they began to have daughters-in-law who could help them and over whom they would have authority. From this psychocultural perspective, "personal growth" constitutes becoming increasingly embedded in familial relationships and responsibilities, *not* in achieving autonomy and independence from others. [25]

In Kakar's (1982, pp. 76–82) developmental model, a woman's "identity crisis" is resolved with her pregnancy and motherhood. Unquestionably, the production of children begins to improve a woman's status in her parents-in-law's home, especially if she bears sons to continue the family patriline. The production of children also increases her responsibilities and moves her further in the direction of potential "matriarch," the manager of household activities and personnel. For Kakar, however, motherhood provides a woman with personal fulfillment not only because it is culturally valued but also because it provides a woman with an exclusive emotional attachment to another person, her infant. Kakar's analysis here is seriously problematic because, as we have seen, the love between mother and infant – like other potential dyadic love relationships – should be contained so as not to threaten the interdependence and cooperation of the larger group. Not only are most mothers too busy to devote themselves exclusively to an infant's care, but they are not supposed to do so. Besides, in joint households there are many other caretakers assisting the mother and vying for the child's attention. Even in the truncated joint households of the New Capital most children were not exclusively cared for by their mothers. Kakar's model, therefore, overemphasizes mother-child bonds and ignores the significance of multiple-caretaking for a girl's identification with other women and with the entire extended family.

Equally problematic is the fact that women's self-descriptions of this stage of life do not fit with the kind of emotional peak that Kakar hypothesizes. The mothers, daughters, and grandmothers that I interviewed described motherhood as the beginning of a new and long period of increased responsibility, which for daughters continued until they were suitably married and for sons continued indefinitely. Several grandmothers pointed out that they were still children themselves when they first became mothers and that they had had to rely heavily on their mothers-in-law. Other new mothers were allowed to return to their natal homes for extended periods in which they were cared for like daughters once again. Only very gradually could a woman achieve a new status by assuming more and more of the household responsibilities and by bearing a number of children. I am reminded of Mrs. Badhei's (Old Town Carpenter) response to my question about what was most satisfying to her as a woman: "Being a household manager," she replied. Her son translated this as "growing the family."

In Hindu society and culture, the emphasis upon fulfilling different roles is not exclusively for women. Men also have a series of roles and life stages through which they must move, and they are also expected to control their personal desires for the sake of the collective whole.[26] Steve Derné (1995) has examined how a set of middle- and upper-status Hindu males, whom he interviewed in Benares, talk about such constraints. These men, he found, continually reiterated the need for group mechanisms to keep "too-strong individual volition" under control. The "real self," according to Derné's informants, is discovered not in following inner impulses and desires but in *controlling* them, which requires submission to social pressure. As a consequence, these men expressed a strong preference for joint family living because, as they explained, the presence of elders would help them to check their antisocial impulses. Furthermore, they frequently expressed concern with honor (*izzat*), which also entailed submitting to social pressure: For example, they considered arranged marriages (submission to parental choice) to be honorable whereas love marriages (self-choice) were not.

By pointing out that men as well as women are subject to role

280

expectations and constraints, I do not wish in any way to underestimate the abuses against women that India's patrifocal family system and ideology can produce and legitimate. Such phenomena as female infanticide and neglect, wife beating, suttee, and dowry deaths are all real and parallel the abuses of women that occur in other patriarchal societies. Just as it is important to document such abuses and to try to do something about them, it is equally important to counteract stereotypes of Indian women as powerless victims of their society or as individuals with no personhood. Female power and authority is real in both secular and sacred contexts. Hindu myths, stories, and songs are replete with images of powerful women who are depicted as morally superior to men – who are the ones who hold the family together and who uphold the social order.[27] For example, Usha Menon and Richard Shweder (1994) have examined narrations by ninety-two female and male Old Town Bhubaneswar residents of a core Oriya cultural symbol, a particular iconic representation of the Great Mother Goddess of Hinduism, Kali. In this manifestation of the goddess, Kali stands with her foot planted on the chest of her husband Shiva, who is lying prostrate on the ground. They conclude:

> The ultimate message of the icon, therefore, is to display the cultural "truth" that it is women who uphold the social order. The more competent narrators, both men and women, articulate this view. They describe wives and mothers as the centrifuges that hold families together. They contrast those roles to those of husbands and fathers who contribute only financially to the welfare of the family, a contribution that most informants do not view as terribly significant to the family's well-being. Curiously enough, this view of women coincides with the Tantric one that also sees women as the power that upholds the universe. The difference is that while the Tantric view sees women achieving this position through the unchecked exercise of power, the narrators in the sample see it as being attained through the moral self-control of such power.
> *(Menon and Shweder 1994, p. 73)*

New Capital women would probably not differ significantly with this view, although I expect they would give more credence to the financial contributions of men – and now some women – to the welfare of the family.

As women move into old age, they gradually remove themselves from the daily household chores and focus more on the spiritual dimensions of life. They are likely to spend more time in prayer in the family's *puja* room and at temples and, for those who are literate, in reading the sacred Hindu epics. Several Old Town and New Capital grandmothers reported that reading the *Ramayana* and the *Mahabharata* gave them much pleasure now that they had reared their children and no longer had to be concerned with the daily management of the household. In 1965–67, one Old Town great-grandmother devoted her days to prayer, often with her two-year-old grandson sitting nearby, observing. In 1987, a New Capital mother had begun to fast and meditate regularly at an ashram (a monastery or place for meditation) in a neighboring town. She would be gone for weeks at a time. Such activities not only are personally gratifying, but they add to the moral status of women and enhance the welfare of the family.

There is no single developmental process for women in India any more than there is one for women in the United States. The preceding discussion is meant to be more suggestive than conclusive. However, it is important to identify ways in which Western psychological models are biased toward a particular construction of the individual in contrast to the more traditional Hindu construction of the individual who is embedded within a complex set of hierarchical, gender-segregated family relationships. It is equally important to counter stereotypes of Indian women as passive, depersonalized individuals who are simply fulfilling predetermined roles. However broad and oversimplified, a general depiction of the psychocultural processes relevant to women's lives is useful for understanding the potential impact on them of contemporary change as India moves from a primarily agrarian society to one that is increasingly industrialized and urbanized.

Plate 25. Old Town Brahmin great-grandmother performs morning prayers with great-grandson watching

Conclusion

Bhubaneswar, an ancient temple town and locus of several previous transformations, is once again experiencing dramatic change. As the site of a recently created capital city and a governing part of the new nation-state, India, Bhubaneswar has had to confront modernity in the form of new educational and occupational opportunities, commercialization of the economy, and new democratic ideals. The patrifocal family system, which is embedded in a complex caste system, is being challenged by these and other socioeconomic forces of change. Accordingly, some of its underlying principles, which affect the roles and lives of women, are being transformed.

As previously noted, sociocultural change is neither uniform nor monolithic; it is a complex and sporadic process. India's family system is not, therefore, being transformed from a monolithic pre-

283

industrial extended system to a similarly monolithic "modern" nuclear one. Many family theorists in the West have misjudged the degree of homogeneity produced by industrialization in the West and, therefore, have incorrectly predicted what would happen in other parts of the world as they industrialized.[28] Their overly simplistic view of family transformation has been seriously questioned by the work of recent researchers such as the historian Peter Laslett.[29] Using English parish records, Laslett has demonstrated the statistical salience of the preindustrial nuclear household, thus challenging the assumption that it was a product of industrialization and modernization. Although there has been some controversy surrounding Laslett's interpretation of these data, other research has documented the diversity of family forms existent in both *pre-* and *post*-industrial Europe.[30] In other words, there appears to be no simple causality in the Western world between industrialization and the nuclear family. Furthermore, the nuclear family is not predominant everywhere in the West. What implications might such research have for thinking about contemporary change in India's family and gender systems?

Such research affirms the approach taken in this study – the need to examine systems of family and gender as they are affected, for example, by caste and class or by place of residence. The Hindu patrifocal family has taken a variety of forms through time and space.[31] Because this has been true in the past, one should assume a variety of outcomes as families adapt to present conditions. As Susan Carol Rogers (1991) has theorized:

> Historical change includes processes of sociocultural reproduction, such that large-scale transformative forces are absorbed and shaped to trace variant trajectories. As a result, (cultural) difference over place remains no less salient than (historical) difference over time. The two kinds of difference do not stand in opposition, but are inextricably intertwined. *(P. 35)*

In her analysis of family organization in a rural French community, Rogers has demonstrated the complex interplay between historical forces of change and the ways in which villagers conceptualize and respond to them. By bringing to bear their cultural understandings of what is appropriate and what is possible, Rogers argues, villagers help to shape processes of change. Furthermore, by creatively reworking and redefining their cultural assumptions, they actively participate in the process of transformation. "Persistent (but not inert) structures, pervasive (but not overwhelming) forces, and the willful (but not not unconstrained) acts of individuals are thus interwoven in a kind of moving tapestry" (1991, p. 45).

A "moving tapestry" is an appropriate metaphor for the complex interplay of historical, social, and cultural forces that both affect and are affected by individual actions. The many tiny, interwoven threads of the tapestry are the products of people – men and women acting individually and in groups – creating, reproducing, and transforming social institutions and cultural beliefs. Critical to my understanding of contemporary change in Bhubaneswar, therefore, has been my ability to observe a stable set of people interacting over a significant period of time in one location in India. These people have provided me with insights into how variants of the Hindu patrifocal family system are being reproduced and transformed, and how, accordingly, gender roles and ideology are being affected. The process is not a revolutionary one, but consists of a series of adjustments to changing socioeconomic conditions that, in time, may produce more radical change in some of India's systems of family and gender.

Caste and Class Differences

There is considerable variation by caste and class status in how families respond to change. In the New Capital, for example, a middle class has emerged that is increasingly oriented toward status based upon educational and occupational achievement. A commitment to women's education has become part of the process of change and adaptation among such families – a process that began in a few urban centers a century ago in India and that has now spread to other cities, towns, and some villages. Sending girls to school began largely as a response to the demands of educated men for better educated wives, but, in India's post-Independence democratic culture, it has for some families become an end in itself. It has also become a part of popular culture, which is now available to rural families via television, videos, and cinema.

The emergence of a class system, with a burgeoning middle class, presents a serious challenge to India's widespread caste system, which assigns every individual, as a member of a specific family and extended kinship group, a place in the local and regional social order. For some Indians, change in this well-ordered, hierarchical social world is threatening, whereas for others it means new opportunities.[32] Thus for one of the Old Town Washerman families in my sample, it has entailed new forms of employment and a level of prosperity previously unattainable. Although still categorized as "Washermen," this family can now lead a middle-class life, which for them has involved the education and employment of daughters and daughters-in-law.

New Capital families, by right of their government employment, were already part of a changing system of social stratification. In contrast, most Old Town families have only recently been exposed to this new status system, and their adjustments have been more cautious and measured. Their commitment to the more traditional components of patrifocal family structure and ideology has largely been retained.

For the very poor, life continues to be a struggle. Many poor families are stigmatized by both their caste and class status. For example, government-employed janitors in the New Capital are Sweepers by caste and continue to be so labeled. It is poverty, however, that has the greatest effect upon systems of family and gender. Poverty encourages different family members to cooperate – often regardless of the principles of patrilineality and patrilocality – in whatever way is adaptive. And poverty dictates that most women work outside the home, further stigmatizing them and their families, who cannot seclude them and thereby attain honor according to traditional patrifocal principles. Whether the increased employment of higher-status women will have a significant effect upon this system of honor, and thereby remove some of these stigma on poor families, remains to be seen.

286

Caste, Class, and Gender

The control of women's sexuality still underlies India's caste, now increasingly class, system of social stratification. How to protect girls until the time of marriage is a major consideration for most families, especially if they send their daughters out of the home to school.[33] To arrange suitable marriages for daughters that will affirm, and preferably enhance, a family's status is still a major obligation of parents and extended kin. To succeed in this endeavor requires that a girl have a good reputation. Not only should she be physically attractive, have some education, and personify the characteristics of a good wife and daughter-in-law, but she should be pure. A daughter's controlled sexuality still symbolizes family honor in India, as it once did in Euro-American culture where the bride's purity was symbolized by her wearing of a white dress on her wedding day. In India, systems of caste, class, and gender continue to be inextricably intertwined.

The dowry system further underscores the interconnection of caste, class, and gender. The increased investment in education for sons and their increased employability has raised families' expectations for dowry at the time of marriage. This places a particularly heavy economic burden upon higher-status families with daughters, especially if they are highly educated daughters who require even more highly educated bridegrooms. Susan Wadley (1994, p. 239), in her longitudinal analysis of change in a North Indian village, reports that families in Karimpur worry more about marrying their daughters than about any other issue. So long as dowry remains an integral part of the marriage system, daughters will be perceived as an economic liability, and there will be pressure to restrict their numbers through abortion, infanticide, and neglect.

The sexual control of women, caste and class, and dowry giving are all interconnected phenomena. In her cross-cultural analysis of virginity, Alice Schlegel (1991) has demonstrated that societies that value female virginity are societies that also practice dowry giving or indirect dowry and gift exchange. Dowry is a way of using property to cement family ties at the time of marriage and, potentially, to raise a family's status by having property and/or a title accompany a girl into marriage. In systems of arranged marriage and dowry, families are, therefore, exchanging property for expanded kinship ties and increased social status. Within such a sociocultural system, valuing virginity operates as a mechanism to limit access by social-climbing, lower-status males to girls from high-status, propertied families, thereby forestalling any paternity claims they might make. Accordingly, the girl's dowry and reproductive powers are preserved for a suitable family. Linking virginity with family honor and instilling this value in daughters helps to ensure that the girls will want to act in appropriate ways. However, in a society like India's, in which girls are believed to be highly sexual by nature and internal impulses are believed to require external control, further mechanisms of social control are needed: The movements of sexually mature girls should be restricted and their activities carefully supervised.[34]

The practice of dowry seems to have become heightened, if anything, in contemporary India. There is evidence from Bhubaneswar and other parts of India that the custom is spreading to poorer and lower-status families, some of whom must go into serious debt to finance a daughter's marriage.[35] Beliefs about dowry are changing, however. Almost every family with whom I spoke in Bhubaneswar expressed disapproval of dowry, asserting with respect to their sons that they had made no dowry demands and with respect to their daughters that they wished to avoid dowry. However, there was also evidence that in most cases property had been exchanged at the time of marriage. What people are saying and what they are doing are in conflict. Perhaps, this augurs change.

Directions of Change

Although change in India's family and gender systems will be neither uniform nor monolithic, there is widespread evidence that the principles of age and gender hierarchy and gender segregation are loosening to make way for a more companionate husband-wife relationship and for an increase in female autonomy. Helen Ullrich's (1987, 1994) longitudinal study of Brahmin families in a South Indian village documents dramatic change within the last generation. There, young village women have succeeded in their demands for schooling and for having an active role in the selection of their husbands. They also strongly prefer postmarital residence in nuclear households where they can be independent of in-laws and have a more intimate relationship with their husbands.

Two other longitudinal studies, while not documenting such dramatic change, indicate similar directions of change. In 1975, Leigh Minturn (1993) returned to Khalapur village in North India to interview women from the high-caste Rajput families that she had studied in 1955. She found that purdah observations had decreased, giving women greater autonomy and freedom of movement. Daughters-in-law were, for example, being allowed to visit their natal families more often. In addition, daughters-in-law were less deferential in the presence of parents-in-law and less obedient with mothers-in-law. They were also beginning to establish separate *chulas* (cooking fires) within joint households over which they could cook exclusively for their own husbands and children.

Although older Khalapur women disliked such changes, which threatened their authority, they did not blame the younger women, but explained that it was "God's will." Nonetheless, they did recognize that such change was associated with the increased education of women and the changing attitudes of sons. Expectations for girls' education in Khalapur had jumped from a girl's being able to read and write letters in 1955 to a girl's completing an elementary school education in 1975. Meanwhile, sons had come to desire that their wives be less restricted. According to Minturn, with increased education and economic affluence, sons had grown less cooperative and more desirous of increased personal control within the joint family.

In 1983–84 Susan Wadley returned to Karimpur, a North Indian village that she had studied in the late 1960s and mid-1970s and that had originally been studied by William and Charlotte Wiser (1971) in the 1920s. Wadley (1994) also documents significant educational change for women, which she associates with the easing of purdah restrictions. Not only is schooling a force for change, she argues, but villagers are learning new definitions of kinship and gender roles via television programs and films. One impact is that

289

families are growing more couple-oriented: Young husbands and wives, for example, are demanding their private space within the joint household – a space that is off-limits to mothers-in-law (Wadley 1994, p. 237).

Changes paralleling those in Bhubaneswar have thus been documented in several different regions of India. In Ullrich's South Indian village there has been little resistance to these changes. In the North Indian village of Khalapur, Minturn reports that Rajput villagers are reasonably philosophical about them. Older Khalapur women complain but are successfully adjusting:

> Women retain their essential values while adapting them to changing realities, and manage this transition without serious disruption. Women still function as healthy individuals and families as intact groups.
>
> One expects that the transition to modernism will continue to be made at a pace that does not fracture social bonds or violate basic values. The key customs of purdah are indeed disappearing, but not too rapidly to allow for the building of new customs, based on altered ideas, to take their place.
> *(Minturn 1993, p. 317)*

In contrast, North Indian Karimpur villagers, Wadley reports, perceive change as "increasing disorder" – disorder of the once well-established caste and gender hierarchies.

> Within the family, sons are challenging parental authority, whereas women's demands for equality are muted. Women are neither asking to govern nor declaring the family an irrelevant institution. But as disorder increases, gender control becomes the focus of greater attention. Control of women becomes the symbolic focus of male control in the community. Yet this inward turning to control within the family is itself challenged by women's education and demands to ease purdah restrictions.
> *(Wadley 1994, p. 5)*

It is not surprising that different sets of villagers are conceptualizing change differently and that their responses to changing conditions vary. We should predict a variety of outcomes in family structure and gender roles as different groups confront the forces of modernization. What is striking, however, is the degree of uniformity that these several longitudinal studies document – movement toward the loosening of familial bonds of authority based upon age and gender hierarchies in favor of increased husband-wife intimacy and the relaxation of purdah restrictions on women. The fundamental question then becomes: To what extent will the patrifocal joint family be able to adjust to these kinds of democratizing changes while retaining the general commitment of family members to the well-being of the collective whole? Will India achieve any better solutions to the dilemma faced in Western societies of how to balance the needs of the family, whether extended or nuclear, with the desire to enhance gender equity and provide women as well as men with personal autonomy? As middle- and upper-status Indian women – who have construed themselves as household managers and whose locus of self-esteem has been principally within the domestic realm – move out into the public world, who will assume responsibility for the daily well-being of the family? Will these women be able to rely on the help of husbands, parents-in-law, and other extended kin in caring for children and the elderly, or will the kinds of familial problems faced by working couples in the contemporary United States simply be duplicated in India? Although Western feminism has achieved significant change for women, these kinds of issues remain largely unresolved.[36]

Throughout this book, I have argued that India's family heritage differs significantly from its Western counterparts both in structure and in cultural ideology. These kinds of differences should produce somewhat different adaptations to contemporary modernization, as has happened in Japan. Because it has begun its contemporary transformation of familial roles and relationships from a more sociocentric, less individualistic, basis than American society, Indian society may be able to achieve a better resolution to the dilemmas posed by change. In both societies, the care and well-being of children, who constitute the future, will depend upon finding creative solutions.

Notes

Chapter One. Introduction

1. Initiated in 1961 by Cora Du Bois, then a professor of Anthropology at Harvard University, the project was to examine processes of rapid urbanization and sociocultural change in an Indian town undergoing transformation from an ancient temple town to a modern state capital. Over some twelve years, fourteen Orissan and American graduate students, representing a variety of academic disciplines, undertook research in Bhubaneswar under the guidance of Professor Du Bois. This research has become known as the Harvard-Bhubaneswar Project and has been synthesized in Seymour 1980.
2. Goode 1963 is one of the most notable contemporary social scientists to make this prediction.
3. LeVine et al. 1994, in their comparison of Gusii (African) and middle-class American child care practices, clearly delineate how systems of child care develop to fit other adaptive needs of a population. As fundamental adaptive processes such as subsistence, reproduction, and communication change, so will socialization practices.
4. There are significant exceptions to patrilineal descent in India. In South India, for example, there are caste groups, such as the Nayars (Fuller 1976), that were formerly matrilineal in descent.
5. Mukhopadhyay 1991, in her analysis of family educational decision making, first delineated the complex of family/kinship features referred to here as "patrifocal family structure and ideology" and which we used in our coauthored and coedited volume, *Women, Education, and Family Structure in India*, 1994. Bennett 1983 describes a similar phenomenon for high-caste Chetri families in Nepal.
6. See, for example, Burton et al. 1992. They propose a "Middle Old World" culture area, comprising North Africa, the Middle East, South Asia, and China, which has all these features.

7. See the "Theoretical Introduction" in Mukhopadhyay and Seymour 1994.
8. Manisha Roy 1972 makes this point in her study of middle-class, urban women in Calcutta, *Bengali Women*. The relevance of familial roles to the psychocultural development of Indian women will be discussed at greater length in Chapter 8.
9. Two popularized accounts of women's lives in India are Bumiller 1990 and Mitter 1991. Several excellent ethnographies are Jeffery 1979; Jeffery, Jeffery, and Lyon 1989; and Sharma 1980. Two recent books from longitudinal studies of villages in North India address changes in women's lives: Minturn 1992 and Wadley 1994. Minturn's book, however, is based upon just one return visit, in 1975, to Khalapur village where she originally studied child-rearing practices in 1955. Wadley's study is concerned with broad socioeconomic changes in Karimpur village and is not focused upon issues of family or gender, specifically. Wadley's most recent visit to Karimpur was in 1983–84. Some results of these two studies will be compared with those from Bhubaneswar in Chapter 8.
10. As a Western woman, however, I was never restricted to the world of women. I could and did interact with the male members of households, many of whom took an interest in my research.
11. An important distinction is that between "household" and "family." In this book, I shall use the term "household" to mean those members of a family residing under one roof who usually share food and other goods, who usually cook together, and who cooperate in child care. The term "family" refers to extended kin who may not necessarily reside together but who consider one another family. See Gray and Mearns 1989 for a discussion of households in different parts of South and Southeast Asia.
12. See D. M. Miller and Wertz 1976.
13. Mitra 1961, vol. 2, p. 113.
14. Miller and Wertz 1976.
15. Mitra 1961, vol. 2, pp. 99 and 101.
16. According to Miller and Wertz 1976, p. 7, the temple's full name is Lingaraja Mahaprabhu Temple, but it was originally called Tribhuvaneshvara (Lord of the Three Worlds) Temple, an epithet of Shiva from which Bhubaneswar gets its name. The temple houses a large stone, eight feet in diameter, that is believed to possess very sacred powers as the lingam of the god Shiva.
17. Quoted in Grenell 1980, p. 35.
18. Grenell, 1980, p. 34.

19. See, for example, Rudolph and Rudolph 1967; Singer 1972; and Seymour 1980.

Chapter Two. Field Methods and Longitudinal Research in Bhubaneswar

1. Language instruction in Oriya was established especially for me and two colleagues by D. P. Patnaik, then the director of the Advanced Center of Linguistics in Poona, Maharashtra state. G. N. Dash, now Reader in Linguistics at Berhampur University in Orissa, was our language instructor.
2. For reviews of the extensive literature on caste, see Kolenda 1985 and Seymour 1996.
3. For example, one of Professor Du Bois's Indian doctoral students – Manamohan Mahapatra – resided in the Old Town and had recorded the different *jatis* residing there. Drawing on his knowledge and some introductions from him, I was able to meet and select from a variety of Old Town families. See Mahapatra 1981 for additional information on Old Town temple families.
4. The civil service hierarchy, with names and salaries, is a public document that I was able to examine and thus determine peoples' relative status.
5. For analyses of sex disparities in North India, see B. D. Miller 1981 and Freed and Freed 1989.
6. See LeVine et al. 1994 for an analytic framework for examining child care practices in relationship to other population-specific characteristics.
7. Naturalistic behavior observations of children and their caretakers were based upon the techniques developed by Beatrice B. and John W. M. Whiting for the Six Culture Study. See B. B. Whiting 1963 and J. W. M. Whiting, Child, and Lambert 1966.
8. See Minturn and Hitchcock 1966 and Minturn and Lambert 1964.

Chapter Three. The Patrifocal Family: Growing Up Female in the Old Town

1. See Bennett 1983, L. Dube 1988, Fruzetti 1982, Mandelbaum 1988, and Schlegel 1991. The relationship of female chastity to family honor is more fully developed in Chapter 8.
2. There is an extensive anthropological literature on how many spheres of activity are genderized in different societies, with women being

associated with the domestic or private sphere and men with the less domestic or public sphere. (See Rosaldo 1974 for an early theoretical discussion, Moore 1988 for a more recent review, and Dubisch 1986 for excellent comparative materials from Greece.) In much of the Muslim and Hindu world, not only are women associated with the domestic sphere, but they are often relegated to it, as is reflected in the practice of purdah (seclusion). This seclusion of women is, in turn, associated with family status and honor. (See Mandelbaum 1988 for a good synthesis of this process for South Asian societies.)

3. See, for example, the extensive case study by Freed and Freed 1985.

4. Jacobson 1970 (p. 485) argues that respect-avoidance relationships between a daughter-in-law and the elder males of her conjugal household function as a distancing technique in "situations of ambivalence, ambiguity and imminence of role conflict" – that is, in the introduction of a new affinal woman into the patrifocal family. They also reduce potential sexual conflict among adult male kin over the new female member of the household. In this age-stratified, hierarchical setting, however, a husband's *younger* brothers are not considered part of the respect-avoidance relationships for a new bride/daughter-in-law. In fact, they are allowed a relaxed and familiar relationship with her – a joking relationship. Radcliffe-Brown (1950, 1952) early on recognized the reciprocal nature of avoidance and joking relationships in his analysis of African kinship systems.

5. There are actually two schools of family law that influence contemporary tradition and practice with respect to the division of property. They are derived from two medieval legal texts, *Mitaksara* and *Dayabhaga* (Basham 1954, pp. 156–158). According to the former, sons and grandsons have rights in family property before the death of the paterfamilias, whereas according to the latter, sons obtain rights to property only upon the death of the father. In Orissa, Bengal, and Assam the division of property has tended to follow the Dayabhaga school of inheritance.

6. Female seclusion and the sexual division of labor and space within the household result in women spending their time primarily with other women. Karlekar 1991 (p. 61), in her examination of nineteenth-century Bengali women's narratives, writes: "Early experiences after marriage, in the personal narratives of women, rarely mention husbands or older male in-laws: it was the unwritten law of the *antahpur* [women's quarters] which dominated their existence."

7. See, for example, Kurtz 1992, Roland 1988, and Trawick 1992. A more theoretical discussion of this issue is found in Chapter 8.

8. Within Hinduism all life transitions are marked by temporary and personal pollution requiring separation and ritual purification. In addition, all people are subject to daily pollution from the bodily emissions of others, that is, from others' secretions and excretions, including menstrual blood. Childbirth produces perhaps the most dramatic emission. Mother and child are therefore secluded from others for a specified period until they can be properly purified and then returned to the household's daily routine. Pollution has to do with the sanctity of life, of the family, and of the temple. One should be cleansed of any pollution before entering into the everyday life of the household just as one would bathe before entering the temple or family *puja* room. (See Shweder 1985 for a discussion of how pollution is conceptualized by Old Town Brahmins.)

9. See Chapter 8 for a discussion of such events as a married son's leaving his father's household without permission.

10. LeVine et al. 1994, in their analysis of African child care practices, have clearly and elegantly articulated these goals of the ethnographer to formulate the cultural model of early child care that constitutes the premises in use by caretakers at any given moment in a society's history. They suggest that such a model has three parts: a moral direction, a pragmatic design, and a set of conventional scripts for action. "This is the cultural software driving parental behavior" (p. 248).

11. On the basis of textual data and psychoanalytic interviews both Kakar 1981 and Roland 1988 have argued that Indian mothers devote themselves to their infants and that infancy is, therefore, a time of total indulgence for the young child. My naturalistic behavior observations of parents and children in Bhubaneswar families, as well as the child-rearing research of others, do not support this generalization. See Kurtz 1992 for a good synthesis of the child-rearing literature.

12. LeVine et al. 1994 cite evidence that the tactile and kinesthetic stimulation of a massage promotes weight gain and metabolic efficiency during infancy.

13. Intermittent or irregular reinforcement encourages the child to keep asking for her mother's breast or other sources of satisfaction. Others have also noted how the mother's intermittent responsiveness to young children sets up a pattern of bargaining or persistent request between mother and child (e.g., Beals 1962; Maduro 1976; Minturn and Hitchcock 1966; and Trawick 1992).

14. Kurtz 1992 theorizes that this is a means by which any exclusive mother-child pair-bond is kept contained so that the child is forced to look to the extended family for satisfaction. Trawick 1992 similarly

297

argues that a mother's love for her child must be kept contained and hidden so that exclusive pair-bonds are negated and the individual looks to the larger group for love.

15. See Seymour 1983 for a fuller account of the diffusion of affect among Old Town family members. Munroe and Munroe 1994, in their cross-cultural analysis of human development, also address this topic.

16. As Munroe and Munroe 1994 point out, a focus upon the "self" and the cultivation of a "self-orientation" is relatively recent in Western history, and in many comparative studies it differentiates American society from smaller, traditional societies. In the Six Cultures Study (B. B. Whiting and J. W. M. Whiting 1975), for example, American children scored 40 percent higher than the children of any other society on seeking attention, seeking dominance, and seeking help.

17. The focus on teaching Indian children kinship terms has been noted by a number of researchers. See, for example, Beals 1962 (p. 21); S. C. Dube 1955 (p. 193); Luschinsky 1962 (p. 167); Minturn and Hitchcock 1966 (p. 132); Nichter and Nichter 1987 (p. 73); and Trawick 1992 (p. 157).

18. See Abbott 1992 for a review of the cross-cultural literature on co-sleeping as well as evidence from the United States. Mother-infant co-sleeping seems to have been the pancultural human pattern for most of human history and may help to protect infants against breathing irregularities that can lead to sudden infant death (e.g., Konner 1981; Konner and Super 1987; McKenna 1986, p. 48).

19. See references in note 13 to others' discussions of teasing behavior with children.

20. Kurtz 1992 emphasizes the importance of renunciation in Hindu culture and personality; Trawick 1992 addresses the importance of containing and hiding such love; and Derné 1994b addresses the ways in which Hindu men view Western-style romantic love as dangerous to the well-being of the joint family. This topic is developed further in Chapter 8.

21. Roland 1988 (p. 236) uses the term "emotional relatedness" and compares "the dominant themes of American early child rearing around self–other differentiation, autonomy, and individuation" with the Indian emphasis upon "we-ness, affective exchange, and empathic sensitivity." The one, he argues, leads to an emphasis upon separation of the American adolescent from her family, whereas the other produces an adolescent who "remains a highly interdependent part of the extended family."

22. See Basham 1954 (pp. 158–177) and Kakar 1981 for a fuller discussion of the Hindu life stages for males and of the Sacred Thread or Twice-Born ceremony for upper-status boys in particular.

23. Wadley 1980 addresses the generally more overt celebration of female puberty in South India than in North India. L. Dube 1988 (pp. 172–174) also asserts that in North India a girl's first menstruation is less marked than in South India. Nonetheless, it is recognized as a significant moment of transition in a girl's life. See Bennett 1983 (pp. 234–246) for a fuller description of menarche rites for upper-caste girls in a Nepali village.

24. See Bennett 1983 and Ferro-Luzzi 1974 for fuller descriptions of menstrual practices and pollution concepts in South Asia.

25. Bennett 1983, L. Dube 1988, and Wadley 1980 all make similar connections between society's concern with controlling women's sexuality and the handling of menstruation.

26. In her analysis of upper-status Bengali women, Manisha Roy 1972 emphasizes the significance of different roles to the psychocultural development of Indian women.

27. See Kakar 1981 and O'Flaherty 1980.

28. This does not mean that women are unable to find ways within this patrifocal system to express resistance to and critiques of those parts of the system which they find constraining, difficult, or unfair. Raheja and Gold 1994 have documented how some North Indian village women express themselves through songs and other oral traditions.

Chapter Four. Variations and Transitions: Being a Wife, Mother, and Daughter in the New Capital

1. For a historical perspective on this phenomenon, see Chapters 1 and 2 by Karuna Chanana and Malavika Karlekar, respectively, in Mukhopadhyay and Seymour 1994.

2. For a fuller account, see Sable 1977.

3. The horizontal movement of literate castes has been noted by Sable 1980 and Freeman 1977.

4. Mukhopadhyay and Seymour 1994 point out that often Indian families that are structurally nuclear should be construed as "joint" because of their shared economic resources with extended kin and because of their commitment to the larger unit. Joint family members may not always be able to reside together, but they visit one another for extended periods of time, send their children to reside with relatives for educational purposes, and ritually celebrate their "jointness." Regardless of household structure, children grow up thinking of themselves as part of an extended family unit.

5. See Seymour 1975a.

6. See Seymour 1975b.

7. See Seymour 1983.

8. An increased reliance on verbal interaction by mothers with their infants and young children has been found to be strongly associated with maternal schooling (LeVine et al. 1994; Richman, Miller, and LeVine 1992). Thus, the behavior of New Capital middle- and upper-status mothers is consistent with an observed cross-cultural pattern of maternal responsiveness.

9. This refers to Margaret Mead's discussion of North American child-rearing practices in the film *Four Families*, produced by Ian MacNeill and Guy Glover in 1959.

Chapter Five. Caste/Class and Gender: To Be Poor and Female

1. Kolenda 1987 (chaps. 1 and 2) has examined factors associated with joint family households in India. Although there is not a clear correlation between caste rank and proportions of joint households, she did find that joint households were least characteristic of local Untouchable *jatis* (p. 77). She found no clear association of joint households with land ownership, suggesting that other factors contribute to whether or not joint households predominate in a particular caste group or region. In Bhubaneswar, many poor, low-caste families found it useful to pool such resources as they had. For example, joint households permitted most adult women to work outside the home, an economic incentive, while one or two remained home to care for children.

2. In their analysis of children's behavior in the Six Culture Study, B. B. and J. W. M. Whiting 1975 identified the mother's workload as a critical factor. In societies where they have heavy workloads, mothers assign more chores to their children, and the children exhibit more responsible behavior. Also, see Seymour 1988 for an analysis of intracultural variation with respect to this phenomenon.

3. Sable (1977, 1980), in his analysis of educational attrition and caste/class status, found that the primary-school attrition rates of low-caste boys in Bhubaneswar were three to four times those of high-caste boys and averaged 69.4%. If analyzed according to father's occupation, they averaged 64.9% for boys with fathers who had low-level occupations. My data indicate similar attrition for boys, whereas poor, low-status girls rarely attended school.

4. See Liddle and Joshi 1986 and Mandelbaum 1988 for good syntheses of this literature.

5. Srinivas 1966 introduced the term "Sanskritization" to refer to the process of sociocultural change in India by which lower-status Hindus adopt the customs, ritual, and ideology of higher-status ones. Srinivas

argues, however, that British rule introduced a new status group to emulate, leading to Westernization and secularization among some high-status groups. He tries to delineate the complex interweaving of these processes in modern India.

Chapter Six. Going Out to School: Women's Changing Roles and Aspirations

1. Women in India tend to enter the "pure" sciences, such as physics, chemistry, and biology. These fields are considered to be less prestigious and male-oriented than applied sciences such as engineering. See Mukhopadhyay 1994 on this phenomenon.
2. See Sable 1977 and 1980.
3. See chapters by Chanana and Karlekar in Mukhopadhyay and Seymour 1994 for a fuller discussion of the early education of women in India. For Orissa's slow economic growth and its slow development of a Western-style school system, see Basu 1974, Maloney 1974, and Rudolph and Rudolph 1972.
4. See Sable 1977 for a fuller discussion of educational institutions in Bhubaneswar.
5. Following British practice, the Indian government keeps a schedule (list) of low-status Untouchable castes and tribal groups so that they can be easily identified and receive special educational incentives and other government benefits.
6. See Papanek 1989 on this phenomenon.
7. In 1987 I collected some of the women's magazines that were available in Bhubaneswar. For example, *Femina*, a *Times of India* publication, contained articles on topics that ranged from Indian movie stars, child care, and household equipment to women's health concerns, feminist poets, and running one's own business. Other magazines, such as *Savvy*, were more clearly directed toward full-time wives and mothers who needed entertainment and advice about sex, child care, and so forth. A full examination of the literature directed toward women in Bhubaneswar would make an interesting study in itself.

Chapter Seven. Change and Continuity in Women's Lives: A Three-Generational Perspective

1. There is evidence that family expenditures on daughters' dowries have been increasing despite the central government's efforts to curtail them. See figures in the Indian feminist journal *Manushi* in an article by Kishwar 1993. For a rural setting, see Minturn 1992 (pp. 118–120). In her 1975

restudy of Khalapur village in North India, Minturn found that among high-status Rajput families dowries had increased in both the number and the value of goods that a daughter took with her at the time of marriage.

2. The employment of middle- and upper-status women is still viewed ambiguously in much of India (Liddle and Joshi 1986), although there is some evidence that some families are beginning to value their daughters' earning power (Blumberg and Dwaraki 1980; Sharma 1986). Although some young men are beginning to desire employable wives, their families do not see a daughter-in-law's earning power as a substitute for dowry. A family's investment in their son's education and employability is still what tends to drive demands for dowry. Therefore, the more educated a daughter, the more educated the husband that must be found for her and the higher the potential demand for dowry by his family. Since a daughter's employability is associated with her level of education, this means that the more employable she is the greater the chance her marriage will require a sizable dowry.

3. See Goody 1973 and 1990 for an elaborate delineation of this argument. There is, however, some evidence of increased control of dowry goods, particularly jewelry, by wives (Government of India 1974; Minturn 1993).

4. Mrs. Das's family comes from a region of southern Orissa and northern Andhra Pradesh where village endogamy is often practiced and where the preferred marriage is between a son and his mother's brother's daughter. Close ties between brother and sister are maintained, and women tend to have higher status than in North India. See Kolenda 1987, Mandelbaum 1970, and Nuckolls 1993.

5. See Basham 1954 and Mandelbaum 1970.

6. See references in note 4.

7. See B. D. Miller 1981 and Freed and Freed 1989.

8. Ullrich 1992, for example, has found in her longitudinal study of Havik Brahmin women in a South Indian village that menstrual taboos have decreased over a twenty-year period as women's educational opportunities have changed. Simultaneously, women's age at the time of marriage has increased together with their control over the choice of marriage partner. Ullrich argues that Havik Brahmin women's roles have changed from that of primarily progenitor to that of companionate wife.

9. See Apffel-Marglin 1994, p. 32.

Chapter Eight. Systems of Family and Gender in Transition

1. Kurtz 1992 reviews in detail the child-rearing literature for different regions of India – Northwest India, East India, and South India. His

review includes studies whose principal focus is child rearing (e.g., Minturn and Hitchcock 1966; Poffenberger 1981; Rohner and Chaki-Sircar 1988; Seymour 1971, 1975b, 1976, 1983), insightful observations by anthropologists not primarily interested in child rearing (e.g., Beals 1962; S. C. Dube 1955; Mencher 1963; Wiser and Wiser 1971), and studies that focus less systematically on child-rearing practices but offer numerous insights into family dynamics (e.g., Luschinsky 1962; Maduro 1976; Trawick 1992). Other studies that address child rearing in India are Freed and Freed 1981 and Poffenberger 1976.

2. See, for example, the work of Lutz 1988 and Riesman 1992; for India, the work of Daniel 1984, Derné 1992, Kakar 1981, Kurtz 1992, Marriott 1988, Roland 1988, Shweder 1985, and Trawick 1992. For cross-cultural research, see the analysis of children's behavior from the Six Cultures Study by J. W. M. Whiting and Whiting 1973 and B. B. Whiting and Whiting 1975. In a recent cultural psychology text Matsumoto 1994 addresses two different construals of the self – the "independent" and the "interdependent."

3. For reviews of these two types of societies with contrasting self-concepts, see Markus and Kitayama 1991 and Triandis 1993.

4. Spiro 1993 has effectively argued this point.

5. Roland 1988 (p. 64) discusses the "private self" that Indians keep "beneath the observance of an overt etiquette of deference, loyalty, and subordination." Ewing 1991 has made a similar point for Pakistani women, using the concept "intrapsychic autonomy."

6. Triandis 1993 has recently made this point.

7. See Kurtz 1992, 1993.

8. See Kurtz 1992, 1993, and Derné 1992, 1994a.

9. Kurtz 1992 has made extensive use of my child-rearing observations to support his thesis regarding an Indian collective identity.

10. See Bellah et al. 1985, Berger, Berger, and Kellner 1973, Durkheim 1949, Kluckhohn and Strodtbeck 1961, Toennies 1957, Turner 1976, and Weber 1947.

11. Triandis 1993 summarizes the factors that are correlated with individualistic versus collectivist societies.

12. See Iwao 1993.

13. These results for Bhubaneswar are corroborated by three other longitudinal studies of Indian villages: Minturn 1993, Ullrich 1994, and Wadley 1994.

14. See Chodorow 1978 and Gilligan 1982.

15. See Trawick 1992 (p. 93).

16. See Derné 1994a. Nonetheless, it is important to note that India has a long tradition of poetry, literature, and art that expresses romantic love,

and Wadley 1994 has documented women's songs that also speak of husband-wife romantic love.

17. Also see Ullrich 1994.
18. This point has recently been well argued by Raheja and Gold 1994 in their analysis of North Indian women's songs and stories that challenge many principles of patrifocal family and gender.
19. See, for example, Minturn 1993 (chap. 9), O'Flaherty 1980, and Wadley 1980, 1994 (chap. 2).
20. Feminist analyses of Judeo-Christian religion and patriarchy as compared with Hinduism make this point. See, for example, Gross 1989.
21. See Bennett 1983, Liddle and Joshi 1986, and Wadley 1980, 1994.
22. See Mukhopadhyay and Seymour 1994 and Raheja and Gold 1994.
23. See Brown and Gilligan 1992 and Gilligan 1982.
24. Also see Roland 1988.
25. See Menon 1994 and 1995.
26. See Kakar 1981.
27. See Wadley 1994 (pp. 40–41).
28. See Goode 1963, Le Play 1871, and Shorter 1975.
29. See Laslett 1965 and Laslett and Wall 1972.
30. See Rogers 1991 (pp. 39–41) for a review of this literature.
31. See Kolenda 1987.
32. See Wadley 1994.
33. See Mukhopadhyay and Seymour 1994.
34. Although this is a widely found view in India – from religious texts to popular cinema – it is principally a male view. When one listens to women's voices, as in this book, one finds that it is not, in the women's view, their own sexual urges that must be guarded against, but the unwanted attentions of men and the disapproval of society if the women are too much in the public domain.
35. The adoption of dowry by low-status castes as they increasingly emulate high-status castes is part of what Srinivas 1966 has referred to as "Sanskritization" – efforts to move up the caste hierarchy by adopting the practices of higher-status groups.
36. The dilemma of how to balance family needs, especially those of children, with some degree of personal autonomy has been the subject of much feminist discourse in the United States, India, and more generally. For the United States, see two excellent anthologies: Dornbusch and Strober 1988 (especially, the chapter by Skold) and Thorne and Yalom 1982.

References

Abbott, Susan. 1992. Holding On and Pushing Away: Comparative Perspectives on an Eastern Kentucky Child-Rearing Practice. *Ethos* 20 (1): 33–65.

Apffel-Marglin, Frederique. 1994. The Sacred Grove. *Manushi: A Journal about Women and Society,* no. 28: 22–32.

Aquino, Belinda A. 1985. Feminism across Cultures. In Madeleine J. Goodman (ed.), *Women in Asia and the Pacific: Towards an East-West Dialogue.* Pp. 317–351. Honolulu: University of Hawaii Press.

Basham, A. L. 1954. *The Wonder That Was India: A Survey of the Culture of the Indian Sub-Continent before the Coming of the Muslims.* New York: Grove Press.

Basu, Aparna. 1974. *The Growth of Education and Political Development in India, 1898–1920.* Delhi: Oxford University Press.

Beals, Alan R. 1962. *Gopalpur: A South Indian Village.* New York: Holt, Rinehart and Winston.

Bellah, Robert N., Richard Madsen, William N. Sullivan, Ann Swidler, and Steven M. Tipton. 1985. *Habits of the Heart: Individualism and Commitment in American Life.* Berkeley: University of California Press.

Bennett, Lynn. 1983. *Dangerous Wives and Sacred Sisters: Social and Symbolic Roles of High-Caste Women in Nepal.* New York: Columbia University Press.

Berger, Peter L., Brigitte Berger, and Hansfried Kellner. 1973. *The Homeless Mind: Modernization and Consciousness.* New York: Random House.

Blumberg, Rhoda G., and Leela Dwaraki. 1980. *India's Educated Women: Options and Constraints.* New Delhi: Hindustan Publishing Corporation.

Brown, Lyn Mikel, and Carol Gilligan. 1992. *Meeting at the Crossroads: Women's Psychology and Girls' Development.* Cambridge: Harvard University Press.

305

References

Bumiller, Elisabeth. 1990. *May You Be the Mother of a Hundred Sons.* New York: Random House.

Burton, Michael L., C. C. Moore, J. W. M. Whiting, and A. K. Romney. 1992. World Cultural Regions. Unpublished paper presented at the annual meeting of the Society for Cross-Cultural Research, Santa Fe, New Mexico.

Chanana, Karuna. 1994. Social Change or Social Reform: Women, Education, and Family in Pre-Independence India. In Carol Chapnick Mukhopadhyay and Susan Seymour (eds.), *Women, Education, and Family Structure in India.* Pp. 37–57. Boulder: Westview Press.

Chodorow, Nancy. 1978. *The Reproduction of Mothering.* Berkeley: University of California Press.

Daniel, E. Valentine. 1984. *Fluid Signs: Being a Person in the Tamil Way.* Berkeley: University of California Press.

Dash, G. N. 1978. The Evolution of Priestly Power: The Gangavamsa Period. In Anncharlott Eschmann, Hermann Kulke, and Gaya Charan Tripathi (eds.), *The Cult of Jagannath and the Regional Tradition of Orissa.* Pp. 157–168. New Delhi: Manohar Publications.

Davis, Susan Schaefer. 1994. Keeping Our Voices: Moroccan Girls Growing Up. Unpublished paper presented at the annual meeting of the Society for Cross-Cultural Research, Santa Fe, New Mexico.

Derné, Steve. 1992. Beyond Institutional and Impulsive Conceptions of Self: Family Structure and the Socially Anchored Real Self. *Ethos* 20: 259–288.

⸻ 1994a. Structural Realities, Persistent Dilemmas, and the Construction of Emotional Paradigms: Love in Three Cultures. In William Wentworth and John Ryan (eds.), *Social Perspectives on Emotion.* Vol. 2: 281–308. Greenwich, CT: JAI Press.

⸻ 1994b. Arranging Marriages: How Fathers' Concerns Limit Women's Educational Achievements. In Carol Chapnick Mukhopadhyay and Susan Seymour (eds.), *Women, Education, and Family Structure in India.* Pp. 83–101. Boulder: Westview Press.

⸻ 1994c. Hindu Men Talk about Controlling Women: Cultural Ideas as a Tool of the Powerful. *Sociological Perspectives* 37: 203–227.

⸻ 1995. *Culture in Action: Family Life, Emotion, and Male Dominance in Banaras, India.* Albany: State University of New York Press.

Dornbusch, Sanford M., and Myra H. Strober (eds.). 1988. *Feminism, Children, and the New Families.* New York: Guilford Press.

Dube, Leela. 1988. Socialisation of Hindu Girls in Patrilineal India. In Karuna Chanana (ed.), *Socialisation, Education, and Women: Explorations in Gender Identity.* Pp. 166–192. New Delhi: Orient Longman.

Dube, S. C. 1955. *Indian Village.* London: Routledge and Kegan Paul.

Dubisch, Jill (ed.). 1986. *Gender and Power in Rural Greece*. Princeton: Princeton University Press.

Durkheim, Emile. 1949. *The Division of Labor in Society*. Glencoe, IL: Free Press.

Ewing, Katherine. 1991. Can Psychoanalytic Theories Explain the Pakistani Woman?: Intrapsychic Autonomy and Interpersonal Engagement in the Extended Family. *Ethos* 19: 131–160.

Ferro-Luzzi, G. E. 1974. Women's Pollution Periods in Tamiland. *Anthropos* 69: 113–161.

Freed, Ruth S., and Stanley A. Freed. 1968. Family Background and Occupational Goals of School Children of the Union Territory of Delhi, India. *American Museum Novitates*, no. 2348, pp. 1–39.

    1980. *Rites of Passage in Shanti Nagar*. New York: Anthropological Papers of The American Museum of Natural History, vol. 56 (3), pp. 323–554.

    1981. *Enculturation and Education in Shanti Nagar*. New York: Anthropological Papers of The American Museum of Natural History, vol. 57 (2), pp. 49–156.

    1982. Changing Family Types in India. *Ethnology* 21 (3): 189–202.

    1985. *The Psychomedical Case History of a Low-Caste Woman of North India*. New York: Anthropological Papers of The American Museum of Natural History, vol. 60 (2), pp. 101–228.

    1989. Beliefs and Practices Resulting in Female Deaths and Fewer Females than Males in India. *Population and Environment* 10 (3): 144–161.

Freeman, James M. 1977. *Scarcity and Opportunity in an Indian Village*. Menlo Park, CA: Cummings Publishing Company.

Fruzetti, Lina. 1982. *The Gift of a Virgin: Women, Marriage, and Ritual in Bengal*. New Brunswick: Rutgers University Press.

Fuller, C. J. 1976. *The Nayars Today*. Cambridge: Cambridge University Press.

Gilligan, Carol. 1982. *In a Different Voice: Psychological Theory and Women's Development*. Cambridge: Harvard University Press.

Goode, William J. 1963. *World Revolution and Family Patterns*. New York: Free Press.

Goody, Jack. 1973. Bridewealth and Dowry in Africa and East Eurasia. In Jack Goody and S. J. Tambiah (eds.), *Bridewealth and Dowry*. Pp. 1–58. Cambridge: Cambridge University Press.

    1990: *The Oriental, the Ancient, and the Primitive: Systems of Marriage and the Family in the Pre-Industrial Societies of Eurasia*. Cambridge: Cambridge University Press.

Government of India. 1974. *Towards Equality*.

References

Gray, John N., and David J. Mearns. 1989. *Society from the Inside Out: Anthropological Perspectives on the South Asian Household*. New Delhi: Sage Publications.

Grenell, Peter. 1980. Planning the New Capital of Bhubaneswar. In Susan Seymour (ed.), *The Transformation of a Sacred Town: Bhubaneswar, India*. Pp. 31–66. Boulder: Westview Press.

Gross, Rita M. 1989. Hindu Female Deities as a Resource for the Contemporary Rediscovery of the Goddess. In Carl Olson (ed.), *The Book of the Goddess: Past and Present*. Pp. 217–230. New York: Crossroad.

Iwao, Sumiko. 1993. *The Japanese Woman: Traditional Image and Changing Reality*. New York: Free Press.

Jacobson, Doranne. 1970. Hindu and Muslim Purdah in a Central Indian Village. Ph.D. diss., Columbia University.

Jacobson, Doranne, and Susan S. Wadley. 1977. *Women in India: Two Perspectives*. New Delhi: Monohar.

Jeffery, Patricia. 1979. *Frogs in a Well: Indian Women in Purdah*. London: Zed Books.

Jeffery, Patricia, Roger Jeffery, and Andrew Lyon. 1989. *Labour Pains and Labour Power*. London: Zed Books.

Kakar, Sudhir. 1981. *The Inner World: A Psycho-analytic Study of Childhood and Society in India*. 2d ed. Delhi: Oxford University Press.

Karlekar, Malavika. 1991. *Voices from Within: Early Personal Narratives of Bengali Women*. Delhi: Oxford University Press.

—— 1994. Woman's Nature and Access to Education in Bengal. In Carol Chapnick Mukhopadhyay and Susan Seymour (eds.), *Women, Education, and Family Structure*. Pp. 59–81. Boulder: Westview Press.

Kishwar, Madhu. 1993. Dowry Calculations. *Manushi: A Journal about Women and Society*, no. 78, pp. 8–17.

Kluckhohn, Clyde, and Frederick Strodtbeck. 1961. *Variations in Value Orientations*. Evanston, IL: Row Peterson.

Kolenda, Pauline. 1985. *Caste in Contemporary India: Beyond Organic Solidarity*. Prospect Heights, IL: Waveland Press.

—— 1987. *Regional Differences in Family Structure in India*. Jaipur: Rawat Publications.

Konner, Melvin J. 1981. Evolution of Human Behavior Development. In Ruth H. Munroe, R. L. Munroe, and Beatrice B. Whiting (eds.), *Handbook of Cross-Cultural Human Development*. Pp. 3–52. New York: Garland.

Konner, Melvin J., and Charles Super. 1987. Sudden Infant Death Syndrome: An Anthropological Hypothesis. In C. Super (ed.), *The Role of Culture in Developmental Disorder*. Pp. 95–108. New York: Academic Press.

References

Kurtz, Stanley. 1992. *All the Mothers Are One: Hindu India and the Cultural Reshaping of Psychoanalysis*. New York: Columbia University Press.

1993. Toward a Cultural Psychoanalysis: Reflection on *All the Mothers Are One*. Paper presented for the panel "Psychoanalytic Relativism: Oxymoron or Truism?" at the Third Biennial Meeting of the Society for Psychological Anthropology, Montreal.

Laslett, Peter. 1965. *The World We Have Lost*. New York: Scribner's.

Laslett, Peter, and Richard Wall (eds.). 1972. *Household and Family in Past Time: Comparative Studies in the Size and Structure of the Domestic Group over the Last Three Centuries in England, France, Serbia, Japan, and Colonial North America*. Cambridge: Cambridge University Press.

Le Play, Frederic. 1871. *L'organisation de la Famille: Selon le Vrai Modele Signale par L'histoire de Toutes Les Races et de Tous Les Temps*. Paris: Tequi.

LeVine, Robert A., Suzanne Dixon, Sarah LeVine, Amy Richman, P. Herbert Leiderman, Constance H. Keefer, and T. Barry Brazelton.

1994. *Child Care and Culture: Lessons from Africa*. Cambridge: Cambridge University Press.

Liddle, Joanna, and Rama Joshi. 1986. *Daughters of Independence: Gender, Caste, and Class in India*. New Brunswick: Rutgers University Press.

Luschinsky, Mildred Troop. 1962. The Life of Women in a Village of North India: A Study of Role and Status. Ph.D. diss., Cornell University.

Lutz, Catherine. 1988. *Unnatural Emotions: Everyday Sentiments on a Micronesian Atoll and Their Challenge to Western Theory*. Chicago: University of Chicago Press.

Maduro, Renaldo. 1976. *Artistic Creativity in a Brahmin Painter Community*. Berkeley: Center for South and Southeast Asia Studies, University of California.

Mahapatra, Manamohan. 1981. *Traditional Structure and Change in an Orissan Temple*. Calcutta: Punthi Pustak.

Maloney, Clarence. 1974. *Peoples of South Asia*. New York: Holt, Rinehart, and Winston.

Mandelbaum, David G. 1988. *Women's Seclusion and Men's Honor: Sex Roles in North India, Bangladesh, and Pakistan*. Tucson: University of Arizona Press.

Markus, Hazel Rose, and Shinobu Kitayama. 1991. Culture and the Self: Implications for Cognition, Emotion, and Motivation. *Psychological Review* 98 (2): 244–253.

Marriott, McKim. 1989. Constructing an Indian Ethnosociology. *Contributions to Indian Sociology*, n.s. 23: 1–40.

References

Matsumoto, David. 1994. *People: Psychology from a Cultural Perspective*. Pacific Grove, CA: Brooks/Cole Publishing Company.

McKenna, James J. 1986. An Anthropological Perspective on the Sudden Infant Death Syndrome (SIDS): The Role of Parental Breathing Cues and Speech Breathing Adaptations. *Medical Anthropology* 10: 9–53.

Mencher, Joan. 1963. Growing Up in South Malabar. *Human Organization* 22: 54–65.

Menon, Usha. 1994. Women's Representations of Midlife: What It Means To Be a Middle-Aged Woman in an Oriya Joint Family. Unpublished paper presented at the annual meeting of the Society for Cross-Cultural Research, Santa Fe, New Mexico.

_____ 1995. Receiving and Giving: Distributivity as the Source of Women's Wellbeing. Ph.D. diss., The University of Chicago.

Menon, Usha, and Richard A. Shweder. 1994. Kali's Tongue: Cultural Psychology and the Power of "Shame" in Orissa, India. In Shinobu Kitayama and Hazel Markus (eds.), *Emotion and Culture: Empirical Studies of Mutual Influence*. Pp. 241–284. Washington, DC: APA Books.

Miller, Barbara D. 1981. *The Endangered Sex*. Ithaca: Cornell University Press.

Miller, David M., and Dorothy C. Wertz. 1976. *Hindu Monastic Life: The Monks and Monasteries of Bhubaneswar*. Montreal: McGill-Queen's University Press.

Minturn, Leigh. 1993. *Sita's Daughters: Coming Out of Purdah*. New York: Oxford University Press.

Minturn, Leigh, and John Hitchcock. 1966. *The Rajputs of Khalapur, India*. New York: Wiley.

Minturn, Leigh, and William W. Lambert. 1964. *Mothers of Six Cultures: Antecedents of Childrearing*. New York: Wiley.

Mitra, Rajendralala. 1961. *The Antiquities of Orissa*, Vols. 1 and 2. Reprint, Indian Studies Past and Present. Calcutta: Firma K. L. Mukhopadhyaya.

Mitter, Sara S. 1991. *Dharma's Daughters*. New Brunswick: Rutgers University Press.

Moore, Henrietta L. 1988. *Feminism and Anthropology*. Minneapolis: University of Minnesota Press.

Mukhopadhyay, Carol Chapnick. 1991. Linking Family Structure and Women's Participation in Science and Engineering: An Indian Case Study. Unpublished paper presented at the annual meeting of the Association of Asian Studies, New Orleans.

_____ 1994. Family Structure and Indian Women's Participation in Science and Engineering. In Carol Chapnick Mukhopadhyay and Susan Seymour

References

(eds.), *Women, Education, and Family Structure in India*. Pp. 103–132. Boulder: Westview Press.

Mukhopadhyay, Carol Chapnick and Susan Seymour. 1994. Theoretical Introduction. In Carol Chapnick Mukhopadhyay and Susan Seymour (eds.), *Women, Education, and Family Structure in India*. Pp. 1–33. Boulder: Westview Press.

Munroe, Robert L., and Ruth H. Munroe. 1994 (reissued). *Cross-Cultural Human Development*. Prospect Heights, IL: Waveland Press.

Nichter, Mimi, and Mark Nichter. 1987. A Tale of Simeon: Reflections on Raising a Child While Conducting Fieldwork in Rural South India. In Joan Cassel (ed.), *Children in the Field: Anthropological Experiences*. Pp. 192–209. Philadelphia: Temple University Press.

Nuckolls, Charles W. (ed.). 1993. *Siblings in South Asia: Brothers and Sisters in Cultural Context*. New York: Guilford Press.

O'Flaherty, Wendy Doniger. 1980. *Women, Androgynes, and Other Mythical Beasts*. Chicago: University of Chicago Press.

Panigrahi, K. C. 1961. *Archaeological Remains at Bhubaneswar*. Bombay: Orient Longmans.

Papanek, Hannah. 1989. Family Status-Production Work: Women's Contribution to Social Mobility and Class Differentiation. In Maithreyi Krishnaraj and Karuna Chanana (eds.), *Gender and the Household Domain: Social and Cultural Dimensions*. Pp. 97–116. New Delhi: Sage Publications.

Poffenberger, Thomas. 1976. *The Socialization of Family Size Values: Youth and Family Planning in an Indian Village*. Michigan Papers on South and Southeast Asia, no. 12, pp. 1–160.

——— 1981. Child Rearing and Social Structure in Rural India: Toward a Cross-Cultural Definition of Child Abuse and Neglect. In Jill E. Korbin (ed.), *Child Abuse and Neglect: Cross-Cultural Perspectives*. Pp. 71–95. Berkeley: University of California Press.

Radcliffe-Brown, A. R. 1950. Introduction. In A. R. Radcliffe-Brown and Daryll Forde (eds.), *African Systems of Kinship and Marriage*. Pp. 1–85. London: Oxford University Press.

——— 1952. *Structure and Function in Primitive Society*. Glencoe, IL: Free Press.

Raheja, Gloria Goodwin, and Ann Grodzins Gold. 1994. *Listen to the Heron's Words: Reimagining Gender and Kinship in North India*. Berkeley: University of California Press.

Richman, Amy L., Patrice M. Miller, and Robert A. LeVine. 1992. Cultural and Educational Variations in Maternal Responsiveness. *Developmental Psychology* 28: 614–621.

Riesman, Paul. 1992. *First Find Your Child a Good Mother: The Construction of Self in Two African Communities*. New Brunswick: Rutgers University Press.

Rogers, Susan Carol. 1991. *Shaping Modern Times in Rural France: The Transformation and Reproduction of an Aveyronnais Community*. Princeton: Princeton University Press.

Rohner, Ronald P., and Manjusri Chaki-Sircar. 1988. *Women and Children in a Bengali Village*. Hanover, NH: University Press of New England.

Roland, Alan. 1988. *In Search of Self in India and Japan: Toward a Cross-Cultural Psychology*. Princeton: Princeton University Press.

Rosaldo, Michelle Zimbalist. 1974. A Theoretical Overview. In M. Z. Rosaldo and Louise Lamphere (eds.), *Women, Culture, and Society*. Stanford: Stanford University Press.

Roy, Manisha. 1972. *Bengali Women*. Chicago: University of Chicago Press.

1975. The Concepts of "Femininity" and "Liberation" in the Context of Changing Sex Roles: Women in Modern India and America. In D. Raphael (ed.), *Being Female*. Pp. 219–230. The Hague: Mouton Publishers.

Rudolph, Suzanne Hoeber, and Lloyd I. Rudolph. 1972. *Education and Politics in India: Studies in Organization, Society, and Policy*. Cambridge: Harvard University Press.

(eds.). 1967. *The Modernity of Tradition: Political Development in India*. Chicago: University of Chicago Press.

Sable, Alan. 1977. *Paths through the Labyrinth: Educational Selection and Allocation in an Indian State Capital*. New Delhi: Chand and Company.

1980. Indian Education: A View from the Bottom Up. In Susan Seymour (ed.), *The Transformation of a Sacred Town: Bhubaneswar, India*. Pp. 157–182. Boulder: Westview Press.

Schlegel, Alice. 1991. Status, Property, and the Value on Virginity. *American Ethnologist* 18: 719–734.

Seymour, Susan. 1971. Patterns of Child Rearing in a Changing Indian Town: Sources and Expressions of Dependence and Independence. Ph.D. diss., Harvard University.

1975a. Some Determinants of Sex Roles in a Changing Indian Town. *American Ethnologist* 2 (4): 757–769.

1975b. Child-Rearing in India: A Case Study in Change and Modernization. In Thomas R. Williams (ed.), *Socialization and Communication in Primary Groups*. Pp. 41–58. The Hague: Mouton Publishers.

1976. Caste/Class and Child-Rearing in a Changing Indian Town. *American Ethnologist* 3 (4): 783–796

1980. Some Conclusions: Sources of Change and Continuity. In Susan Seymour (ed.), *The Transformation of a Sacred Town: Bhubaneswar, India*. Pp. 257–273. Boulder: Westview Press.

References

1983. Household Structure and Status and Expressions of Affect in India. *Ethos* 11 263–277.

1988. Expressions of Responsibility among Indian Children: Some Precursors of Adult Status and Sex Roles. *Ethos* 16 (4): 355–370.

1996. Caste. In David Levinson and Melvin Ember (eds.), *The Encyclopedia of Cultural Anthropology*. Vol. 1:177–181. Lakeville, CT: American Reference Publishing Company.

Sharma, Ursula. 1980. *Women, Work, and Property in North-West India*. London: Tavistock Publications.

1986. *Women's Work, Class, and the Urban Household: A Study of Simla, North India*. London: Tavistock Publications.

Shorter, Edward. 1975. *The Making of the Modern Family*. New York: Basic Books.

Shweder, Richard A. 1985. Menstrual Pollution, Soul Loss, and the Comparative Study of Emotions. In Arthur Kleinman and Byron Good (eds.), *Culture and Depression: Studies in the Anthropology and Cross-Cultural Psychiatry of Affect and Disorder*. Pp. 182–215. Berkeley: University of California Press.

Shweder, Richard A., and Nancy C. Much. 1987. Determinations of Meaning: Discourse and Moral Socialization. In William W. Kurtines and Jacob Gewirtz (eds.), *Moral Development through Social Interaction*. Pp. 197–242. New York: Wiley.

Singer, Milton. 1972. *When a Great Tradition Modernizes: An Anthropological Approach to Indian Civilization*. New York: Praeger.

Skold, Karen. 1988. The Interests of Feminists and Children in Child Care. In Sanford M. Dornbusch and Myra H. Strober (eds.), *Feminism, Children, and the New Families*. Pp. 113–136. New York: Guilford Press.

Spiro, Melford E. 1993. Is the Western Conception of the Self "Peculiar" within the Context of the World Cultures? *Ethos* 21, (2): 107–153.

Srinivas, M. N. 1966. *Social Change in Modern India*. Berkeley: University of California Press.

Thorne, Barrie, and Marilyn Yalom (eds.). 1982. *Rethinking the Family: Some Feminist Questions*. New York: Longman.

Toennies, F. 1957. *Community and Society*. East Lansing: Michigan State University Press.

Trawick, Margaret. 1992. *Notes on Love in a Tamil Family*. Berkeley: University of California Press.

Triandis, Harry C. 1993. Collectivism and Individualism as Cultural Syndromes. *Cross-Cultural Research* 27 (3–4): 155–180.

Turner, Ralph. 1976. The Real Self: From Institution to Impulse. *American Journal of Sociology* 81: 989–1016.

References

Ueno, Chizuko. 1984. The Individualist versus the Communalist Version of Feminism. Unpublished paper presented at the National Women's Studies Association Conference, Rutgers University, New Jersey.

Ullrich, Helen. 1987. Marriage Patterns among Havik Brahmins: A Twenty-Year Study of Change. *Sex Roles* 16 (11/12): 615–635.

——— 1992. Menstrual Taboos among Havik Brahmin Women: A Study of Ritual Change. *Sex Roles* 26 (1/2): 19–40.

——— 1994. Asset and Liability: The Role of Female Education in Changing Marriage Patterns among Havik Brahmins. In Carol Chapnick Mukhopadhyay and Susan Seymour (eds.), *Women, Education, and Family Structure in India*. Pp. 187–212. Boulder: Westview Press.

Wadley, Susan S. 1994. *Struggling with Destiny in Karimpur, 1925–1984*. Berkeley: University of California Press.

——— (ed.) 1980. *The Powers of Tamil Women*. Foreign and Comparative Studies/ South Asian Series, no. 6. Maxwell School of Citizenship and Public Affairs, Syracuse University.

Weber, Max. 1947. *The Theory of Social and Economic Organization*. Glencoe, IL: Free Press.

Whiting, Beatrice B. 1963. *Six Cultures: Studies of Child Rearing*. New York: Wiley.

Whiting, Beatrice B., and John W. M. Whiting. 1975. *Children of Six Cultures: A Psycho-Cultural Analysis*. Cambridge: Harvard University Press.

Whiting, John W. M., and Beatrice B. Whiting. 1973. Altruistic Behavior in Six Cultures. In Laura Nader and Thomas W. Maretzki (eds.), *Anthropological Studies* 9: 56–66.

Whiting, John W. M., Irving L. Child, and William W. Lambert. 1966. *Field Guide for a Study of Socialization*. New York: Wiley.

Wiser, William H., and Charlotte Viall Wiser. 1971. Rev. and enl. ed. *Behind Mud Walls, 1930–1960, with a sequel: The Village in 1970*. Berkeley: University of California Press.

Index

Apffel-Marglin, Frederique, 87–88
arranged marriage
  see marriage
authority
  in patrifocal family, xvii, 8, 55, 272–74
autonomy
  of females in contemporary India, 288–89
  increase for women in, 271

Bhubaneswar
  description of contemporary, 2–3, 13–30
  educational opportunities, 2–3, 28–29, 102–3, 187–88
  heritage of Buddhist and Jain religions in, 17
  social complexity of contemporary, 11–12
  see also New Capital, Bhubaneswar; Old Town, Bhubaneswar
boys
  changes in educational levels for, 180–95
  educational goals of New Capital, 138–40
  education of low-status poor, 170–73
  middle and late childhood in poor families, 167–69
  opportunities for education of low-status, 170
  responsible acts, 170–71

caste system
  adopting practices of higher-status groups, 177–78, 304n35

arranged marriage related to status in, 109–10
caste status in, 35
control of women's sexuality under, 8, 37, 287–88
dilemma related to marriage (1989), 198, 203
groups in new socioeconomic order, 109
Hindu paradigm for, 35
inheritance of caste status, 35
jatis, 35–36
occupational and ritual identity in, 35–36
transition to class from, 108–9
variation in response to change by, 285–86
varna, 35, 58
see also outcaste status
childbirth
  changes in observance of pollution related to, 252–57
  changing practices related to pollution, 116–17
  ritual pollution of mother and child after, 71, 116–17
  women's discussion of restrictions following (1989), 247–52
child care practices
  in absence of patrilocal residence, 125–36
  bathing, 72, 73–74, 131–32
  in Bauri (outcaste) families (1965–67), 153
  effect of changing, 270
  infant indulgence, 72, 75–76
  in low-status families, 161–66

315

Index

nurturant acts (*continued*)
directed toward children, 125–26, 132–
  33, 158–59
by mothers and other caretakers, 78

occupations
  hereditary, 36
  linked to caste structure, 35–36
  of Old Town castes, 60–61, 155
Old Town, Bhubaneswar
  Bauri settlement (1965–67), 149–52
  caste-related occupations, 35–36, 60–
    61, 150, 152, 154–55
  changes in educational levels, 180–
    95
  child-rearing practices, 72–85
  description of contemporary, 18–30
  educational level (1965–67), 61–62
  families chosen for study, 37–39, 41–
    42
  household division of labor, 66, 152–
    53
  outcaste (Bauri) family in (1965–67),
    149–55
  public presence of women (1987), 179–
    80
  research techniques, 45–50
Oriya language, 17, 33–34
outcaste status
  Bauri families in Old Town (1965–
    67), 149–52
  dowry, 177, 222
  educational opportunity for, 170–73,
    208–9
  food availability for families in, 150,
    152
  Sweeper families in New Capital
    (1965–67), 147, 155–57
  of Washerman families in Old Town
    (1965–67), 146, 155

parents
  arranged marriage as obligation of,
    287
  concern of New Capital parents for
    education of children, 125–30, 139
  control of married children by, 201
  demand for dowry system, 302n2
  education levels of Old Town and
    New Capital, 61–62, 104–6
  role in patrifocal family system,
    xvii
  teaching and allowing self-reliance,
    131–34

patrifocal family system
  in absence of patrilocal residence,
    115–16
  abuses against women in, 281
  based on age and gender hierarchy
    of authority, 272–74
  bride's responsibility in, 55, 96–97
  challenges to and transformation of,
    142–43, 200–1, 283–85, 288–91
  containment of pair-bonds, 272–74
  contemporary conditions for women
    to oppose, 267
  delegation of parental care to sons
    and daughters-in-law, 218–19
  description of, 8–9
  development of girls' self-esteem in,
    277–78
  differences in education for sons and
    daughters, 186–88
  differences in expectations for sons
    and daughters, 247–52
  division of labor among women, 66
  effect of employed and educated
    women on, 202
  forms of joint, 4–5
  gender hierarchies, 64
  implications with changes in
    women's roles, 202
  interdependence in, 100–1, 134, 268
  keeping men together in joint fami-
    lies, xvi
  for low-status, poor women and fam-
    ilies, 145–47
  male-based hierarchy and authority
    system, xvii, 8, 55, 272–74
  men as earners, and women as de-
    pendents, 193
  motherhood in, 97–100
  of parental choice and authority,
    xvii
  purdah observed in, 63–64
  sexual segregation in, 56–57
  structural principles of, 154
  subordination of individual in, 57,
    70, 100, 134, 280
  transitions in, 110–18
  welfare of extended family as prior-
    ity in, 8, 266–67
  wife's attention to needs of hus-
    band's extended family, 267
patrilineality, Indian family system, 8,
  54–55
patrilocal residence
  with absence of, 114–16

320